BEHAVI
DECISION MAKING

THE SCOTT, FORESMAN SERIES IN ORGANIZATIONAL BEHAVIOR AND HUMAN RESOURCES

Lyman W. Porter, Editor

Published:

Baskin/Aronoff	*Interpersonal Communication in Organizations*
Carroll/Schneier	*Performance Appraisal and Review Systems*
Griffin	*Task Design: An Integrative Approach*
Pinder	*Work Motivation: Theory, Issues, and Applications*
Schneider	*Staffing Organizations*
Stone	*Research Methods in Organizational Behavior*
Taylor	*Behavioral Decision Making*
Wexley/Latham	*Developing and Training Human Resources in Organizations*

BEHAVIORAL DECISION MAKING

Ronald N. Taylor

George R. Brown Professor of Administration
Rice University

Scott, Foresman and Company
Glenview, Illinois
Dallas, Tx. Oakland, N.J. Palo Alto, Ca. Tucker, Ga. London

Library of Congress Cataloging in Publication Data

Taylor, Ronald N., 1938–
Behavioral decision making.

(Scott, Foresman series in organizational behavior and human resources)
Bibliography: p.
Includes index.
1. Decision-making. I. Title. II. Series.
HD30.23.T39 1984 658.4'03 84-5521
ISBN 0-673-16645-7

SCOTT, FORESMAN SERIES IN ORGANIZATIONAL BEHAVIOR AND HUMAN RESOURCES

Printed in the United States of America.
1 2 3 4 5 6—EBI—89 88 87 86 85 84

To EuJane, Sharon, David, and Stephen

Acknowledgments

Adapted from H. I. Ansoff, CORPORATE STRATEGY. New York: McGraw-Hill, 1965. Courtesy of McGraw-Hill Publishing Company.

"Morphological Matrix for Inventing Powered Vehicle" by J. E. Arnold, CREATIVE ENGINEERING SEMINAR, Stanford University, Summer 1959.

From J. D. Bransford and M. K. Johnson, "Contextual Prerequisites for Understanding: Some Investigations of Comprehension and Recall," JOURNAL OF VERBAL LEARNING AND VERBAL BEHAVIOR, 1972, 11, 718. Courtesy of Academic Press and Marcia K. Johnson.

From D. C. Dearborn and H. A. Simon, "Selective Perception: A Note of the Departmental Identification of Executives." SOCIOMETRY, Vol. 21, 1958. Courtesy of the American Sociological Society and Herbert A. Simon.

From A. W. Drake and R. L. Keeney, DECISION ANALYSIS. Cambridge, Mass.: Massachusetts Institute of Technology, 1978. Courtesy of the Center for Advanced Engineering Study, Massachusetts Institute of Technology.

From M. Driver and T. Mock, "Human Information Processing, Decision Style Theory, and Accounting Information Systems," THE ACCOUNTING REVIEW, 1975. Courtesy of the American Accounting Association.

Adapted by permission of the publisher and author from "The Influence of Strength of Drive on Functional Fixedness and Perceptual Recognition" by Sam Glucksberg in JOURNAL OF EXPERIMENTAL PSYCHOLOGY. Vol. 63, 1962. Copyright © 1962 by the American Psychological Association.

From E. F. Harrison, THE MANAGERIAL DECISION-MAKING PROCESS. Boston: Houghton Mifflin, 1975. Courtesy of Houghton Mifflin.

From P. H. Lindsay and D. A. Norman, AN INTRODUCTION TO PSYCHOLOGY. New York: Academic Press, 1977. Courtesy of Academic Press.

From "The Old Sailor" in NOW WE ARE SIX by A. A. Milne. Copyright 1927 by E. P. Dutton & Co., Inc. Renewal, 1955 by A. A. Milne. Reprinted by permission of the publisher, E. P. Dutton, Inc., Methuen Children's Books, and McClelland and Stewart Ltd.

From A. P. Sage, "Designs for Optimal Information Filters" in P. Nystrom and W. H. Starbuck (eds), HANDBOOK OF ORGANIZATIONAL DESIGN, Vol. 1. Oxford: Oxford University Press, 1981. Courtesy of Oxford University Press.

From HUMAN INFORMATION PROCESSING by Harold M. Schroder et al. Copyright © 1967 by Holt, Rinehart and Winston, Inc. Reprinted by permission of Holt, Rinehart and Winston, CBS College Publishing.

From "Heuristic Simulation of Psychological Decision Processes" by Robert D. Smith in JOURNAL OF APPLIED PSYCHOLOGY, Vol. 52, No. 4, 1968. Copyright © 1968 by the American Psychological Association. Reprinted by permission of the publisher and author.

From "Probability Encoding in Decision Analysis" by Carl S. Spetzler and Carl Stael von Holstein in MANAGEMENT SCIENCE, Vol. 22, No. 3, November 1975. Copyright © 1975 by The Institute of Management Sciences. Reprinted by permission of The Institute of Management Sciences and Carl Spetzler.

Exhibit from "Utility Theory—Insights into Risk Taking" by R. O. Swalm in HARVARD BUSINESS REVIEW, November/December 1966. Copyright © 1966 by the President and Fellows of Harvard College; all rights reserved. Reprinted by permission of the Harvard Business Review.

From R. N. Taylor, "Nature of Problem Ill-Structuredness: Implications for Problem Formulation and Solution," DECISION SCIENCES, 1974. Courtesy of the American Institute for Decision Sciences.

Reprinted by permission of the publisher from "Can Leaders Learn to Lead?" by V. H. Vroom in ORGANIZATIONAL DYNAMICS, Winter 1976, p. 19. Copyright © 1976 by AMACOM, a division of American Management Associations. All rights reserved.

CONTENTS

FOREWORD

The Scott, Foresman Series in Organizational Behavior and Human Resources embodies concise and lively treatments of specific topics within the broad area indicated by the Series title. These books are for supplemental reading in basic management, organizational behavior, or personnel courses in which the instructor highlights particular topics in the larger course. However, the books, either alone or in combination, can also form the nucleus for specialized courses that follow introductory courses.

Each book stresses the *key issues* relevant to the given topic. Thus, each author, or set of authors, has made a particular effort to "highlight figure from ground"—that is, to keep the major issues in the foreground and the small explanatory details in the background. These books are, by design, relatively brief treatments of their topic areas, so the authors have had to be carefully *selective* in what they have chosen to retain and to omit. Because the authors were chosen for their expertise and their judgment, the Series provides valuable summary treatments of the subject areas.

In focusing on the major issues, the Series' authors present a balanced content coverage. They have also aimed at breadth by the unified presentation of different types of material: major conceptual or theoretical approaches, interesting and critical empirical findings, and applications to "real life" management and organizational problems. Each author deals with this body of material, but the combination varies according to the subject matter. Thus, each book is distinctive in the particular way in which a topic is addressed.

A final word is in order about the audience for this Series. Although the primary audience is the student, each book in the series concerns a topic of importance to the practicing manager. Managers and supervisors can rely on these books as authoritative summaries of the basic knowledge in each area covered by the Series.

The topics included in the Series to date have been chosen on the basis of their importance and relevance for those interested in management and organizations. As new appropriate topics emerge on the scene, additional books will be added. This is a dynamic Series both in content and direction.

Lyman W. Porter
Series Editor

PREFACE

The intent of this series of books is to highlight key issues in broad areas of organizational behavior and to provide a balanced coverage of the important advances in theory, research and application related to the issues identified. The focus of the present volume is the behavioral aspects of decision making in organizations.

Preparing a book on this topic involved making a number of choices regarding the audience to address, the approach to take, and the material to cover. It may be useful to the reader if I begin the volume by stating three of the choices I made as I deliberated concerning what it should accomplish.

(1) The book is intended to be read and used by "students" interested in decision making in organizations—students in the classroom, performing research on decision making, or applying the techniques of decision making to the solution of applied problems. It is hoped that the book will be used in the classroom in at least two contexts for advanced undergraduate and graduate students. The book attempts to provide a central theme for courses on managerial decision making, perhaps supplemented by appropriate readings drawn from original research reports or other sources. The book also may be used to present the decision making component for organizational behavior courses. Much of the material presented in the book was gleaned from my experiences in teaching managerial decision making and organizational behavior.

It is also hoped that the book will stimulate research and writing which spans the boundary between managerial decision making and organizational behavior. The New Directions in Decision Making Conference (Braunstein & Ungson, 1982) held at the University of Oregon clearly pointed out the advantages of exchange of ideas among researchers in these fields. Landmark *Annual Review of Psychology* chapters on decision making (Slovic, Fischhoff & Lichtenstein, 1977; Einhorn & Hogarth, 1981) and organizational behavior

(Cummings, 1982; Staw, 1984) have signaled the importance of understanding decision processes in organizational contexts. Hence, a further objective of the volume is to attempt to link the literatures on managerial decision making and organizational behavior; hopefully, making those working in each field even more aware of the strengths and limitations of the other field.

A detailed presentation of specific techniques for making decisions is beyond the scope of this book. This is not intended to be primarily a book on decision analysis or other specific strategies for making applied decisions. Excellent treatments of specific decision-making techniques have been provided by authors such as Moore and Thomas (1976), Brown, Kahr and Peterson (1974), Churchman, Auerbach, and Sadan (1975), Keeney and Raiffa (1976), and Goodman, Fischhoff, Lichtenstein and Slovic (1978). Yet, it is hoped that readers interested in tips for applied decision making will find the strategies for improved decision making derived from theoretical and empirical research contributions to be useful in their own decision-making activities.

(2) Since the book is intended to be read by people with a variety of backgrounds, I have attempted to describe briefly some of the central issues in behavioral decision making with a minimum of technical detail and jargon. In order to link organizational behavior with decision making the literature from each field is selectively discussed in some depth by focusing on major issues which have implications for both fields. These issues are highlighted and a balanced coverage of advances in relevant theory, research, and techniques pertaining to each issue is presented. Where possible, the issues are described without recourse to formulas and with illustrative examples. As each issue is discussed, sources of further, more detailed, information that may be useful to each of the types of students mentioned above are suggested.

(3) In order to facilitate the systematic and balanced coverage of the major issues related to behavioral aspects of decision making, the issues examined in this volume are presented within a framework representing the decision-making process. Literature pertaining to each issue is discussed and, drawing upon the insights provided by examining relevant behavioral theory and research, implications for advancing our understanding of the issue are developed. For example, to understand the difficulties imposed upon decision making by the informational demands of highly complex decision problems, it is necessary to examine the research literature on human information processing. Such an examination reveals both the contributions made by researchers concerned with this topic and aspects of human information processing which have been neglected by researchers. The contributions may provide insights into ways to im-

prove decision making; the neglected areas may identify topics for future advances in theory, research and practice.

The decision to write this book and the form it ultimately took were influenced by a great many students and colleagues. Although I cannot acknowledge all of these influences here, a few of the people most instrumental in my writing this book should be mentioned. Professor Marvin Dunnette was influential in stimulating my interest in the field of decision making. A great many colleagues have shaped the material presented in this book and many of these influences are reflected in the citations. I am particularly grateful to Professor Kenneth MacCrimmon for the stimulation provided by many discussions of issues in managerial decision making and his insightful comments on the manuscript. Series Editor Dr. Lyman Porter has encouraged me, shaped the book through its various revisions, and has patiently awaited the completed manuscript. It also has been rewarding to benefit from the expertise of Scott, Foresman, particularly the encouragement and guidance of Roger Holloway, James Boyd, and Darcie Sanders.

Financial support for this book was provided by a Social Sciences and Humanities Research Council Leave Fellowship. For her expert typing of the manuscript, and their tolerance of tight deadlines and many revisions, I am grateful to Colleen Colclough and Mabel Yee. Possibly the greatest influence on this book, however, has come from interaction with students in my courses on Managerial Decision Making and Policy Analysis. I acknowledge this debt and hope they will continue to influence me as much in the classroom as I influence them.

Ronald N. Taylor

INTRODUCTION TO BEHAVIORAL DECISION MAKING 1

As individuals, as organizations, and as a society we are faced with the necessity of coping with difficult decision problems. Individuals must choose among careers, marriage partners, and make other decisions with far-reaching personal implications. Organizations must invest in new products, issue credit, and decide where to locate production facilities. Societies must cope with staggering problems concerning energy, employment, health services, and relationships among nations. Yet all of these choices will be made by fallible humans with sharply limited abilities compared to the bewildering array of information with which we are being bombarded. Not only is it essential to improve decision-making effectiveness, but in view of the serious consequences for all those people affected by decisions, there is considerable urgency in doing so. This provides the stage for our discussion of behavioral decision making and its potential contributions to understanding and improving decision-making effectiveness.

BEHAVIORAL DECISION MAKING AND ITS IMPORTANCE

What, then, is behavioral decision making, and why is it important both to students of decision making and to decision makers? Behavioral decision making attempts to understand how people make decisions and how they can make decisions more effectively. In doing so, particular attention is given to the human behaviors involved in decision making, frequently expressed in the form of patterns of behaviors which are found to be typical of most people. An example of this would be the observed tendency of humans to be conservative in revising opinions when presented with new evidence. In this book we will attempt to highlight some of the major theoretical advances in behavioral decision making, to summarize evidence developed by researchers related to these theories, and on the basis of this understanding of how decisions are made, to suggest strategies for making better decisions.

Theoretical Importance

Decision-making activities have provided the focus for considerable theoretical and research attention, both in the behavioral sciences and in other disciplines. Many contributions have been made by psychologists interested in cognitive processes and are characterized by an emphasis on the capabilities and limitations of humans in processing information and making choices. Yet there is a growing awareness that organizational and social influences affecting choices are at least as important as the characteristics of the individual decision maker. While this development is relatively recent, the preliminary advances made toward placing the individual decision maker in the context of organizations and societies are discussed in this book.

Another theoretical development in decision making is shown by attempts to merge the behavioral and quantitative aspects of decision making. Frequently, the behavioral and quantitative aspects of decision making have been viewed as dichotomous, with the rigorous formulation of the quantitative approaches being irreconcilable with the descriptive theories of the behavioral sciences. For this reason, decision making typically has been taught, in the past, from either a quantitative or a behavioral viewpoint. Today, however, many universities offer decision-making courses which cover both behavioral and quantitative topics.

Practical Importance

In practice, decision makers have also reflected this split in orientation, emphasizing either a rigorous decision-analytic approach or an approach based on subjective judgments and experiences. While many books have been written on managerial decision making, they typically ignore the behavioral aspects of the topic. Some notable exceptions are the discussions by Lee (1971), Shull, Delbecq, and Cummings (1970), and Radford (1975). On the other hand, behavioral scientists have done little to relate the developments in their fields to the concerns of applied decision makers.

The approach taken in this book is that material from many fields can contribute to our understanding of the decision-making process, but that their influences are not equal in understanding every issue in decision making. The quantitative approaches offer a great variety of rigorous techniques for assisting decision makers in dealing effectively with the challenge of evaluating and choosing among alternative courses of action. The behavioral sciences are applicable to understanding the behavioral aspects of many decision processes, but are particularly relevant to problem specification, generating alternative courses of action, and decision implementation. By drawing upon both quantitative and behavioral viewpoints, this book will provide a stronger foundation for improving applied decision making.

DEFINING DECISION MAKING AND DECISION MAKER

A number of theoretical viewpoints have been employed in attempting to define what is meant by decision making and to determine who makes decisions in organizational contexts. At one extreme, an individual decision maker—typically identified as a *manager*—can be the focus, and choices can be examined in the light of the resulting consequences for the organization. Other viewpoints suggest that it is misleading even to speak of decision making in attempting to explain the functioning of organizations.

What Is Decision Making?

Simon (1960) has gone so far as to equate decision making with management. He has expressed the view that decision making is an essential part of the administrative process. In fact, "a theory of administration should be concerned with the processes of decision as well as with the processes of action" (Simon, 1957, p. 1). From this perspective, decision making is an inescapable part of a manager's everyday activities, and the ability to make effective decisions is essential to all functions of management. Similar viewpoints have been expressed by others:

> The decision problem is that of selecting a path which will move the system—individual, computer program, or organization—from some initial state to some terminal state. (Feldman & Kanter, 1965, p. 614–615)

> We will define decision making as: a conscious and human process, involving both individual and social phenomena, based upon factual and value premises, which concludes with the choice of one behavioral activity from among one or more alternatives with the intention of moving toward some desired state of affairs. (Shull, Delbecq, & Cummings, 1970, p. 31)

These definitions of decision making indicate that it involves reaching a conclusion, which implies deliberation and thought and suggests a conscious act. A natural reaction or an unconscious act would be more accurately labeled a habit or reflex act (George, 1964). A similar distinction has been made by Ofstad (1961); he has stated that the unconscious process preceding action should be called *compulsion* rather than *decision*. The viewpoints reported above suggest that decision making involves conscious choices among alternatives made by organizational participants—generally by managers.

Other views of decision making in organizations specify that it is not appropriate to describe decision making in terms of choices made by organizational members. Instead, decision making is an organizational process that is shaped as much by the interactions of organizational members, as it is by the contemplation and cognitive processes of individual organizational members (Sayles, 1964). Choices are made within the social and political contexts of organizations and their environments. To adequately describe decision-making behaviors, it is important that alternate theories of decision making in organizations be developed to take the social and political influences into account. The behavioral aspects of managerial decision making traditionally have been examined from a "rational actor" perspective (Allison, 1971), in which a decision represents a single person or people with shared values evaluating alternative courses of action and making choices. Additional insights can be obtained by viewing decision making from organizational and political perspectives.

Finally, other theorists have suggested that organizational activities can be explained without recourse to the concept of decision making. The *nondecisional* theories, such as the one proposed by Weick (1977), hold that labeling these activities as *decision making*, produces a spurious sense of orderliness and purposiveness. Instead, it would be more accurate to view the outcomes that frequently are attributed to a decision as, in fact, results of a host of interwoven influences—and not as the consequences of deliberate choices made by organizational members.

There has been little exchange of ideas across theoretical positions to date, although the literature pertaining to each viewpoint is voluminous. For example, the techniques developed by decision analysts have proved to be useful in choosing appropriate solutions to many problems facing organizations (e.g., for selecting marketing strategies, investment opportunities, and so forth). Theories of organizational processes have proliferated, many of which have implications for understanding how courses of action are adopted by organizations. Also, theory and research on the behavioral aspects of human information processing and decision making are central to understanding decision making in organizations. The approach taken in this volume is that, while it is convenient to focus upon decision making by individuals or groups in organizations to take advantage of the well-developed—and, at times, quantitative—theories and techniques pertaining to decision making, this approach is not sufficient to explain how decisions are made in organizational contexts. Organizational processes, both social and political, also must be considered. Hopefully, this approach will advance our understanding of decision making by drawing relevant theory, research, and strategies from each viewpoint and stimulating the exchange of ideas across these fields.

Who Is a Decision Maker?

We will use the term *decision maker* to refer to an individual, a group, an organization, or even an entire society. Decision making occurs at each of these levels. While the nature of decision problems differs across levels of decision making, decisions made at each level essentially follow the process that characterizes choices made by individual decision makers. Allison (1971) has shown that a better understanding of decisions made by nations can be achieved by including the influences of organizational processes and politics in the model. Through analysis of cases, such as the decision to drop the atomic bomb on Japan during World War II, he has demonstrated that the analysis becomes more complete as additional influences are included. Clearly, the impact of the decision context upon a decision maker must be taken into account if we hope to understand how decisions are made.

Yet, individual decision making has a place even in organizational and political contexts. For example, one must decide whether to vote for a bill, propose an amendment, or apply political pressure. As Keeney and Raiffa (1976) have described, if individuals have choices to make they are decision makers. Thus, there are many decision problems in the public sector in which decision makers can be viewed as a well-specified, unitary, identifiable entity, and the paradigm of decision analysis is appropriate for analyzing these problems.

INTEGRATING DESCRIPTIVE AND NORMATIVE APPROACHES

Behavioral decision making represents an integration of descriptive and normative approaches to decision making. Generally, the behavioral scientist's concern for human information processing and choice capabilities has led to descriptive, as opposed to normative, theories of decision-making behavior. Descriptive theories of human behavior can be distinguished from normative theories in that descriptive theory describes what people actually *do,* while normative theory specifies what they *should do.* Making a rigid distinction between descriptive and normative theories, however, can be misleading. There is much overlap of interest between normative and descriptive viewpoints; and the contributions of many people concerned with descriptive aspects of decision making have markedly influenced the normative decision analysts. These contributions are summarized by Edwards (1954, 1961), Slovic & Lichtenstein (1971), Fischer & Edwards (1973), and Slovic, Fischhoff, & Lichtenstein (1977).

If, however, people *do* make the decisions they *should* make (as decision theory would specify), normative and descriptive theories merge into one. For example, a normative model is proposed for a decision situation. Let's say that Bayes' theorem is used to prescribe how much people should change their opinions about the proportion of red balls in an urn as they are allowed to draw additional balls from the urn. Bayes' theorem provides a quantitative measure of the amount of change in prior opinions that theorists believe *should* follow exposure to additional information of known value. Experiments generally have found that people do not change their opinions as much as the evidence provided by the sample of balls would indicate that they should. Hence, they have been called *conservative* opinion revisers.

Since empirical research on human behavior has shown that people do not behave as the model predicts, the discrepancy is attacked from both sides as investigators attempt to bring normative theory and observed behavior into agreement. Researchers try to devise experiments which will overcome possible "flaws" in prior studies. Perhaps the experimental situation appears "artificial" to subjects or makes excessive demands upon their ability to process or aggregate information. Or, the appropriateness of the Bayes' theorem for representing human opinion revision may be questioned. We don't expect people to have perfect perception, memory, and calculational abilities, so the model should be degraded to correspond to the limited abilities of real experimental subjects. In brief, attempts are made to align Bayesian and actual human opinion revision.

It is important to compare normative and descriptive theories pertaining to various decision-making phenomena, since normative theories may rest upon assumptions that fail to accurately describe actual behaviors. It is misleading to propose a normative theory specifying that people maximize expected utility if they are unable to process the large amounts of information that confront them in complex decision situations. Taking human capabilities into account is even more important when systems are designed to aid decision making. Knowledge of human ability to process information and make decisions is essential in applications such as human engineering (fitting a job to the person). Man-machine systems that fail to take this into account will not work. Similarly, research has shown that management information systems can be improved by considering the attributes of information users in the design of information systems. (Mason & Mitroff, 1973).

Understanding decision-making processes can be advanced by considering the interplay among theories (normative or descriptive) and research. Normative theories can be made descriptive by stating their propositions as illustrative of what decision makers actually do and then testing these propositions by empirical research. Descriptive theories can be made normative by using them as bases for prescribing what decision makers should do in various situations. Research is frequently used to test the accuracy of descriptive theories in reflecting actual decision behaviors; and, at times, empirical research can lead to new or refined descriptive theories. Exhibit 1.1 illustrates the complex interplay of theory and research in advancing our understanding of decision making.

EXHIBIT 1.1 Relationships Among Theories and Research

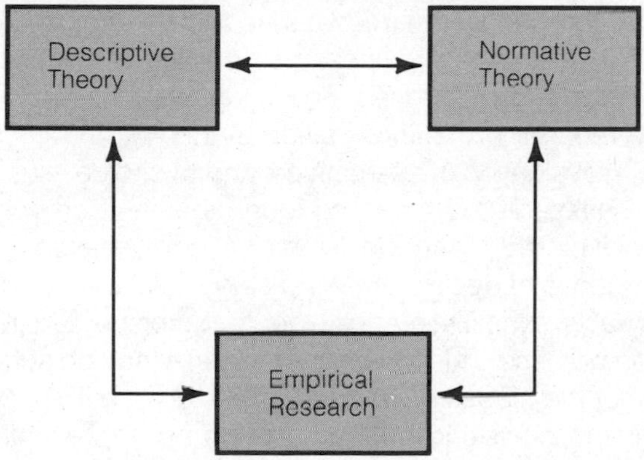

One challenge for behavioral decision making is to derive and test normative strategies from behavioral theories and empirical research. The decision tree developed by Vroom and Yetton (1973) to specify strategies for involving subordinates in the decision making of their superiors represents one attempt to develop such a normative model. These normative strategies, if they are to be of value, must be solidly grounded in the theory and research of the field. In addition, the limited attention devoted to deriving normative theories from descriptive theory and research may reflect the difficulty in specifying direction of causal relationships in research using a correlational design. For example, to conclude that an employee-centered style of supervision produces work groups with higher levels of productivity is unwarranted if the descriptive research finding is based upon the analysis of correlations between supervisory style and productivity. In such a study it would be equally justifiable to conclude that certain types of work groups, which are also characterized by high productivity, produce employee-centered supervisory styles in their leaders. Hence, attempts to prescribe normative strategies from correlational research findings are hampered by the inability to infer direction of causality among variables.

MAJOR ISSUES IN BEHAVIORAL DECISION MAKING

Management decision theorists have proposed many lists of steps, stages, or phases in the decision-making process. Witte (1972) conducted research to determine whether distinct stages do occur in decision making and if they follow the sequence described in many discussions of decision making. He concluded that the decision processes he examined, dealing with data processing equipment, did involve a number of different operations that tended to occur at different points in time. His research divided the decision process into ten equal time intervals and then noted the level and type of activity that occurred in each time interval. The sequence of five phases generally proposed as descriptive of decision activity—1) problem recognition, 2) information gathering, 3) developing alternatives, 4) evaluation of alternatives, and 5) choice—was not supported by his research. Rather, he found that the decision process consisted of a plurality of subdecisions, which also failed to show the regular sequence of decision-making stages. Activities generally attributed to each of the five stages were found dispersed throughout the decision process. This suggests that there may be some truth to the claim that the *stages* of decision making were invented for the convenience of decision analysts, and do not represent a natural condition of decision making.

The central features of decision making have been summarized by Simon (1960) in the following manner: "Decision making comprises three principal phases: finding occasions for making a decision; finding possible courses of action; and choosing among courses of action" (p. 1). To this list it is important to add that the chosen course of action must be appropriately implemented. Hence, the issues in behavioral decision making which are highlighted in this volume are:

What is known about the behavioral processes involved in specifying decision problems?

How are problems diagnosed and their causes attributed?

What are the behavioral processes underlying the selection or development of appropriate solutions for ill-structured and well-structured problems? What is known about creativity in decision making?

What behavioral processes are involved in making choices in complex decision situations? How are probabilistic judgments made in uncertain decision situations?

How can understanding of decision making in organizational contexts be advanced by expanding the analysis to incorporate the social and political aspects involved in decision-making groups, in situations characterized by conflict, and in implementing decisions?

DECISION ENVIRONMENTS AND LEVELS OF ANALYSIS

Attempts have been made to systematically describe the environments in which decisions are made by individuals, groups, and organizations. In this section some of these classification systems are sketched. The nature of the decision environment, of course, depends upon the level of analysis represented by the "decision maker," but the classification systems described here can be used to illustrate some key aspects of decision environments.

Enacted Environments

All decision making takes place within an environment which influences the selection of objectives, bounds the search, constrains the selection of alternatives, and directly affects the acceptance of an implemented course of action. Moreover, how an individual perceives particular stimuli in the environment is important because these perceptions become the basis for decision-making behavior. Yet, how stimuli are perceived and given meaning depends as much on the decision maker as on the environment. Weick (1977) has suggested that organizations can be viewed as *enacted* or perceptually constructed by individuals in a manner which makes sense to the individual. Decision environments are subjective and reflect the particular cognitive, perceptual, and emotional state of an individual at one point in time.

Decision Consequences

Keeney and Raiffa (1976) proposed that decision problems can be described in terms of the consequences of decisions. This is of interest to our concern for describing decision environments, because the consequences they include are determined, in large part, by the decision environment. Their dichotomy of problem types represents both the number of attributes a decision problem has and the amount of uncertainty regarding its consequences. Class 1 decision problems, which have certain and unidimensional consequences, can be solved by choosing the feasible alternative that maximizes the given single objective function and are of little interest for managerial decision making. Class 2 decision problems, in which there is certainty and more than one descriptor, can be viewed as complex value analysis under certainty. The basic problem is one of ranking a set of consequences when each consequence is described by performance values on many attributes. This requires use of subjective trade-offs. Class 3 decision problems involve uncertainty, but only one descriptor, and require analysis of risk and utility. Class 4 decision problems represent consequences which are both uncertain and multidimensional. While the techniques appropriate for the other three classes may be used, in Class 4 decision problems, additional techniques are needed to cope with the difficulties introduced by interactions between uncertainty and multidimensionality.

Clearly, decision environments can be described in many ways, but two dimensions which are central to the literature of decision making are the complexity and uncertainty (MacCrimmon & Taylor, 1976). When a decision maker has only partial knowledge of the variables relevant to a decision, the decision is characterized by uncertainty. One may be uncertain about any of a number of aspects of the decision problem—what the problem is, whether one should attempt to solve the problem, what resources are available for its solution, and how exogenous events may affect the outcomes of decision-making efforts. In essence, then, decision making under conditions of uncertainty involves an inadequate information base upon which to make a decision. Typically, decision making under uncertainty requires information acquisition. Complexity in a decision situation, on the other hand, frequently occurs when a decision maker is confronted with too much information relevant to a problem. Decision makers can be overwhelmed by the voluminous information base required by the decision problem. Complexity requires a decision maker to cope with both the multiplicity of factors to be considered and the interconnections among these factors.

Finally, decision-making situations involve consideration of the social and political influences on decision-making activities. Social and political influences can arise from the need to involve many people in decision-making activities and to consider the preferences and values of each person. For example, frequently decisions made in organizational contexts must be implemented by many members of the organization. In considering the social and political aspects of decision situations, multiple-person decision making is examined—both under conditions of conflict among the parties to a decision and when conflict does not occur.

Open Systems

The environment can be viewed as an open system within which the decision maker in a formal organization functions as one element, receiving inputs from the environment and dispensing processed outputs to the environment. The inputs from the environment can be information, energy, and materials, while the outputs can be decisions. This concept of the decision environment is shown in Exhibit

1.2, which depicts decision makers bounded by their memberships in one or more groups that are, themselves, circumscribed by the formal organization. Harrison (1975) stated that "the decision maker must cope with exogenous forces of politics, economics, society, and technology. The impact of these factors is moderated somewhat by the permeable boundaries of the two larger aggregates within which choices are made. The initial impacts are felt first at the organizational level; secondary effects penetrate at the group level; and the decision maker himself receives only the tertiary impacts from the environment" (pp. 85–86). Within the organization, the three levels are interdependent, and the decision maker's choices are bounded by the larger aggregates of which they are a part, by time and cost constraints, and by their own cognitive limitations. Decision makers with greater cognitive ability will be able to reduce the blocking effects of the permeable boundaries by more extensive information acquisition.

EXHIBIT 1.2 A Decision-Maker's Environment

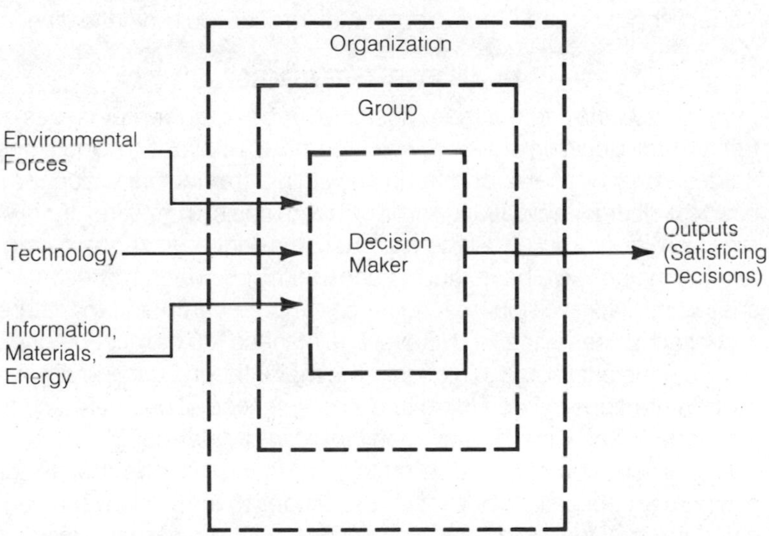

Source: Harrison, E.F. *The managerial decision making process.* Boston: Houghton-Mifflin, 1975, 41.

Environmental "Textures"

Another system for describing decision environments has been advanced by Thompson and McEwen (1969). They suggested that organizations make decisions in environments characterized by four types of "textures": 1) the placid, randomized environment; 2) the placid, clustered environment; 3) the disturbed, reactive environment; and 4) the turbulent field. Organizations can dominate their environments, be dominated by their environments, or fall between these positions. The decision strategy adopted by the organization depends upon the texture of its environment, and can range from competition, to bargaining, to coalition formation.

Organizations in placid environments can make decisions on the basis of power to both adapt and attain their objectives. In the disturbed, reactive environment, competitive strategies are necessary for successful decision making, and in the turbulent field, decision making is seriously hampered by a great deal of uncertainty and coalitions may be sought. Decision makers, therefore, should both take into account the inputs of the environment in arriving at a decision, and consider the effects of that choice on the environment. In particular, decision makers should be aware of the uncontrollable external variables that shape their choices by influencing objectives and aspirations, channeling the search, and limiting the range of relevant alternatives. In addition, the decision environment determines the effectiveness of an implemented decision; it is unlikely that a choice made without regard for environmental forces would be effective.

PLAN FOR THE BOOK

This volume attempts to expose the reader to some key issues of behavioral decision making which appear relevant to decisions made in organizations, and to do so within a framework which may suggest useful implications for improved decision-making theory, research, and practice. Since we must be selective in choosing material to include, we have tried to choose topics which represent issues central to decision-making theory and research and to feature recent advances in the field. Coverage of these topics must be brief, but we have attempted to highlight the major theoretical and empirical contributions to each topic and to suggest additional references for readers who wish to pursue any topic in greater detail.

Any discussion of decision making presents an opportunity, or perhaps an obligation, to expose the reader to material from a variety of fields. Other fields, such as psychology and managerial economics, are represented to the extent that we are aware of their relevant contributions and when their material is clearly appropriate for advancing our understanding of the issues under discussion. Viewing decision making from more than one disciplinary perspective permits us to reconcile contributions to understanding decision making derived from a variety of approaches, theories, and methods of research and to draw strategies for improving decision-making theory, research, and practice from a wider base.

The emphasis of this volume, however, is on human behavior and we are primarily interested in the behavioral sciences' contributions to understanding decision making. The behavioral topics covered include bounded rationality, problem perception, cognitive models of choice, Bayesian approaches to judgment and decision, man as an intuitive statistician, multiattribute and multiobjective decision making, group decision making, and decision implementation.

In analyzing behavioral aspects of decision making, we will proceed by highlighting some of the major issues in decision-making behavior, examining major advances in behavioral theory and research pertaining to each issue, and discussing their implications for improving decision-making theory, research, and effectiveness. In Chapter 2 we look at the behavioral aspects of problem identification, formulation, and diagnosis. The influence of perception in problem formulation and reformulation is examined, and the implications of these processes for understanding problem specification and diagnosis are explored. Chapter 3 examines the behavioral aspects of developing and evaluating alternative solutions. Here the behavioral aspects involve creativity in generating alternatives; and research on creativity stimulation methods for individuals and groups is discussed in an effort to identify the "active features" that contribute to creativity. Also, issues in modeling and evaluating alternative solutions (including value and utility) are examined. Chapter 4 looks at the behavioral aspects of evaluating and choosing in decision situations where consequences are complex, and, at times, multidimensional. Here the behavioral issues of central importance are cognitive limitations and biases which contribute to bounded rationality of decision makers, and cognitive models of judgment and choice.

In Chapter 5 we discuss the behavioral processes involved in decision situations in which the consequences are uncertain. This requires introducing the concepts of probability and risk. Here the effectiveness of human probabilistic judgment is examined, and risk-taking behaviors of individual and group decision makers are analyzed. Chapter 6 deals with the social and political aspects of organizational decision making, in which multiple decision makers typically pursue preferences that may be in conflict. Alternate approaches for explaining decision making in organizations are explored, as well as theory, research, and strategies for pooling information and the preferences of multiple decision makers are examined. Also the impact of group influences in understanding decision implementation processes is discussed. Finally, Chapter 7 points out some of the unresolved behavioral issues pertaining to behavioral decision making and suggests additional useful areas for future advances in theory, research, and practice.

2 UNDERSTANDING DECISION PROBLEMS

Before decisions can be made it is necessary to identify just what are the problems that need solving, to arrange the problem so that it can be understood, and to determine the cause or causes of the problem. The task of a decision maker is further complicated, in that typically a great many problems must be dealt with simultaneously and priorities for attempting to solve them must be set. Problem solving, then, can be viewed as comprised of two components: *understanding* (processes for comprehending problems), and *solving* (processes for resolving problems) (Hayes, 1978). The processes for understanding decision problems are discussed in this chapter; the subsequent chapters deal with problem solution.

Relatively little theoretical and research attention has been devoted to processes involved in *understanding* decisions. As Edwards (1954) pointed out some time ago, decision-making theory and research generally have focused on the activities which take place at the moment of choice (the choice point) and have tended to ignore both the activities which led up to the choice point and what happened after the choice had been made. While Edwards' comment was directed toward predecisional information search (which subsequently received more research attention), his point still holds true for the predecisional activities involved in identifying, prioritizing, formulating, and diagnosing decision problems. It seems likely that one reason for the limited research attention devoted to the events which occur prior to choosing is that many of these activities appear difficult to observe objectively and describe quantitatively. Hence, the processes involved in problem understanding do not lend themselves easily to investigation by the methods which traditionally have been used in decision-making research. The limited amount of research evidence that has been developed pertaining to problem identifying, prioritizing, formulating, and diagnosing is surveyed in this chapter.

IDENTIFYING DECISION PROBLEMS

Problem identification has sometimes been called *problem finding.* However, this term is misleading since it seems unlikely that busy managers will need to search for problems. A multitude of urgent matters generally are brought to their attention. Identifying decision problems has been depicted in the decision-making literature as the task of perceiving "gaps" between the existing state and the desired state of the decision makers in some context (Newell, et al., 1958; Reitman, 1964). Decision makers faced with the task of reducing the weight of an automobile component, for example, may identify the problem in this manner:

> **Existing State:** The current standard production steel air cleaner assembly used on 1980 and earlier Apex automobiles.
>
> **Desired State:** A lighter weight air cleaner assembly for the 1981 Apex automobile with the same or improved performance in filtering, efficiency, capacity, silencing capabilities, temperature control, and ease of adaptability to changing under-hood engine configurations.

The problem of designing a lighter air cleaner would be described as an "anticipated opportunity" in Ansoff's (1965) taxonomy of ways in which existing and desired states can change to produce decision problems. That is, the desired state changed while the existing state remained the same. Therefore, decision makers facing this situation have sought out an opportunity, rather than being forced to respond to changing conditions. He also described a type of problem in which the existing state changed while the desired state remained constant (e.g., a disequilibrium occurs in a production system) as comprising a "threat" to the decision makers. His final type of problem occurs when both existing state and desired state change simultaneously; for example, when a research and development department generates an idea for a new product.

Identifying problems as gaps is a central feature of the Kepner and Tregoe (1965) problem-analysis program in which problem-analysis activity is initiated by noting a deviation from some previously determined objective. This approach implies that conditions of disequilibrium occur to produce the deviation and, as MacCrimmon (1974) has stated, "it is difficult to see how it could be used more generally, for example, in problems involving structural changes or in open-ended problems (e.g., controlling inflation)" (p. 450).

Models for Identifying Problems

Pounds (1969) has proposed three models of managers' problem "finding" processes; these models suggest ways in which problems can be brought to the attention of decision makers. "Historical models" are based on the assumption that recent past experience is the best estimate of the immediate future, and depict managers identifying problems as departures from the trends that they have learned to expect (e.g., May sales are down 15 percent from April sales). These models tend to be much simpler than the managers' world. Hence, discrepancies which arise between the model's predictions and what actually takes place cause many false problems to be identified and true problems to be missed. Pounds has pointed out the gains in accuracy of identifying problems which can result from a more systematic and accurate "planned model."

Planning models involve making annual projections of operating variables for the coming year and less detailed projections for the next five years. In some instances planning models have provided the basis for problem identification through management by objectives (MBO) programs. While, at least for large-scale problems, formal use of planning models appears to be a better approach to identifying problems than are the historical models, Pounds found that the planning model contributed relatively little to problem finding in the organization he studied. Historical models had a greater influence on the problem-identification activities of managers. A final type of problem identification model is called "other peoples' model," and suggests that many problems arise from discrepancies perceived by people other than the decision makers. Customers identify problems involving product quality and bosses set standards which may identify problems for subordinates.

Biases in Identifying Problems

The research on behavioral decision making has explored two major types of bias that can hamper problem identification—informational bias and perceptual bias. The informational bias occurs when information reaches decision makers in a misleading or distorted manner. Perceptual bias can be attributed to limitations in perceptual abilities of decision makers. These two types of biases in identifying problems are discussed below.

Informational bias. The informational base used to identify problems can contain biases which may mislead decision makers. This topic has received some research attention in the context of communication upward in organizational hierarchies (Cohen, 1958). The MUM effect (keeping *M*um about *U*ndesirable *M*essages to the recipient) has been studied by Rosen and Tesser (1969). In their experiments subjects were found to be more reluctant to communicate information perceived by them as negative for the recipient than to communicate positive information. While this study did not involve communication up the hierarchy of an organization, when the information may reflect adversely upon the job performance of a subordinate, it would seem to be an even stronger effect.

Another way in which information tends to be distorted is through *uncertainty absorption* (Woods, 1966). As information is acquired, it is passed along to the various decision-making units involved. During transmission it tends to lose some of its uncertainty and attains a false aura of precision. Units further along the line of transmittal, where decisions must be made, frequently are not informed of the high degree of uncertainty that actually exists. Although this distortion appears to be very pervasive in organizations, no published research has been directed toward understanding either its causes or the influences it may exert upon problem finding or other aspects of decision making.

Perceptual bias. The important role of perceptual processes in identifying problems is evident when we consider that there are no decision problems which are necessarily problems for everyone. A military conscription policy limiting eligibility for draft to 18-year-olds may be viewed by those facing the prospect of military service as far from ideal and a decision problem that should be addressed. To other people in the society, however, it may be completely satisfactory and not a decision problem. If the rules pertaining to eligibility for draft are changed, thus requiring other age groups to serve in the military forces, then those people who find themselves facing military service under the revised regulations may perceive that a decision problem exists—but they may have different desired states. Indeed, each of the decision makers will perceive the problem from the perspective of their own beliefs, values, and resources.

Perception can be thought of, in general terms, as the total process of receiving and interpreting information from either the decision makers' external or internal environment. *External* and *internal* in this sense mean with respect to the body itself. The decision makers selectively filter information. To the environmental stimuli are added their prior experiences which are relevant to the immediate problem. The process of receiving and interpreting information concerning the existing and desired states that identify a problem is greatly influenced by the decision makers' perceptual characteristics.

The perception of problems is a selective process. Information is selectively perceived, in part, because the decision makers are not capable of assimilating all of the stimuli to which they are exposed. In addition, decision makers have revealed systematic tendencies to seek or avoid certain types of information from the stimulus field. For example, research using the Rokeach Dogmatism Scale (Rokeach, 1960) supports the view that dogmatic decision makers (i.e., with closed belief systems) are characterized by limited information input (e.g., Block & Petersen, 1955; Brengelmann, 1959); this has been interpreted as reflecting a defense mechanism which shields the decision makers from information which may threaten their self-images (Long & Ziller, 1965). In addition to being selective in attending to stimuli, the decision makers attempt to order the stimuli into a meaningful set of subjective classifications. Stimuli are interpreted, using their past experience and knowledge, and these interpretations form the basis for actions directed toward attaining their objectives.

Considerable evidence exists to indicate that decision makers either consciously or unconsciously distort their perceptions of the uncertain aspects of their decision environment. Psychological experiments have demonstrated that high levels of uncertainty can produce considerable anxiety, and that individuals tend to ignore the more uncertain features of their environments in an effort to reduce anxiety (Rokeach, 1960). An illustration of the tendency to ignore potentially hazardous, but uncertain, aspects of the decision environment is shown in White's (1964) report of how people living on flood plains may disregard relatively infrequent flood threats. Similarly, Cyert and March (1963) described how business firms tend to neglect consideration of sources of uncertainty, perhaps in an implicit avoidance strategy. Decision makers frequently act as if events are more certain than they actually are. For example, Carter (1971) demonstrated several attempts of a computer software firm to reduce perceptions of uncertainty. And, although there is abundant evidence to suggest that it is not true, business firms have shown a tendency to behave as though interest rates, unemployment policy, and other aspects of their decision environment will remain in the future at the same levels that they had been in the past (Cyert & De-Groot, 1970).

Research into interpersonal perception, which has examined the use or misuse of learned perceptual categories, is relevant to problem finding when decisions about other people are being made. In addition to perceptual defense, which was illustrated in the above discussion of dogmatic personality, there are two main ways in which the decision maker's perceptual processes tend to systematically distort information about other people—selective perception and stereotyping.

Selective perceptions of managers were examined by Dearborn and Simon (1958) in an effort to identify the influence of departmental affiliations on the types of problems managers viewed as most urgent in a case study. The managers were classified for the study as representing sales, production, accounting, and a miscellaneous group made up of personnel, public relations, and other department members. The managers were asked to specify the major problem that faced the new president of a steel company. Since the problem to be selected was also described as the most urgent problem, which may not be the same as the major problem, some confusion may have been introduced into the responses. Nevertheless, as can be seen in Exhibit 2.1, the managers tended to identify problems from their own departments as the major ones. These results are consistent with the operation of a selective perception by which managers see problems related to their own training and objectives as the most important problems.

EXHIBIT 2.1 Selective Perception of Executives

DEPARTMENT	TOTAL NUMBER OF EXECUTIVES	SALES	"CLARIFY ORGANIZATION"	HUMAN RELATIONS
Sales	6	5	1	0
Production	5	1	4	0
Accounting	4	3	0	0
Miscellaneous	8	1	3	3
Totals	23	10	8	3

Source: Dearborn, D. C. & Simon, H. A. "Selective perception: A note on the departmental identification of executives." *Sociometry*, 1958, 21, 143.

Stereotyping involves making decisions about other people on the basis of a prominent characteristic (e.g., sex, race, age). The advantage of stereotyping, when it permits accurate judgment of other characteristics or behaviors of the person, is that it very efficiently categorizes information. The danger of stereotyping, when it is based on false premises, is that it leads to a distorted view of problem characteristics. Stereotyping on the basis of age, race, and sex in work organizations has received some research attention. The research approach used was similar to that of the studies of decision making in the employment interview (see Mayfield, 1964, for a useful review of these studies); it involved having subjects make decisions about hiring, promoting, or otherwise dealing with a person described in a dossier or shown in a film.

Terborg and Ilgen (1975) have described a typical study in which hiring decisions were made on the basis of information contained in matched pairs of dossiers, which differed only in that one in each set had a male name and the other a female name. The dossier with a male name was more likely to be hired. It seems evident from these studies that older workers, females, and minority-group workers are victims of negative stereotypes in the workplace. These stereotypes can be troublesome in identifying problems in organizations; for example, attempting to predict the capabilities of employees on the basis of inaccurate stereotypes is likely to lead to misperceptions in setting levels of performance.

Motivation and Identifying Problems

Motivational levels also influence the manner in which problems are identified. Stress and information overload affect a decision maker's state of attention and ability to cope with the information demands of a decision task. Aspiration levels also influence decision making through the setting of standards which decisions must achieve, or target levels which trigger decision-making activity. Each of these aspects of motivation is discussed in turn.

Stress and overload. Decision makers must be motivated to identify problems, and motivation in this context generally has been depicted as the decision maker's level of stress. The impact of environmental stress, which is felt to operate upon the individual's level of arousal, is reflected by the Yerkes-Dodson Law shown in Exhibit 2.2. This curve describes the optimum arousal level for a task, and

EXHIBIT 2.2 The Yerkes-Dodson Law of Optimal Arousal Level for Task Performance

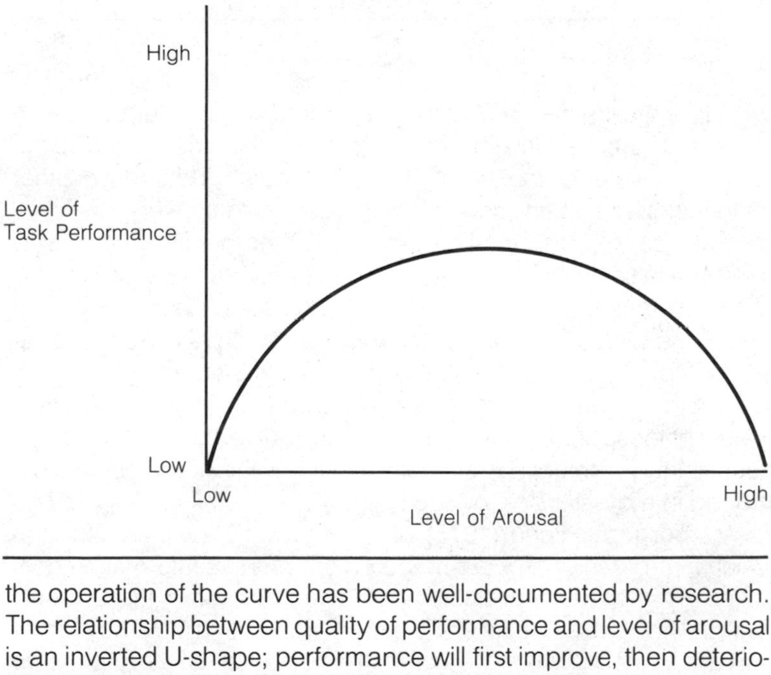

the operation of the curve has been well-documented by research. The relationship between quality of performance and level of arousal is an inverted U-shape; performance will first improve, then deteriorate as arousal increases from its lowest to highest levels. The best performance by decision makers would occur under conditions of intermediate levels of stress. Remove all stress, and the people become bored and lose alertness. Or they may exhibit some of the hallucinations and cognitive deficit sometimes reported in studies of sensory deprivation. Individuals would also be expected to do poorly at very high levels of stress. Increase the information load to the point where it is impossible for the individuals to keep up with the demands placed upon them, and performance again deteriorates. A person's best performance and the conditions of work that are reported as most challenging, stimulating, and conducive to maximum effort are found between these extremes.

Investigations of motivational effects on problem solving have taken one of two approaches. Either subjects with different levels of general arousal (usually measured by a test of general anxiety) are identified and these differences are correlated with problem-solving performance, or conditions designed to produce different levels of arousal are created (e.g., giving stress-inducing instructions or offering money for superior performance).

An attribute of the decision environment moderating the relationship between stress and task performance is the difficulty of the task. As the difficulty of the decision is increased, a lower level of arousal is likely to be optimal. The rationale is that the motivational level must be high enough to arouse the correct habits, but not so high as to bring additional competing habits into play. So the effect of arousal would be expected to differ depending upon the habit strength of the responses (Spence, 1956).

Glucksberg (1962), for example, used two difficulty levels of the candle problem, shown in Exhibit 2.3 (next page), to study the interaction of task difficulty and motivational level. Motivation was manipulated through instructions; in the *low-arousal* condition, individuals were given neutral instructions, whereas in the *high-arousal* condition, they were told they could get money for fast solutions (up to $20). High arousal impaired solution of the difficult box-filled version, but increasing arousal had no effect on performance with the easy, box-empty version.

One explanation of the relationship between stress and task difficulty in determining problem-solving performance involves taking into account both the stress produced by the decision environment and the chronic anxiety level of the problem solvers. A number of studies have indicated that performance on problem-solving tasks (including anagrams and insight problems) is not directly related to individual differences in general anxiety (e.g., Mendelsohn, Griswold, & Anderson, 1966).

However, if subjects are differentiated on the basis of test anxiety (the tendency to become anxious in test situations) rather than on general anxiety, high test-anxious subjects usually perform more poorly (e.g., Harleston, 1963); Russell & Sarason, 1965). Sarason (1961) found that stress-inducing instructions impaired the performance of high-anxious subjects to a greater extent (by telling subjects that anagrams measured intelligence, the performance difference favoring low-anxious subjects was increased). Yet, Russell and Sarason (1965) found that giving neutral and stressful instructional conditions had no effect. Since both optimal level and arousal for the tasks and the levels produced by the experimental manipulations may have differed in the studies, this lack of agreement in the findings may not be contradictory.

EXHIBIT 2.3 The Candle Problem. The subject is shown a candle, a book of matches, and a box of tacks on a table; the instructions are to fasten the candle to the wall so that it burns properly. In the box-full condition, tacks are in the box; in the box-empty condition, tacks are on the table. The challenge is to see the box as a candle supporter rather than as a container for tacks.

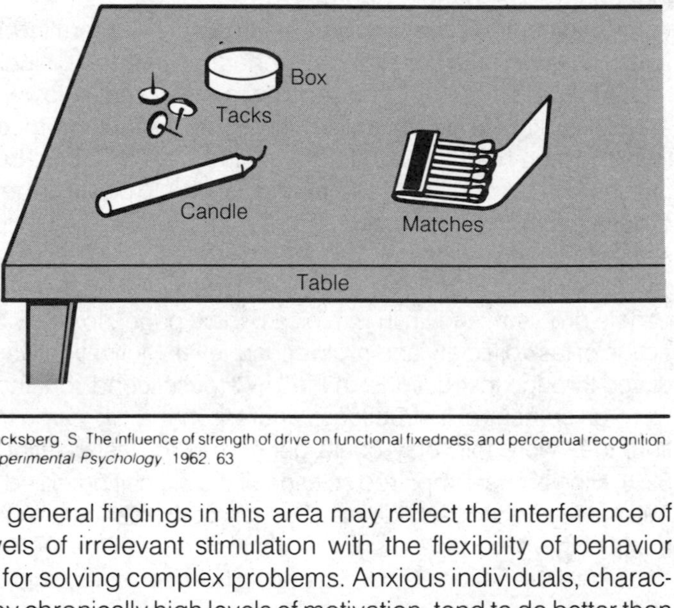

Source: Glucksberg, S. The influence of strength of drive on functional fixedness and perceptual recognition. *Journal of Experimental Psychology*, 1962, 63.

The general findings in this area may reflect the interference of high levels of irrelevant stimulation with the flexibility of behavior needed for solving complex problems. Anxious individuals, characterized by chronically high levels of motivation, tend to do better than low-anxiety individuals on simple learning tasks such as classical conditioning. The high level of motivation apparently helps in this case. On complex learning tasks they do no better, or perhaps worse, than low-anxiety individuals, particularly on tasks requiring novel responses (Cofer & Appley, 1964).

Aspiration level. If problems are to be correctly identified, desired states must be set at appropriate levels. The desired state can be viewed as a level of aspiration held by a decision maker; that is, a threshold the decision maker attempts to attain (Siegel, 1957).

Therefore, level of aspiration determines the standard against which the existing state in a decision problem is judged. In this manner, potential problems are identified. Problem solving is initiated when the perceived gap between a desired state and an existing state surpasses a minimal threshold of deviation and seriousness. Therefore, aspiration levels held by decision makers figure prominently in initiating decision-making activity. Helson's (1948) hypothesis of par generally has been used to depict the impact of aspiration level on task performance. According to this theory, individuals set standards for themselves—usually the standards are below their capability—and they attempt to meet, but not exceed, these standards. Setting aspiration levels too low means they can be easily achieved, but they do not serve as appropriate standards in problem recognition; nor do they effectively motivate performance. Setting aspiration levels too highs simply leads to frustration when decision makers are unable to attain them. Aspiration levels also figure importantly in determining the effectiveness of corporate strategy decisions, as has been demonstrated by Hansberger (1969).

It is misleading to view states which define problems as representing a single dimension—representing profit maximization, for example—as the only objective of the firm in classical theory. In actuality, both firms and individual managers pursue many goals, and each goal can suggest deviations from standards which specify problems. Firms try to achieve profitability, market share, return on investment, and a great many other goals (Drucker, 1963; Johnsen, 1968; Carter, 1971).

SETTING PRIORITIES FOR SOLVING PROBLEMS

The many dimensions of existing and desired states which confront decision makers imply many gaps and problems corresponding to these gaps. Although Cyert and March (1963) have suggested that attention can sequentially shift from one gap to another, in an effort to identify problems while not exceeding the decision makers' information-processing capacity, it is clear that cognitive limitations prevent decision makers from dealing with many different things at the same time (Miller, 1956; Simon, 1957). Hence, decision makers must monitor stimuli to detect problems and set priorities for solution attempts among the problems they identify.

Assessment of the importance and urgency of problems suggests that problems which are urgent and important should receive high priority, and problems which are of low importance and not urgent should be given low priority. Problems which are urgent, but of low importance (and vice versa), challenge the decision makers' ability to set priorities. Pounds (1969) found that, when they were asked, "Which problems do you usually get to first: time deadline, big payoff, or personal interest?'' forty-three of the fifty-two managers he questioned said, ''Time deadline.''

Drucker (1963) has noted that threats (i.e., the existing state changes while the desired state stays the same) are more readily perceived than opportunities (i.e., the desired state changes and existing state remains constant). Consequently, threats may become the overwhelming concern of inefficient managers and may lead to decision strategies characterized by avoidance, crisis management, and firefighting rather than aggressive confrontation of problems.

However, the one-factor models for determining problem-solving priorities implied by these behaviors do not appear to be very effective. Phillips (1969) specified both need for a solution and perceived solvability as essential prerequisites for emergence of problem-solving activity. Logically, one would expect effective decision makers to choose among the problems competing for their attention on the basis of the size of the gap that is perceived, the degree to which the problem seems to be solvable, the urgency of its solution, and, in general, just how important the reduction of such a gap is in achieving the decision makers' further ends.

FORMULATING OR REFORMULATING PROBLEMS

Frequently, problems cannot be solved in the form in which they are found by a decision maker. Rather, it is necessary to restructure the decision problem in some manner prior to its solution. In this section models for formulating problems are examined, as well as issues involved in reformulating *discovery problems* (in which the structure of the problem becomes apparent only after solution attempts have begun); finally, issues in decomposing into subproblems are explored.

Models for Formulating Decision Problems

The manner in which the problem is represented can make a great difference in the success of decision making. Some problems are difficult to understand by simply examining the problem characteristics; they can best be understood by trial and error attempts to solve them (jumping in). Another approach for understanding a problem is to decompose a complex problem to achieve a simpler form. In this section we discuss issues related to each of these approaches to understanding problems by formulating or reformulating them.

Representing problems. Understanding problems can be aided by clearly representing their features. Representations of problems can be elaborate models or can be quite simple; they can be useful at various points in the decision-making process. While

Churchman, Ackoff, and Arnoff (1957) have suggested that model building is most useful after a problem has been formulated, Pounds (1969) saw model building as an essential step in problem definition. Pounds explained this position by saying, "It is impossible to know, for example, that cost is too high unless one has some basis (a model) which suggests it might be lower. This basis might be one's own experience, the experience of a competitor, or the output of a scientific model. Similarly, one cannot be sure that his distribution costs will be reduced by linear programming until a model is constructed and solved which suggests that rescheduling will lower costs" (p. 129).

Reformulating discovery problems. Making decisions frequently requires "jumping into" the problem by attempting to solve the problem before it has been clearly formulated. By attempting trial and error solutions, the decision maker can learn about the problem—what are the operators, how troublesome are the constraints, and how interconnected are the aspects of the problem. This approach is quite helpful with very large problems that contain either too many components to deal with at one time or those in which the decision maker cannot look far enough ahead to determine the consequences of incorrect solutions (Simon, 1973). Hayes (1978) has called these *discovery problems.* "A discovery problem is the sort of ill-defined problem in which the problem solver's attempts to solve the problem reveal that the initial formulation of the problem was inadequate" (p. 213). Most management problems are discovery problems, and involve changing the problem formulation as a result of experience in attempting to solve them.

Decomposing into subproblems. When large problems contain subproblems that are not highly interconnected, Simon (1961) has suggested that it is useful to reformulate the problem through decomposition. For example, a watchmaker will be more productive if he puts together preassembled subparts than if he assembles an entire clock one part at a time (Simon, 1961). In addition to the complexity of the assembly task, it is also likely that the watchmaker will be interrupted during the task; each of these problem features contributes to the benefits of factoring into subproblems. On the other hand, when the subparts are highly interconnected, the difficulties in coordinating may outweigh the advantages of decomposing.

Decomposition into subproblems is shown in the movement of a military unit:

Actual State

A field artillery cannon battery is in position, engaged in providing fire support to the infantry battalion to which it is assigned as direct support. The battery commander is called to battalion headquarters and notified that the infantry will be moving laterally and forward and, consequently, his battery must move a considerable distance (approximately forty kilometers) and be in position, ready to fire, no later than 2000 hours. The battery must be prepared to operate on its own, without resupply for at least two days. It is now 1430 hours.

Desired State

The battery must be in the new position, ready to fire within five hours (2000 hours). It must be supplied with ammunition, fuel, and food for the next two days.

Other Information

Restrictions on radio transmission allow use only in emergencies. The battery has limited ability to preserve perishable foodstuffs and is low on ammunition and fuel.

Reformulation of Problem

The problem can be broken down into several subproblems:

1. The problem of refueling, rearming, and drawing rations for two days prior to leaving present position. These rations should be mostly C-Rations, since they do not require refrigeration.
2. The problem of preparing the main force of the battery for movement. This includes maintenance of equipment, feeding of personnel, etc.
3. Formation of a reconnaissance party and the movement to the advance area where the selection of primary and alternative positions will take place.
4. Coordination of battery movement plan before reconnaissance due to radio usage restrictions.
5. Coordination of final guidance of main body into advance position for a rapid occupation.
6. Coordination with supported infantry battalion via fire support officer and battery forward observers.
7. Coordination with battalion for movement times, routes of march, resupply, etc.

Simon (1969) has pointed out that factoring large problems facilitates their solution by permitting the subproblems to be solved in parallel by one or more decision makers. For example, specialization and division of labor are based upon this principle and can be used most effectively when the decision-making unit is made up of individuals who have different capabilities. Although much research has been conducted on decomposition in task design, relatively little education has been devoted to its use in decision-making tasks.

Biases in Formulating Decision Problems

Finding and formulating a problem for solution requires that the constraints which bound the problem be considered. Decision makers' perceptions of attributes in the problem would be expected to determine the extent to which they recognize a problem and the nature of the constraints associated with the problem. Yet, the influence of the decision makers' perceptual processes as a source of constraint on problem solving has received relatively little systematic attention.

Problem-solving sets. Through such mechanisms as *psychological set,* the previous decision-making experiences of individuals can shape the constraints perceived for subsequent problems. *Transfer effects* refer to the influence of decision makers' previous experiences on the way they respond to a current problem. Prior experiences can either facilitate (i.e., positive transfer) or inhibit (i.e., negative transfer) decision making. For example, a promotional campaign used successfully with one product may also prove successful with another product. Conversely, the behavior of a businessperson accustomed to a highly affiliative secretary may be offensive to a replacement.

One type of transfer of learning is a *problem-solving set.* A problem-solving set is usually specific to a single decision rule (punt on fourth down) or strategy (allow participation of subordinates in making managerial decisions). Therefore, it is a more restricted learned response than the broad notion of "learning to learn" or "learning to solve problems." Response sets which influence problem-solving approaches have been reported in describing the satisficing decision maker (Simon, 1960), as well as in examining decision-maker traits such as cognitive styles (Benbasat & Taylor, 1978), dogmatism (Rokeach, 1960), and risk-taking propensity (Kogan & Wallach, 1964).

Theories of problem-solving sets. Bourne and his associates (1979) provide a good review of the information-processing and associative-learning theories' views of the development of problem-solving sets. These theories differ sharply in the mechanisms posited to underlie formation and operation of sets. The information-processing viewpoint has little to say about how problem-solving sets are initially formed, but it describes how a program representing such sets can be modified by experience. Solution attempts and their outcomes are cognitively stored, and a subproblem encountered a second time in the course of a solution attempt will be remembered as "tried and failed," and thus will not be tried again. Learning of premises through generalization occurs by remembering which solutions have proven successful in the past for particular decision problems.

A key heuristic of this theory is trying methods in order of their probabilities of success now (based on their success with previous problems). Newell, Shaw, and Simon (1965) have shown that these programs based on problem-solving sets can be highly effective in solving problems. Research on the Logic Theorist (a program for proving theorems in symbolic logic) has shown that the storage of previously proven theorems produces profound changes in the problem-solving capabilities of the Logic Theorist. Information-processing theory, then, has dealt primarily with describing how an existing organization of problem-solving processes operates, and little is known about how to specify the manner in which an organization should be changed in order to improve decision making.

The associative-learning approach to explaining the operation of problem-solving sets can be contrasted to the information-processing viewpoint because it uses classical and instrumental conditioning principles and operates through such cognitive processes as transfer, set, and functional fixedness. In associative-learning theory, problem solving can be described as stimulus-response associations that are established—and subsequently operate—according to the principles of conditioning. Essentially, problem solving is viewed by the associative approach as a rearrangement of the hierarchy of response sets due to reinforced (successful) applications of certain responses (solution attempts) in previous problem-solving experiences. Both of these theories of problem identifying and formulating predict that prior experiences of decision makers result in learned responses which predispose them to apply previously successful solutions to any future problems that are perceived as identical.

Generally, problem-solving sets have been regarded as undesirable in decision making, but they actually have the potential to either help or hinder the decision maker. It depends upon the applicability of the set to the problem. The set *use participative management* would be an aid in situations where it was critical that subordinates accept a decision, but would be a hindrance in situations where it was unimportant that subordinates accept a decision and the decision must be made rapidly. Great efficiencies can be attained when solving well-structured problems by correctly identifying a problem as similar to another and using standard solutions that have been developed for the first (Taylor, 1975). This type of problem is examined below.

Reformulating Problems by Manipulating Constraints

Problem structure typically has been formulated as a continuum ranging from *ill-structured* to *well-structured* problems (Simon, 1960; Minsky, 1961). Well-structured problems frequently can be solved as they are found, but ill-structured problems must be reformulated before they can be solved. In solving well-structured problems, the decision makers are given all the elements required for their solutions—a clear starting point, a clear end point, and techniques for bridging the gap between these points. On the other hand, ill-structured problems do not provide the elements needed to solve them, and decision makers must learn more about the problems in order to close the open constraints. Closing the open constraints accurately may lead to solutions, but imposing or closing constraints inappropriately may make the problems impossible to solve (Reitman, 1964; Taylor, 1975).

Implicit vs. explicit constraints. Problem constraints can be either implicit or explicit. Implicit constraints are informally held, frequently without the decision makers' awareness of the impact on their behavior. Stereotypes concerning male and female job applicants may represent implicit constraints held by some employment interviewers. Other constraints may be explicitly stated (e.g., hire only college graduates).

If they are justified, implicit constraints can facilitate problem solving, but it is difficult to verify them as long as they are implicitly held. Explicitly held constraints, on the other hand, are formally stated by decision makers (at least to themselves) and can be examined to determine the extent to which they are justified and contribute to accurate decision making. While any implicit stereotypes held by employment interviewers would be very difficult to test for validity (i.e., their contribution to correctly predicting success on the job), explicit constraints on hiring decisions can be validated and consistently applied by many interviewers. One approach to reformulating problems is through explicitly stating constraints and determining, where feasible, their justification. As problem solving progresses such constraints could then be opened or closed.

Well-structured vs. ill-structured problems and solution strategies. It is important to consider the nature of problem ill-structuredness in reformulating ill-structured problems. Reitman (1964) has identified problems according to a three-component vector; the initial state (A), the terminal state (B), and the transformation (→). A problem is *defined* by describing the problem attributes as a vector (A,B,→). Using Reitman's problem taxonomy, the initial state is usually described in terms of the current state of the decision makers or the resources available. Next, the terminal state is described as the target or goal they desire to attain. Finally, the transformations (operators) are processes by which the decision makers can move from initial state to terminal state.

Lee (1971) pointed out that this three-component structure closely resembles the notion of a transformation as used by Ashby (1956) and others. The three-component vector (A,B,→) can be interpreted as a generalization of the stimulus-response-stimulus unit which has been used in MacCorquodale and Meehl's (1954) cognitive theory of learning. It also resembles the analytic conceptions Allport (1955) has used in describing cognitive structure in terms of ongoings and events.

Whether a decision problem is viewed as well-structured or ill-structured depends on the extent to which the decision makers are familiar with the initial state, terminal state, and operators. Familiarity with a problem can be as a result of such experiences as prior problem-solving experience, education, or awareness of the availability of such resources as a program library. It is essential that decision makers recognize that a familiar problem has previously been solved (MacCrimmon & Taylor 1976). The influence of the decision makers' familiarity with each component of a problem on their perception of problem structure has been discussed by Taylor (1974), and is depicted in the typology shown in Exhibit 2.4.

EXHIBIT 2.4. Types of Problem Constraints

PROBLEM TYPE		INITIAL STATE	TERMINAL STATE	TRANS-FORMATION
Type I	Resource Specification Problems	Unfamiliar	Either	Either
Type II	Goal Specification Problems	Either	Unfamiliar	Either
Type III	Creative Problems	Either	Either	Unfamiliar
Type IV	Well-Structured Problems	Familiar	Familiar	Familiar

Source: Taylor, R. N. "Nature of problem ill-structuredness: Implications for problem formulation and solution." *Decision Sciences,* 1974, 5, 633.

On the one hand, there are decision problems in which the decision makers are unfamiliar with the initial state (Type I, Resource Specification Problems), the desired state (Type II, Goal Specification Problems), the set of relevant operators for solving the problem (Type III, Creative Problems), or some combination of these three components. These are situations with which we may be partially familiar and which we must reformulate by appropriately closing the open constraints associated with the unfamiliar components. On the other hand, in some problems all three of these components are familiar to the decision makers (Type IV, Well-Structured Problems).

By modifying problem structure through opening or closing constraints, it is possible to prescribe an approach to problem reformulation which is appropriate to each type of problem structure. This discussion is simplified to emphasize the underlying processes in problem reformulation. A complete exposition of problem formulation must deal with such additional issues as the degree to which decision makers are unfamiliar with each component, the various combinations of elements which are unfamiliar, and the more realistic approach involving ascertaining the complete problem prior to considering reformulation. The four classes of decision problems described by Taylor (1974) are summarized below.

Resource specification problems. Resource specification problems are characterized by an unfamiliar initial state and either familiar or unfamiliar terminal state and operators. Career counseling in order to acquaint job seekers with their own capabilities represents an example of this type of problem. In reformulating these problems, emphasis is placed on completely specifying the initial state, or current resources, of decision makers. Two approaches frequently are used: the decision makers may seek further information regarding the current state or, in the absence of such information, may project backward from the familiar desired state to develop transformations which will lead to the initial state (Feldman and Kanter, 1965; Miller, Galanter, and Pribram, 1960). To get the decision makers where they want to be, such transformations can be applied in reverse. As Fischhoff (1969) has stated, hindsight provides a different view of a problem than does foresight. By hypothetically placing ourselves in the perspective of having a solved problem, we may gain insights into its solution. This appears to operate on the basis of the individual's tendency to make sense of outcome knowledge by integrating it into what is already known.

Closing constraints regarding initial states frequently involves examining the desired solution and considering what previous step must have been taken to have arrived there. From that step, the step immediately prior to it is determined, and so on, hopefully back to the starting point represented by the unfamiliar initial state. In playing chess, for example, a player might notice that winning is certain from a particular position on the board, then proceed by determining how that position can be produced from another position; in a sense checking to see if the current position can be generated by working backward from the winning position. Working backward has proved to be helpful in dynamic programming (Bellman & Dreyfus, 1962) and in solving visual problems such as deciding routes from one location to another on a map.

Goal specification problems. Goal specification problems confront decision makers with a familiar initial state, but a terminal state that they have not encountered before. Planning and goal setting problems are of this type. The unfamiliar terminal state is the focus for problem reformulation, and this can proceed by setting a goal or acquiring knowledge of available goals. The decision makers' amount of knowledge generally determines how decision situations of this type will be handled. For example, if the initial state is very familiar, but the desired state or operators are unfamiliar, incremental moves out from the current position may be tried, testing to see if the movement is in the right direction (Lindblom, 1959). How familiar the transformation is depends upon how close the different terminal state is to terminal states that have been confronted in the past. When only slight differences are perceived, standard operators, if available, should be applied.

Using successive limited comparisons decision makers may attempt to take only small steps (increments) away from the existing state toward the desired state. Since few objectives need to be considered, this approach is useful in reformulating problems in which objectives are difficult to specify. In fact, to use this approach it is not necessary even to perceive a problem as a gap between initial and desired states. Decision makers focus on differences between the consequences of the current policy or state and the consequences of the alternative actions or policies under consideration.

Margin-dependent choice suggests that it is only necessary to state how much of one value decision makers are willing to sacrifice, at the margin existing in a given situation, to achieve an increment of another value (e.g., inflation vs. unemployment). Therefore disjointed incrementalism (Braybrooke and Lindblom, 1963) does not require goals to be specified as completely as do the more formal approaches to decision making (in which all alternative courses of action must be ranked in order of preference). Yet, to use the principle of margin-dependent choice, it is necessary to compare on a common scale the major possible outcomes of many incrementally different decision alternatives. Typically, disjointed incrementalism involves the simultaneous development of means and ends and a series of analyses and evaluations to shift policies incrementally. The major uses of this approach have been in governmental policy decisions.

Creative problems. Creative problems are either problems which the decision maker has not solved before, or for which the familiar solution is no longer available. An example of this type of problem is developing a new fuel for powering automobiles when faced with depleted supplies of petroleum. The task is to discover ways to successfully close constraints with regard to selecting an appropriate operator (e.g., names for a new product, rapid transit concepts, etc.). More alternative solutions must be developed; in addition they must be *creative.* Creativity and techniques for stimulating creativity are discussed in the next chapter as we explore ways to generate creative decision alternatives.

Well-structured problems. In some well-structured problems the decision maker already is familiar with the initial state, terminal state, and successful operators. In this case the problem has been previously solved and that solution will be used again. Other well-structured problems become well-structured by reformulating. Primary well-structured problems are of the routine type that the decision maker has solved in the past, and the same solution is used again. Personal habits and business SOPs (Standard Operating Procedures) are routine solutions to well-structured problems.

When the problem is correctly identified as well-structured, no problem reformulation is needed, and the standard solution should be used. Yet, a tendency to use routine responses which are not fully appropriate to the problem has frequently been observed. The much-criticized lack of adaptability of bureaucratic SOPs represents the operation of unjustified constraints. When problems have been inaccurately perceived as well-structured, it would be advisable to open the unjustified constraints and attempt to find a solution of higher quality than the standard response.

DETERMINING PROBLEM CAUSES

Diagnosing problems requires determining causal relationships among the variables in the problem. While our discussion of the manipulation of problem constraints above included some of the issues typically associated with problem diagnosis, it is useful to focus now upon two processes specific to finding the cause of problems. These are: 1) distinguishing the immediate problem from the total problem matrix, and 2) examining changes in the decision environment or the decision maker which may have caused the problem.

Distinguishing the Immediate Problem from the Total Problem Matrix

Reitman (1964) has suggested that problem diagnosis can be furthered by carefully distinguishing the immediate problem from the rest of the total problem situation. While many factors may be present in the problem situation, not all are causally linked to the problem. Kepner and Tregoe (1965) have described an approach to problem analysis in which a decision maker systematically attempts to describe the out-of-control part of the decision situation and the in-control part. After determining what "is" and "is not" part of the problem, the decision maker looks for the factors in the decision situation that will explain the "is" part and discriminate it from the "is not" part. The factors which most completely explain the deviation are considered to be the causes of the problem.

Changes Cause Problems

In addition to identifying what is or is not part of the problem, Kepner and Tregoe (1965) have suggested that changes in desired and existing states must be the result of other changes in the decision situation. Therefore, a fruitful place to look for the causes of a problem is in changes in other features of the problem situation (personnel, materials, procedures, etc.). In some instances the decision maker may have made changes which caused the present problem (e.g., implementing previous solutions may cause subsequent problems); in other instances the problems are caused by factors in the decision environment (e.g., a new pay system for the organization may cause employee morale to decline). Therefore, changes are systematically probed until an equilibrium restoring action can be found.

SUMMARY

Issues in understanding decision problems have been examined briefly in this chapter. The major processes in understanding problems are specifying the problems, formulating problems into a structure which will facilitate solutions, and diagnosing problems to determine their causes. Problems are typically described as ''gaps'' between initial states and desired states as viewed by a decision maker. The perceptual and motivational processes of individuals influence the types of problems they identify, the urgency they give to solving various problems, the manner in which they formulate problems, and their attempts to diagnose problems.

Problems can be well-structured, or they may exhibit ill-structuredness due to their novelty for a decision maker. Well-structured problems are familiar to the decision maker and are most efficiently solved by standard responses. SOPs and program libraries are appropriate ways to solve well-structured problems. The danger, however, is that problems may be incorrectly viewed as well-structured and the standard responses may be ineffective. Ill-structured problems can be reformulated by appropriately manipulating problem constraints. Three types of ill-structured problems were examined and issues in reformulating them were discussed. Reformulation of *resource specification problems* can proceed by working backward and using means-end analysis. *Goal specification problems* can be reformulated by goal setting; some of the difficulties they present can be bypassed by use of disjointed incrementalism. *Creative problems* require that new and novel solutions be developed; Chapter 3 discusses the issues involved in developing creative decision alternatives. Two remaining issues related to problem diagnosis—distinguishing the immediate problem from the total problem matrix and identifying changes as causes of problems—were discussed.

Problem *understanding* has received very limited attention in the research literature and almost no theories have been proposed to explain the processes involved in this very important aspect of decision making. Theoretical and research advances clearly have been made in the study of perception, motivation, and other psychological processes which are logically related to problem solving. As yet, however, it is difficult to generalize these advances to complex problem-solving environments. On the other hand, techniques have been prescribed for problem *understanding.* Yet, seldom do these techniques rest upon a solid research basis to explain why the techniques work, the conditions under which they are appropriately used, and the extent of their contributions to problem understanding. This is in sharp contrast to the substantial contributions which have been made toward development of normative and descriptive theories and research related to problem *solving.* Clearly, problem *understanding* remains an important aspect of decision making which urgently requires theoretical and research attention.

3 CONSIDERING ALTERNATIVE SOLUTIONS

A decision maker must choose among the courses of action that are available; these have been called *alternative solutions, decision alternatives,* or merely *alternatives.* In depicting problems as "gaps" between initial and desired states, alternatives are the operators which may resolve the gap. Alternatives may involve actions (e.g., order coffee with cream, or open a new plant). In effect, however, a decision may be to take no action (e.g., leave things as they are). Refraining from reaching a decision also is an alternative, and the consequences of "no decision" can be evaluated. Alternatives can be single actions (e.g., play the Ace) or can be complex consequences of activities (e.g., declare war).

Alternatives vary tremendously in complexity, ranging from as simple as which ball point pen to purchase to the highly complex alternative sites for a new manufacturing plant. Yet, some common features which are involved in generating and evaluating the quality of any type of alternative can be identified. In this chapter, we will highlight some of the central issues in generating alternatives, describing their attributes, and evaluating their quality. In well-structured problems standard alternatives are routinely applied; ill-structured problems in which appropriate solutions are unknown to the decision maker require that creative alternatives be generated. Preparing a framework for choice among alternatives requires that the decision maker's goals be reflected in decision criteria and that the quality of alternatives be measured along the dimensions represented by the criteria. Finally, the notion of rational choice is explored and the choice modes available to decision makers are explained.

USING ALGORITHMS AND HEURISTICS IN WELL-STRUCTURED PROBLEMS

Routine solutions to various types of problems are analogous to computer programs (March & Simon, 1958) in that they can be specified in advance and called forth as each problem arises. The storage of standard solutions in organizations is much like the operation of a program library, except that it may exist solely in the minds of the organization's members. At times, written records may exist in the form of standard operating procedures or organizational manuals. The processes through which standard operating procedures operate in government and private organizations were discussed by Cyert and March (1963). Essentially, standard programs are designed to minimize variability in organizational performance by insuring that all people in a particular job will carry out a standard series of operations (Cyert & MacCrimmon, 1968).

Algorithms and Heuristics

Standard solutions may involve either *algorithms* or *heuristics.* Algorithms are sets of standard procedures that guarantee solutions to problems. For example, the rules of mathematics are algorithms. In complex decisions, however, algorithms can seldom be developed. Even in the game of chess, which is characterized by perfect information, since all moves and their consequences can be specified (Von Neumann & Morgenstern, 1944), an algorithm cannot be used because the computational requirements are prohibitive.

Heuristics, on the other hand, are extremely useful in solving complex but well-structured problems. The word *heuristics* is derived from the Greek *heuriskein* meaning to find or discover. Heuristics provide general decision rules, or "rules of thumb," to assist in developing workable models of systems which are within the capabilities of humans and machines. They provide procedures for seeking solutions that are relatively easy to use and, although perhaps not the best or optimal solution, good enough. Common heuristics for playing chess are "leave the opponent with the least possible number of replies" and "control the center of the board" (Newell & Simon, 1972).

Using Heuristics in Applied Decisions

Management offers many opportunities to observe heuristics being used by decision makers. Routine rules guide such activities as cost estimation, inventory management, manpower allocations, and production scheduling. It is possible to capitalize upon the tendency of human decision makers to use heuristics by attempting to duplicate these heuristics in computer programs. Hence, the processes used in human decision making can be better understood, and managerial decision making can be made more efficient by substituting a computer program for the human decision maker. Well-known examples of the application of heuristics to management decisions are Clarkson's (1962) investment portfolio selection study, Slovic's (1969) study of stockbroker evaluations of stocks, and Kuehn and Hamburger's (1963) heuristic program to determine warehouse location.

Much of the study of thinking and problem solving involves searching for the heuristics people use. Frequently, this line of research employs verbal protocol analysis, in which individuals talk aloud, in an attempt to describe their thought processes, as a problem is solved. Smith (1968) used this method to develop a computerized simulation of the heuristics used by a psychologist in making personnel selection and classification decisions. The psychologist's verbalizations of thought were recorded as descriptions of job applicants (e.g., psychological tests and job and personal data) were evaluated. The verbal protocol was analyzed to identify heuristics used and a computer program was written to simulate these heuristics.

Heuristics used by the psychologist served to reduce the complexity of the twenty scores derived from psychological tests, plus the personal and job-related information about job applicants. For example, the psychologist was found to divide the problem into four components corresponding to the four psychological tests. He chose mental ability as the first area to investigate. Next, he examined the clerical aptitude scores, followed by emotional stability scores. Personality profiles were the last to be examined. Exhibit 3.1 (page 40) shows part of the heuristic program reflecting the manner in which he evaluated intelligence and ability test scores. Many of the biases in human judgment identified by cognitive psychologists (e.g., use of simple decision rules) can be viewed as the operation of heuristics—although frequently they are ineffective heuristics.

Another example of the use of heuristics as standard solutions is reported in Kaufmann's (1960) description of the detailed sets of routine responses prescribed for rangers in the U.S. Forest Services. A seven-volume *Forest Service Manual* listed the things Rangers are authorized, directed, and forbidden to do.

> Four of the seven volumes—those dealing with General Administration, Fiscal Control, National Forest Protection and Management, and Acquisition of Lands—are issued to Rangers. . . . They run to more than 3,000 pages, and it is difficult to think of anything likely to happen on a Ranger district that will not fall fairly unequivocally into one or another of the hundreds of categories catalogued in this Manual. . . . The provisions describe what is to be done, who is to do it, how (and how well) it should be performed, when (or in what sequence)

> each step should be taken, where the action should take place, and even explain the "why" of the policies—the reasons for their adoption, the objectives they are to attain. (Kaufmann, 1960, pp. 95-96).

Thus, many decisions are made for the rangers. One advantage of the standardization of responses to problems for all rangers is the ease of transferring rangers from one district to another. The danger in prescribing standard responses to decision problems which are perceived as well-structured, however, is that failure to accurately identify the nature of the problem would be likely to lead to unsuccessful solution attempts. Also, the prescribed responses to decision situations listed in the *Manual* must be tested to ensure that they actually do represent effective solutions, and the *Manual* must be continually updated as new problem situations arise.

The concepts underlying heuristic programs are general, but the heuristics themselves are usually specific to one decision situation. Yet, progress has been made in developing heuristics for a variety of decision problems (Simon, 1969), and encouraging theoretical advances have been made in this field (Newell, 1970). Newell and Simon's (1972) excellent review of developments in the field of heuristics is recommended for readers desiring further information.

DEVELOPING CREATIVE SOLUTIONS: THEORIES, RESEARCH, AND TECHNIQUES

The core of the decision-making process is choosing among alternatives, and one of the essential ingredients of this process in handling ill-structured problems is generating alternatives to be evaluated. Maier (1931) described this situation as requiring that elements of the problem be related or integrated in a manner which is unfamiliar to the decision maker and has labeled it *productive problem solving.* Guilford (1956) has proposed a similar classification of *divergent thinking,* which moves outward, rather than zeroing in on the "right" answer. A divergent-thinking general could be expected to think of a great many different battle plans, but might be unable to choose the best plan and take effective action. In contrast, *convergent thinking* tends to focus upon careful evaluation of a small set of problem solutions. Since a decision maker cannot always be expected to have facility in both divergent and convergent thinking, it may be useful to arrange decision-making teams composed of people who have facility with each type of thinking.

What Is Creativity?

Definitions of creativity vary in complexity from "the ability to formulate new combinations from two or more concepts already in the

EXHIBIT 3.1 Heuristic Decision Map for Intelligence and Ability

Variables Shown on Chart

KOTIS Scores for accuracy and speed on Otis Test

NGIFR Degree of decision making responsibility required on job

KSETCA Score on Clerical Ability Test

LAGE Age

LEXPER Years of previous experience

KWASH Scores on Washburne Test

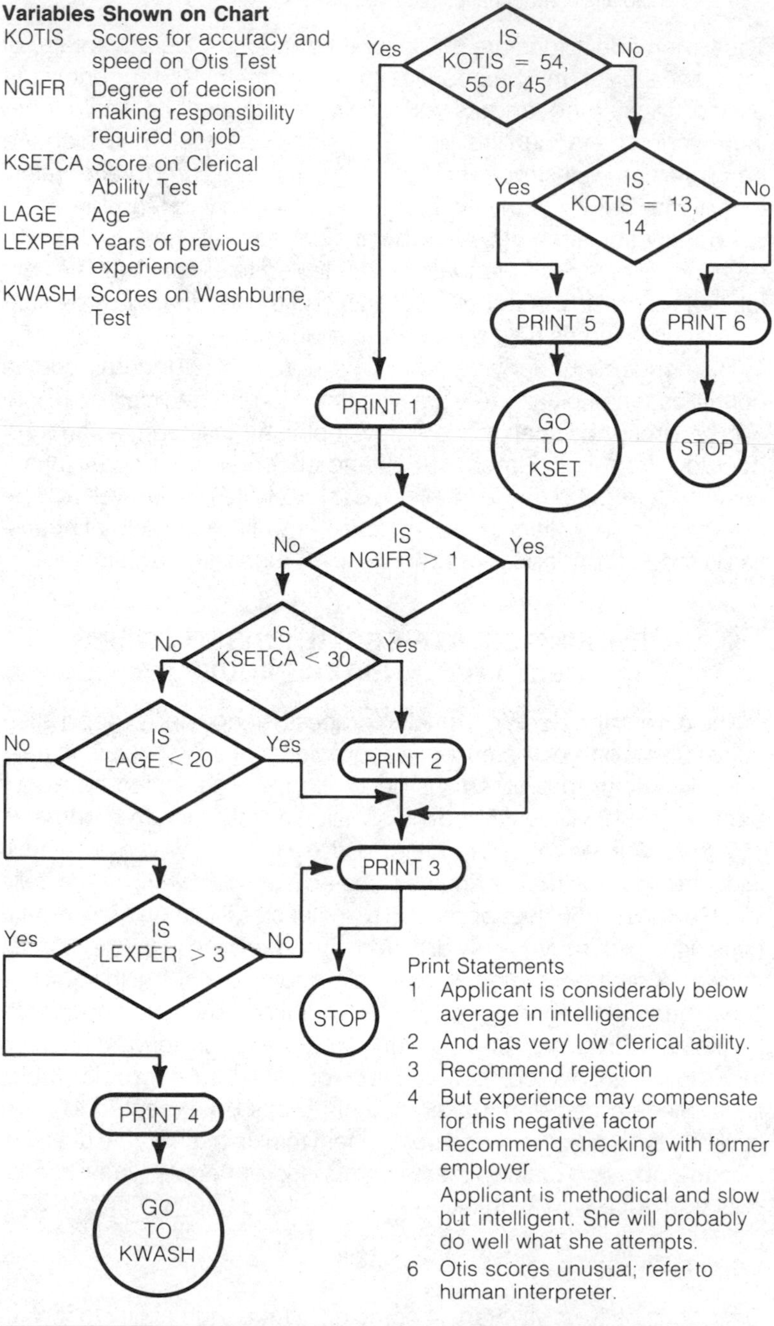

Print Statements

1 Applicant is considerably below average in intelligence

2 And has very low clerical ability.

3 Recommend rejection

4 But experience may compensate for this negative factor Recommend checking with former employer

Applicant is methodical and slow but intelligent. She will probably do well what she attempts.

6 Otis scores unusual; refer to human interpreter.

Source: Smith, R.D. Heuristic simulation of psychological decision processes. *Journal of Applied Psychology*, 1968, 14, 327.

mind" (Haefele, 1962, p. 5) to "a process that results in a novel work that is accepted as useful, tenable, or satisfying by a significant group of people at some point in time" (Stein, 1974, p. xi). Creative decision alternatives must be *original* (statistically improbable or infrequent), *relevant,* and *practical* (Bourne, et al., 1979).

Some Conclusions from Research on Creativity

The study of creativity appears to hold a fascination for researchers. Whiting (1958) reported that Helmholtz was one of the first to propose that creativity be systematically investigated by scientists. Much of the subsequent research has attempted to identify the characteristics of creative people (artists, scientists, architects, and others have been studied) (Cattell, 1963; MacKinnon, 1962; Taylor & Barron, 1963). Cattell and Butcher (1968) provide a thorough review of the research devoted to understanding the nature of creativity in the arts and sciences.

A number of introspective accounts by artists and others in jobs involving creative achievement have suggested that their creativity springs from an "unconscious process." Frequently, they have dramatized the influence of trancelike states and visions which inspired their creative achievement. In contrast, Rossman's (1931) questioning of 710 successful North American inventors, and information obtained from patent attorneys and research directors, presented a very different picture of the creative process. In response to inquiries regarding both the nature of the creative process and the characteristics of the inventors, creative achievement was described as a methodical, systematic process.

Creative achievements and age. At what age is creative achievement the greatest? To answer this question creative production in fields such as science, literature, art, and music was investigated. Although outstanding creative achievement can occur at any age, the research shows that the thirties are the golden age of creative achievement in most fields. For example, Lehman (1953) analyzed published data reporting the ages during which major creative achievements were made in a number of fields. To give an idea of how this research was conducted, let's consider the field of chemistry. The names of 244 deceased chemists who had made outstanding contributions to their field were obtained and the dates of their major contributions were noted. These data were tabulated to show the number of contributions during each five-year period of their lives. The production rate rose steadily to a peak in the thirty-four–thirty-nine year interval, then declined. Only in the case of leaders in government and military organizations were creative achievements found to occur later in life, typically in the years between fifty and seventy.

Why are creative contributions typically made at a relatively early age? We cannot be certain from this type of evidence, of course, but several explanations have been suggested. Younger people may be more flexible and open to new ideas. Health, sensory facilities, and physical vigor change with age and may influence creative achievements. Situations in life change and increased domestic and financial demands may take their toll on creative achievement. Older workers may find themselves with administrative responsibilities which limit the time they can devote to more creative endeavors. However, although explanation is not clear, the pattern of creative achievements shifting with age is quite apparent.

Creativity as a personal trait. Creativity as a personal trait has been the focus of a great deal of research. Thurstone (1951) speculated that creativity is not the same as academic intelligence. A number of studies have factor analyzed scores on batteries of psychological tests designed to measure aspects of creativity. One such study (Guilford, 1956) attempted to investigate four areas of thinking—(1) reasoning, (2) creativity, (3) planning, and (4) evaluation. Many tests were administered to a sample of student officers and air cadets in an effort to identify patterns of relationships among the test scores. Among the factors which emerged with greatest relevance for creativity were originality, conceptual foresight, sensitivity to problems, and several fluency and flexibility factors. Despite the great many research studies of this type which have been conducted, however, very little progress has been made in linking creativity as a personality trait with external evidence of creative accomplishment.

Determinants of creative achievement. In an interesting series of case studies of living scientists made during the 1950s, Roe (1953) clinically assessed psychological tests and demographic data for outstanding biologists, physicists, anthropologists, and psychologists. Although the large volume of data cannot be easily summarized, several implications for creative achievement emerged. Most of these scientists came from high socioeconomic backgrounds and from families which placed a great value on education. Most had been gifted children and had been accelerated in school. Differences in abilities were noted among the various types of scientists; for example, the numerical test was found to be too easy for the physicists, and the theoretical physicists achieved higher scores on the verbal test than did the experimental physicists. Yet, there were wide variations in verbal test scores within each group and it appeared that, once a minimum level of ability was achieved, the degree of verbal ability was not highly related to achievement.

Interviews with the scientists about their childhoods yielded some of the most interesting information concerning the development of creative achievement. Themes of strong inner drive, absorption with work, withdrawing from other interests, and desire for prestige frequently were reported. In some cases, a feeling of "apartness" from others which led to greater concentration on their work was mentioned.

It seems clear from these and other data that creative achievement typically requires some minimum level of ability, opportunity, and encouragement to pursue an education, and a concentration of interests and efforts in work pursuits.

Implications of Creativity for Applied Decisions

It appears quite likely that highly creative people can be identified who can then become involved in making creative decisions. For example, advertising agencies try to hire creative people for developing advertising campaigns, and research and development departments seek creative inventors and scientists. In this book, however, the focus is upon improving the creative ability of any decision maker. In the present discussion of the role of creativity in generating decision alternatives, then, the focus is upon the ways in which creativity can be fostered. Accordingly, we will examine three approaches for stimulating creativity and analyze the features of these approaches which appear to aid in generating creative alternatives. While there are many other techniques for fostering creativity, the approaches we will examine here illustrate important issues in stimulating creative thinking. The voluminous research devoted to evaluating these approaches—particularly brainstorming—makes a thorough review of the literature infeasible, but we will attempt to highlight the major research contributions. The three approaches we will examine are brainstorming, Synectics, and morphology.

Brainstorming

Brainstorming is a method devised by Osborn (1963) which can be used either by groups or "nominal groups." In nominal groups the group members work alone for at least part of the time, then reach a group decision either by group discussions or by statistically combining their individual decisions. Although brainstorming provides little structure for the group working together to develop a list of alternative solutions to a decision problem, a series of rules are given to encourage free expression of ideas. The rules are (Osborn, 1963):

1. **Don't criticize the ideas of others.**
   Criticism is ruled out while ideas are being suggested. As Osborn (1963) stated: "Allowing yourself to be critical at the same time you are being creative is like trying to get hot and cold water from one faucet at the same time. Ideas aren't hot enough; criticism isn't cold enough. Results are tepid" (p. 156). The quality of the ideas that have been listed can be evaluated later.
2. **Free-wheel.**
   Think of wild things. Even off-beat, impractical suggestions are useful since they may trigger creative ideas from other panel members.
3. **Suggest as many ideas as possible.**
   The greater the number of ideas, the greater the likelihood that some will be creative. It is easy to eliminate ideas that are not useful at a later time.
4. **Try to combine and improve ideas that have been suggested.**
   Panel members should not only contribute their own ideas; they should try to improve or build upon ideas of other people. One way to do so is to combine two or more ideas into an even better idea.

The early claims made for brainstorming and its popularity over the past twenty years have led to attempts to evaluate its effectiveness in producing both a large number of decision alternatives and high-quality alternatives. Findings of these studies regarding *attributes of decision makers* and *decision environments* that influence the effectiveness of brainstorming are discussed in this section. Attributes of decision makers which have been researched in the context of brainstorming include the number of decision makers (individuals vs. groups, and number of group members), and the cohesiveness of the group. Attributes of the decision environment which have been researched include task instructions ("use your imagination" and "avoid criticism"), a change in decision context, and extended work sessions.

Are groups more effective than individuals in brainstorming? There seems to be little doubt that the pooled efforts of individuals working in isolation (nominal groups) are superior to brainstorming groups in the production of both unique and high-quality ideas (Taylor, et al., 1958; Dunnette, et al., 1963; Bouchard, 1969).

With regard to the total number of ideas produced, the research evidence is mixed. Findings from a study by Cohen and his associates (1960) were in line with Osborn's original assumption, namely that the presence of other group members will stimulate the production of ideas in the brainstorming sessions. In contrast, other researchers (Taylor, et al., 1958; Dunnette, et al., 1963) found that the pooled efforts of four individuals working alone resulted in more ideas than did the actual brainstorming groups. Using a timely problem concerning what an individual could do about the escalation of the war in Vietnam, Dillon, Graham and Aidells (1972) also confirmed the superiority of nominal over real groups in generating distinct ideas.

Shaw (1971) suggested a possible resolution to this contradiction in the effect of length of the brainstorming session. He cites a study by Milton Rosenbaum which found that, when work periods are extended, groups tend to produce a greater number of ideas in brainstorming than do individuals. This implies that groups tend to produce indefinitely, whereas individuals may run dry.

These studies must also be reconciled with the findings of a study by Barnlund (1959) that, on a task involving ability to draw logical conclusions from given arguments, group decisions arrived at through a process of cooperative deliberation were superior both to decisions obtained by pooling individual answers of group members (majority rule) and to those by individuals working alone. Vroom and Maier (1961) have suggested that group interaction may be more important in evaluating alternatives and making choices than it is in the brainstorming task of generating alternatives.

How large should brainstorming groups be? With regard to the impact of the number of group members on brainstorming effectiveness (the dependent variable was the number of distinct ideas produced), Bouchard and Hare (1970) found that the relative superiority of nominal groups over real groups increased with group size. Similarly, Bouchard, Barsaloux, and Drauden (1974) found that seven-person nominal groups outperformed four-person nominal groups, but in real groups effectiveness was unrelated to group size. Possibly, difficulties presented by interpersonal interactions among members of larger real groups cancel out the advantages of having more people to suggest ideas.

What types of people are the best brainstormers? In one of the few studies investigating the impact of the characteristics of participants in brainstorming, Bouchard (1969) found that scores on both the *interpersonal effectiveness* and *sociability* scales of the California Psychological Inventory were related to group-brainstorming effectiveness. He concluded that ''high scoring subjects in the brainstorming groups have well-developed social skills, are outgoing, enterprising, original, verbally fluent, fluent in thought, somewhat aggressive, dominant and controlling, and yet are concerned with feelings of others. They possess self-assurance and are spontaneous, expressive and enthusiastic'' (p. 26).

Although studies investigating the effectiveness of brainstorming strategies have used both groups of individuals who were well acquainted and those who were apparently strangers, the most direct evidence of a possible mediating effect of group cohesiveness upon brainstorming group effectiveness is provided by Cohen, et al. (1960). Under brainstorming instructions cohesive groups performed better in generating alternatives than did noncohesive groups.

Does criticism inhibit brainstorming? Instruction to avoid criticism while generating decision alternatives is an appealing feature of brainstorming methods. The inhibiting effect of criticism appears very strong. A study by Manski and Davis (1968), for example, found that telling subjects to be practical as well as original resulted in fewer uses for objects being given, but no decrease in the number of creative uses. The central question appears to be not whether criticism will inhibit original thinking, but whether the brainstorming instructions are sufficient to overcome the inhibiting effect. Both Dunnette, et al. (1963) and Taylor, et al. (1958) expressed their concern that subjects perceived a threat of criticism despite the instructions to be nonevaluative.

Does changing the decision context improve brainstorming? Instructions can be used to specify or change the context of the decision, a feature contained in most strategies for generating creative decision alternatives. Instructions to imagine themselves in a particular situation and to list uses for a given item in that situation were compared with instructions to subjects requiring only that they list uses (Manski & Davis, 1966). Subjects given the changed context produced more uses, more original uses, and more creative (original and practical) uses. The authors suggest that the improved performance may be the result of requiring the subjects to consider previously unrelated ideas contiguously. As is pointed out in discussing other techniques for generating alternatives, the change of context is an extremely effective feature which provides the major ingredient of these techniques.

Do longer work sessions improve brainstorming? Another feature of the work environment in brainstorming to be examined here is the effect of extending the work session. When ample time to generate alternatives is available, extending the session appears advisable. Although evidence regarding the practicality of ideas is lacking, the originality of responses has been found to increase as subjects continue working—at least this is true for the kinds of tasks which are typically studied in investigating originality (e.g., giving uses for objects, listing plot titles, free associating). Since early responses tend to be more stereotyped or common than later responses (Wallach & Kogan, 1965; Wilson, et al., 1953), the later responses appear to hold greater promise of creativity.

Can people be taught to be more creative? A major psychological block to creative solving is *functional fixedness.* Functional fixedness means that the ordinary use of an object tends to inhibit its use in an unusual way (e.g., Divesta & Walls, 1967). Ijiri, Jadicke, and Knight (1966) have discussed methods to help accountants cope with functional fixedness when adjusting to new accounting methods. The suggestions involve alerting accountants to the danger of transferring the interpretation given to an accounting index in one system to another system. Other approaches to dealing with transfer of learning which may inhibit adaptation to new situations use originality training.

The Maltzman Originality Training Procedure (Maltzman, 1960), which presents a stimulus repeatedly and requires subjects to give a different association for each presentation, has been shown to increase originality of responses on a subsequent free-association test and on listing uses for objects (Maltzman, et al., 1960). The Maltzman technique may be useful in facilitating creative responses, but it appears that, of the great many ideas potentially available, only a few are practical. This may explain why it seems relatively easy to increase originality, but much more difficult to increase creativity. This is likely to be disappointing to individuals wishing to improve the creativity of potential courses of action available to decision makers; after all, for most practical decisions, original ideas are of little value unless they also are creative (i.e., relevant and practical).

Synectics

A creative problem-solving approach developed by Gordon (1961) and Prince (1962) differs considerably from brainstorming. It is much more highly structured and encompasses the entire decision-making process in eight phases ranging from problem statement through solution. While it specifies ways both to generate creative alternatives and to recommend solutions to management, its major emphasis appears to be stimulating creative thought regarding solutions to management problems. It is an elaborate program, with careful selection and training of group members to work under an experienced leader.

Synectics usually requires the assistance of an outside expert to select a group of about six people representing a variety of experiences and functional areas in the organization. This group is committed for one week each month for a year to a live-in training session. In addition, top management must be willing to permit the group to operate independently from other units of the organization. In spite of the scope of this effort and the patience required of management to wait for up to a year for the group to become established and functioning before tangible outcomes are realized, Synectics has been widely used and appears to show promise as an approach to developing and evaluating creative decision alternatives.

Synectics is a total program of creative techniques, including use of deferred judgment, record keeping, selection of group members on the basis of creative ability, and placing in cohesive problem-solving groups. Yet, its major device for stimulating creative thought is the use of analogies. Analogies help us to "make the familiar strange and the strange familiar" and provide a new perspective on problems. Gordon (1961) suggested that problem solvers need to use four types of analogies. *Personal analogies* involve taking the role of persons or objects in the problem (e.g., a missing murder weapon) to free the problem solver from looking at the commonplace in a commonplace way. *Direct analogies* require making direct comparisons to partially similar objects or processes from nature (e.g., the ability of chameleons and flounders to change color). *Fantasy analogies* (e.g., demons and elves) require that ideal solutions to a problem, no matter how farfetched they may appear, be imagined and then adjusted to make them more feasible. Finally, *symbolic analogies* (e.g., mathematical models) require that the problem situation be modeled using any symbols that appropriately represent the objects and relations in the situation.

With this approach, alternatives are evaluated as they are generated. The problem solvers free-associate with ideas and images until one happens upon appropriate analogy. From that point, the problem situation is developed parallel to the development of the analogy. A formal leader is designated from the group and given special training; the formal leader coordinates the efforts of the group and communicates with management to gain acceptance of the solutions proposed by the group. The complexity of the Synectics program makes a systematic evaluation difficult; despite this lack of formal evaluation it has been widely accepted by organizations.

Morphology

Morphology is designed to achieve the change of viewpoint crucial to creative thinking by relating previously unrelated ideas. The Davis and Manske (1966) study cited above suggested that this approach will facilitate creativity in generating alternatives, yet there is little evidence of the effectiveness of the technique for deliberately producing contiguity.

Morphological analysis was developed by Zwicky (1957). Although the technique was first used in the field of astronomy, its use has spread into applications in nearly every field of human endeavor. The work of Allen (1962) was especially instrumental in clarifying and explaining the use of this technique. It provides a structured approach for systematically relating attributes of decision alternatives to suggest a large number of new alternatives. This is illustrated by "Getting Something from One Place to Another Via a Powered Vehicle" (Arnold, 1962, p. 256). Three major variables or attributes are defined and used as axes. They are the type of vehicle used, the media in which the vehicle operates, and the power sources. Each of these major attributes has its subattributes listed along the relevant axis as shown in Exhibit 3.2 on page 50.

Alternatives are generated by selecting combinations along the axes. For example, one method of solving the problem could be a chair which is belt driven and travels through the air (as seen on many ski slopes). The prime advantage of the morphological method, given in this case that there are only three major attributes, is that it generates *all* of the major decision alternatives. Thus the importance of a complete listing of attributes cannot be overemphasized if this method is to be successfully used.

Decision makers, therefore, follow a systematic program that will generate a large number of alternatives. Although most of these will be worthless, a few may be novel and important. There is no guarantee that anything creative will emerge, and the procedure is highly inefficient. Yet, whenever there are unique combinations that can be generated, this exhaustive approach will find them and the decision maker will be made aware of any unusual combinations.

Although Zwicky (1969) makes sweeping claims regarding the effectiveness of morphology, only two published studies have evaluated morphology as a creativity stimulation technique. Warren and Davis (1969) operationalized morphology by explaining to subjects that: "A good way to think of variations and improvements for something is first to analyze the 'thing' into its various dimensions, then to combine the values of these dimensions into new arrangements. The very large numbers of ideas found in this fashion may be good themselves, or may act as hints in producing still other ideas" (p. 210). In a problem requiring improvements in a doorknob, morphology users produced a greater number of creative ideas than did checklist users or control subjects.

In a study of the effectiveness of morphology for generating plot titles of stories (Stratton & Brown, 1970), subjects were asked to construct an idea table with one column for each major division or theme in the story. Within each column, subjects listed all related information from the story. Thus, all information related to the plot was systematically explicated, and all possible combinations of major and minor details were examined as potential titles. The number of superior solutions produced by subjects using morphology was significantly greater than for the control subjects, but not significantly greater than for subjects trained in judgment techniques. The technique has shown some success in stimulating creativity in simple

EXHIBIT 3.2 Morphological Matrix for Inventing Powered Vehicle

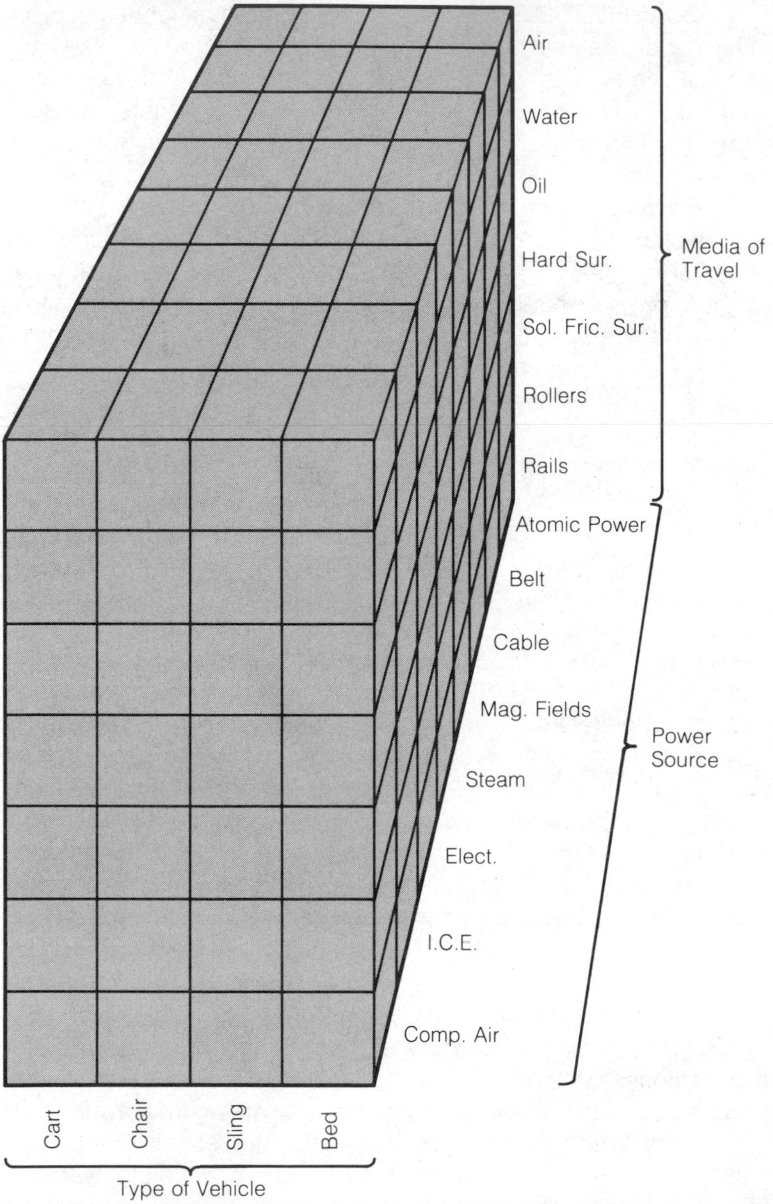

Source: Arnold, J.E. Useful creative techniques. In S. Parnes and Harding (eds.), *Creative thinking,* N.Y.: Scribners, 1962, 256.

problems, but the application of morphology to management problems has not been systematically examined.

Toward More Effective Creativity Stimulation Techniques

Whether, in fact, brainstorming, Synectics, or morphology is the *most* effective means of generating creative alternatives has not been investigated. Brainstorming is the only technique that has received much research attention. The other techniques have received too little attention for us to make any conclusive statements about their effectiveness. Understanding of these techniques can be advanced by: 1) finding better ways to operationalize the techniques, 2) determining appropriate problem types for each technique, and 3) selecting active features from each technique and eclectically combining these features into new techniques.

To elaborate upon the last suggestion, aspects of the techniques which appear to encourage creativity in alternative generation can be incorporated into eclectic programs that may be potentially more effective than the existing techniques. Yet, much more research is required to determine the effectiveness of the various features of these techniques. Among the features that can be drawn from these techniques are those intended for *facilitating group interaction* (use of leader, selecting members for cohesive "mix," developing cohesiveness through interaction), *for encouraging creativity* (changing viewpoint, withholding evaluation of alternatives, extending the work period), for *selecting potentially creative individuals* and developing their ability, and for *facilitating organizational acceptance of the ideas* produced by the group. Brainstorming, Synectics, and morphology are contrasted on these features in Exhibit 3.3. (See page 52.) Rather than researching the effectiveness of the brainstorming or Synectics approaches, understanding the dynamics of generating creative alternatives would seem to advance more rapidly and surely if systematic research were focused upon the contribution made to an eclectic strategy by each of its components.

The Creative Organization

To this point we have considered creativity in individuals and groups. The research evidence summarized above indicates that highly creative individuals can be identified and placed in decision-making positions which call upon their creative abilities. It also is clear that techniques exist for stimulating decision makers to become more creative. Another important question related to decision making in organizations is whether organizations differ in their creativity. The existing research evidence provides very little help to us in answering this question.

Steiner (1965) edited a book which attempted to draw together the available evidence to describe a "creative organization." The organization that emerged is highly adaptive, loosely organized, and has

Exhibit 3.3. Comparisons of Features of Creativity Stimulating Techniques

TECHNIQUE	GROUPS OR INDIVIDUALS	FACILITATING GROUP INTERACTION				ABILITY CONSIDERED	
		Use of Leader	Developing Cohesiveness	Mix of Members	Structured Interactions	Selection	Training
BRAINSTORMING	Groups and "Nominal Groups"	No	No	No	Rules	No	Learn Rules
SYNECTICS	Groups	Emerge From Group	Live Together	Yes	Yes	Yes, But Crude	Yes
MORPHOLOGY	Individuals	N/A	N/A	N/A	N/A	No	Yes

TECHNIQUE	ENCOURAGING CREATIVITY				RELATING TO ORGANIZATION	
	Change Viewpoint	Withhold Evaluation	Relate Ideas	Extended Work	Dual Organization Structures	Interface Designated
BRAINSTORMING	"Be Original"	Yes	"Build on Ideas"	Can Be	No	No
SYNECTICS	Analogies	No	Some	Long Sessions	Yes	Yes
MORPHOLOGY	No	Yes	Yes	No	No	No

a minimum of rigid procedures. Some of the characteristics of a "creative organization" as defined by Steiner are:

—diversified and decentralized structure
—encouragement of interaction with outside sources
—open communication channels
—separate production and creation functions
—encouragement of risk-taking
—emphasis on basic research

Unfortunately, little has been done in the last fifteen years to advance our understanding of how organizations can contribute to the creativity of their members.

THE ROLE OF GOALS AND OBJECTIVES IN EVALUATING ALTERNATIVE SOLUTIONS

It is a challenging task to compare several courses of action and finally select one action to implement. At times the task may prove too challenging:

> So he thought of his hut . . . and he thought of his boat,
> And his hat and his breeks, and his chickens and goat,
> And the hooks (for his food) and the spring (for this thirst)
> . . . But he never could think of which he ought to do first.
>
> And so in the end he did nothing at all,
> But basked on the shingle wrapped up in a shawl,
> And I think it was dreadful the way he behaved,
> He did nothing but basking until he was saved!
>
> *The Old Sailor,* Milne, 1927

Difficulties in choice are presented by complexity in decision alternatives. The limited information-processing capacity of a decision maker is strained by considering the implications of even one course of action, yet choice requires that implications of many courses of action be visualized and compared. If the alternatives are complex ones, there is no clear way to compare them. Moreover, unknown factors always intrude upon the problem situation; seldom are outcomes known with certainty. At times, outcomes depend upon reactions of other people who may not even know what they will do. It is no wonder that decision makers sometimes postpone choices for as long as possible and then decide without attempting to consider all the implications of the decision.

The systematic study of decision making provides a framework for choosing courses of action in complex, uncertain, or conflict-ridden situations. The choice of possible actions and the prediction of expected outcomes derives from a logical analysis of the decision situation. In this section we will describe a basic element in the analysis of decision alternatives and choice—the goals and objectives that guide decision making. In subsequent sections we will examine key issues related to a decision maker's preferences regarding alternatives, criteria for choice, and choice modes.

Objectives are important both in identifying problems and in evaluating alternative solutions. The role of objectives in identifying problems was discussed earlier. Evaluating alternatives requires that a decision maker's objectives be expressed as criteria that reflect the attributes of the alternatives relevant to the choice.

Do Goals Guide Decision Making?

Recent attention has been addressed to the assumption of the prior existence of a set of goals and a well-defined, stable, and consistent preference ordering among goals. The preexistence of goals in organizational decision making has been challenged (Weick, 1977; March, 1972). Weick has proposed that the organization can best be understood as an "enacted" entity which "can never know what it thinks or wants until it sees what it does" (p. 278). This point of view suggests that it is possible for outcomes to occur without decisions having been made. Upon observing a set of events one may attempt to make sense of them by, retrospectively, positing a decision to account for the events. Similarly, the "garbage can" model of choice (Cohen, March, & Olson, 1972) questions both the preexistence of goals to direct decisions made in organizations and the orderliness of decision-making activities. The "garbage can" model views decision making in organizations as simply outcomes resulting from a random merging of four relatively independent "streams" of elements—(1) problems, (2) solutions, (3) participants, and (4) choice opportunities. Hence, decisions made in organizations are merely events produced by the "somewhat fortuitous confluence" of these streams of elements (p. 3).

Discovering Goals

Other writers have acknowledged the existence of goals which guide decision-making behaviors in organizations, but deplore the unquestioning acceptance of existing goals (Argyris, 1973). March (1972) has called for greater concern for discovering and evaluating goals. Argyris has stated that goals in the traditional model of decision making tend to perpetuate the status quo. This is because goals which are consistent with the existing beliefs in an organization tend to be uncritically accepted; then primary attention is given to behavior which is in line with the established goals.

It has been suggested that organizations should consciously strive to find "new" goals and "better" goals to guide decision making (March, 1972), and attempt to overcome the preoccupation of traditional decision-making approaches with how "good" decisions are made. It is equally important to consider how "good" goals are found.

Two strategies exist for finding new goals to direct choices made in organizations—imitation and playfulness. New and valuable goals may be identified by imitating (i.e., duplicating) behaviors of other people or organizations. Organizations may adopt the behaviors of industry leaders, and managers may try to emulate other managers whom they admire. In doing so, organizations and individuals may find goals for themselves that would not otherwise have occurred to them. However, it is important to select appropriate models to imitate, and little guidance has been given in selecting the models. Playfulness requires that the rational imperatives for consistency be temporarily suspended by relaxing the rules in order to explore the possibility of alternative rules. This suggestion reflects a belief that a strict insistence on purpose, consistency, and rationality seriously limits a decision maker's ability to find new purposes. If the decision process is seen as a time to test new hypotheses about goals, then experimenting with new goals may lead to discovering interesting combinations of values.

Although little is known about the activities that initiate and guide decision-making activity, it is important to learn more about them. As Connolly (1977) expressed this issue, "the individual's formulation of the problem he faces, the priority he assigns to it relative to his other work, the solution criteria he applies, the extent and direction of the information he finally puts out, are all plausibly related to the events which initiate his information-processing activity" (p. 261).

Arranging Objectives in a Hierarchy

Evaluating decision alternatives typically requires that the multiple objectives of the decision maker be taken into account. Some members of the set of multiple objectives may be more important (or given higher priority) than others, but all objectives should be reflected in the choice. In some cases, one objective may act as a constraint on others—particularly when resources spent to attain one objective may reduce the resources available for attaining other objectives. We shall consider multiple-objective decision making in the next chapter since it deals with choice among highly complex courses of action.

Objectives can be viewed as representing a hierarchy. As Granger (1964) said, "There are objectives within objectives, within objectives. They all require painstaking definition and close analysis if they are to be useful separately and profitable as a whole" (p. 63). Objectives can be reduced to subobjectives to facilitate decision making. For example, our earlier problem of designing a lighter air cleaner for an automobile can be reduced to four subobjectives:

1. Design an air cleaner assembly made out of *lighter* materials. Examples of such materials would be aluminum, plastic, or paper.
2. Design an air cleaner to perform the same function as the present air cleaner, only *smaller*.
3. Use the same design as the present air cleaner, but use *thinner* materials to perform the same function.
4. Design an air cleaner to perform the same function as the present air cleaner, but with *fewer parts*. An example would be the disposable air cleaner or a bimetal temperature system.

Each of these subobjectives can be reduced to even smaller objectives. All of the smaller objectives are influenced by the available resources in machines and people, the cost of the program, the time to completion, the acceptability of the project to the separate car divisions, and technology. Also, the smaller objectives can be reduced to various combinations of efficiency requirements, capacities for filtering, silencing requirements, temperature control problems, and versatility for change in future applications.

Moreover, it is possible to work back up the hierarchy of objectives to gain greater understanding of the decision problem. A general theme can be extracted from the subobjectives (1—4) derived from the original objective. The reformulation of the objective states that we should design an air cleaner that is *simpler,* that is more *compact,* and that *uses less* of everything. Basically we want an air cleaner that uses *less material* and *takes less time* to assemble.

Evaluating the Quality of Objectives

Granger (1964) proposed six criteria for testing the validity of objectives. They are:

1. Is it a guide to action? It should facilitate decision making by helping managers select the most desirable courses of action.
2. Is it explicit enough to lead to specific actions? While "to increase sales" may not suggest specific actions, "to increase our share of the snowmobile market by 10%" does.
3. Does it suggest ways to measure and control effectiveness? Objectives should suggest ways to implement them and tools to assess their attainment.
4. Is it challenging? Objectives should be ambitious enough to require reaching beyond the decision maker's usual level of effort. Objectives that are too easy to attain fail to differentiate the quality of alternatives. Yet, objectives that are too ambitious may not be attainable by feasible courses of action.
5. Does it reflect internal and external constraints? Objectives should be compatible with the external constraints (e.g., legal and competitive restrictions) and internal constraints (e.g., financial resources) specific to the decision maker's situation. Thus, objectives of personnel managers in different units of an organization may substantially differ.
6. Can it be related to both the broader and the more specific objectives at higher and lower levels of the decision maker's organization? Objectives for a decision problem should be relatable to the objectives of other decision

makers in the organization. Also, specific objectives in a hierarchy of organizational objectives should not conflict with its broad objectives.

Alternatives typically are evaluated in terms of the attractiveness of their outcomes for the decision maker; with the course of action which the decision maker believes will lead to the most favorable outcomes being chosen. March and Simon (1958) have proposed a taxonomy of alternatives based on their anticipated outcomes:

1. Good alternatives. If accepted, they are likely to lead to a positively valued outcome for the decision maker.
2. Bland alternatives. If accepted, they are unlikely to result in either a positively valued or a negatively valued outcome for the decision maker.
3. Mixed alternatives. If accepted, they are likely to result in *both* positively valued and negatively valued outcomes for the decision maker.
4. Poor alternatives. If accepted, they are likely to produce a negatively valued outcome for the decision maker.

Level of Aspiration and Objectives

Attributes of decision makers and their environments also may influence standards for evaluating alternatives. Decision makers' adaptation or aspiration levels appear to have an important influence on the levels at which standards are set. Helson's (1948) hypothesis of par, which was described in Chapter 2, represents a pervasive tendency for scales of subjective judgment to show a neutral point or adaptation level. The neutral point for judging the intensity of a stimulus depends upon the previous experience with similar stimuli and upon the current situation. An interesting aspect of the formulation is its emphasis upon the tendency of aspiration level to reflect previous experiences and current environmental conditions—as do the scales of subjective judgment from which it is drawn. The impact of three conditions upon the level of aspiration in decision making are briefly sketched below.

Specific goals. Setting specific goals has been found to be effective in motivating individuals to perform at higher levels. Bryan and Locke (1967), for example, found that groups with specific goals were able to match the performance of initially more highly motivated groups who were told merely to "do your best." Subsequently, Locke (1967) was able to demonstrate that some of the increased motivation previously attributed to the effect of differential knowledge of results was actually due to the mechanism of goal setting.

The basis for this increased motivation has as yet not been systematically investigated, but in one interesting line of research, Arrowood and Ross (1966) found that expanding effort, or even anticipating such effort, to prepare for a possible future outcome tends to increase belief that it will occur. Possibly, at least part of the impact of goal setting is due to the increased attention given to a specific subset of the potential outcome. Little is known, however, about the basis of the increased motivation produced by goal setting, nor has this mechanism been explored systematically to determine its impact on decision-making behavior.

Feedback. Since the consequences of decisions are generally viewed as having an incentive value in motivating decision makers, it seems plausible that decision makers may set more appropriate standards, and be more strongly motivated to resolve the problems they face, when they are provided with objective knowledge of results compared to their own previous performance and the performance of others. Two types of feedback exist: *intrinsic feedback,* a natural consequence of the movement itself (e.g., moving your hand and receiving kinesthetic cues from the muscles and joints of the hand about the rate of movement and position) and *augmented feedback,* artificial or external cues from the environment, extrinsic to the organism (e.g., a verbal report by an experimenter of how close the hand is to the goal), in which an external source is providing feedback about the consequences of the movement.

It seems clear that the motivation to perform a task can be improved through use of augmented feedback. This improvement is reflected in increased performance not only when the added feedback is present, but also when conditions are returned to normal. Smode (1958) was one of the first to systematically study this issue, using a tracking task in which two groups of subjects learned to keep a randomly varying needle centered by rotating a dial. For two sessions, one group was given normal feedback—in the form of a verbal report after each trial—of the length of time the needle had been on target. The other group was given augmented feedback by means of a counter on which their score was indicated. From the first trial the group with augmented feedback gave much higher performances, which suggests that the effect of the additional feedback was to motivate the subjects to work harder during each trial. While evidence from studies of task performance generally supports the motivational effect of augmented feedback (e.g., verbal report from the experimenter of subjects' performance), the issue does not appear to have been investigated for decision-making tasks.

Prior success or failure. The generally accepted conclusion from experiments investigating the effect upon aspiration level of the decision maker's experience of success or failure in prior decisions (Cofer & Appley, 1964) is that successful performance leads to an increase in the standard of excellence, while failure decreases standards set for future decisions. Bourne, et al. (1979) provided several interpretations of the operation of failure on aspiration level—increased level of arousal magnifying the difficulty of subsequent tasks, increased number of competing responses, or reduced expectancy of success. The latter mechanism would be expected to lead to less effort expended or less appropriate solution attempts; perhaps operating as Streufert, et al. (1968) suggest through failure producing overly complex integrative (strategically and pragmatically related) solutions.

Other research findings with implications for decision strategies involving level of aspiration are that level of aspiration can be varied by arranging the task to suggest that a high performance level is expected, or by providing instructions indicating that other individuals have performed it well. Mace (1953), for example, improved performance in an aiming task simply by adding more concentric rings within the established periphery, thus making what previously appeared to be good performance look mediocre. The experimenter may also vary performance by manipulating the instructions to indicate that good scores have been obtained by others. Conclusions drawn from investigating the influence of prior success or failure experiences on subsequent levels of aspiration suggest that decision making can be improved by providing realistic outcome experiences.

The impact of these conclusions would appear to be lessened by Feather's (1967) finding that past experiences of success or failure seem to have less influence on setting future targets for decision makers who have a high need for achievement (i.e., desire to achieve success and avoid failure). Decision makers who have a high need for achievement may be expected to occupy many key managerial positions.

IDENTIFYING PREFERENCES FOR ALTERNATIVE SOLUTIONS

Optimization is an underlying principle of decision making; all other things being equal, the alternative with the greatest *value* should be chosen. Yet, in most decisions it is not a simple task to determine the value of alternative courses of action. Assigning values to decision alternatives, even in the absence of extreme complexity or uncertainty in the decision situation, is challenging since values are subjective and specific to the preferences of a decision maker. Also, values must be represented by standards (criteria) against which alternatives can be judged, and a decision maker's diverse values are difficult to reflect on a common scale. In this section, we will examine how preferences for decision alternatives can be assessed either directly or indirectly. Special problems raised by considering multiple objectives and the values of more than one decision maker are discussed in Chapters 4 and 6, respectively.

Direct Assessment of Preferences

Direct approaches may involve simply asking decision makers to state their values (usually in numerical form) or using ranking or rating scales. For example, utility functions can be drawn by decision makers or derived by constructing indifference curves for pairs of attributes to show the trade-offs they are willing to accept (e.g., work effort for earnings) in choosing a course of action.

MacCrimmon and Toda (1969) have described a method for determining trade-offs directly by asking questions requiring subjects to indicate "equivalences." The questions are asked in the following manner:

> Most nations of the world are currently confronted with the difficult problem of jointly combatting inflation and unemployment. Unfortunately, many of the measures to reduce the inflation rate lead to an increase in unemployment, while many of the measures to reduce unemployment rate lead to an increase in inflation. . . . Although the consequences of each course of action would be uncertain, assume, for simplicity, that we would know for sure what level of unemployment and what rate of inflation would result from the actions. The current policy leads to an inflation rate of 8% and an unemployment rate of 8%. . . . At what new inflation rate, paired with a new unemployment rate of 6%, would you feel indifferent toward the new policy and the one currently in effect? (MacCrimmon & Siu, 1974, pp. 682–3)

While the direct assessment of preferences seems efficient, this type of question is very difficult to answer. Consequently, decision makers asked to directly state their preferences may not have the motivation and ability to do so accurately.

Indirect Assessment of Preferences

Indirect assessment of preferences is inferred from decision makers' choices. In the example above, questions can be asked in a less demanding, indirect manner. The subjects could be asked if they would accept a 17 percent inflation rate if the unemployment rate was reduced to 6 percent. If the answer is no, then this establishes an upper bound on inflation rate. Next, the subjects could be asked if a 7 percent inflation rate would be acceptable. A lower bound on inflation rates is set if the subjects say yes. By taking intermediate values, between 7 and 17 percent, you can get tighter bounds and reach an equivalence point that reflects the highest inflation level that the subjects would accept in exchange for lower unemployment levels.

Standard gamble method. Other indirect methods for assessing preferences, usually for weights or utilities, rely on a comparison between a gamble and a sure thing. This approach introduces probabilities into the choices. Von Neumann and Morgenstern called this the *standard gamble method* for assessing utilities. For example, the utility of one attribute from a set of twelve attributes describing three automobiles being considered for purchase (e.g., price, gas mileage, number of passengers accommodated) could be assessed in the following manner. Automobile A has the *best* level of all twelve attributes. Automobile B has the *worst* level of all twelve attributes. Automobile C has an *intermediate* level on one attribute, and the worst level for all others. State a probability (p) such that you are indifferent between receiving C for sure versus receiving a gamble wherein you will obtain A with probability (p) and B with probability (1-p). What is the value of p that makes you indifferent?

Variable-probability and fixed-probability methods. In the variable-probability method, the task is to name a probability that makes the sure thing (Automobile C) indifferent to the gamble. Another method, using fixed probabilities, requires that the probabilities for the gamble be held constant at (½, ½), and the decision maker must name an intermediate value on one attribute of the sure thing which leads to indifference. The answer to each question yields one point on a utility curve; thus, several responses are needed to estimate the shape of the curve for each attribute. More will be said about multiattribute utility analysis—its use and validity—in the context of coping with complex decision situations in the next chapter.

DETERMINING COSTS, BENEFITS, AND UTILITIES

A basic issue in evaluating decision alternatives is assessing values and costs incurred as a consequence of choosing each alternative. The value of alternatives can be expressed in many nonmonetary ways. For example, the implications of actions for consumer attitudes, market share, and satisfying the social responsibilities of an organization may be important consequences of a decision.

Costs and Benefits

It is advantageous, however, to specify the value of alternatives in monetary terms and, frequently, this involves cost-benefit analysis. Cost-benefit analysis reflects what is gained and what is given up by taking one or another alternative course of action. The difference between the gain and loss can be used in situations which permit gains and losses to be measured in strictly monetary terms. If costs are

are fixed, decision makers may attempt to maximize benefits or income. If, on the other hand, benefits or income are fixed, the course of action that will solve the problem with the lowest cost will be selected.

Considering the costs and benefits resulting from a decision serves to focus the decision maker's attention upon both positive and negative outcomes. Little systematic attention has been given to distinguishing between positive and negative decision outcomes. Yet, outcomes that are above some neutral point are generally called gains, pleasures, or benefits; outcomes that are below this point are considered to be losses, pain, or costs. In their conceptualization of need for achievement, McClelland (1961) and Atkinson and Feather (1966) contrasted the need to strive for success with the need to avoid failure. In experiments on gambling behaviors, a similar distinction between gains and losses has been observed; gamblers tended to focus more upon losses than gains (Slovic & Lichtenstein, 1968).

Utility

The psychological value a decision maker associates with an alternative—the perceived usefulness of its outcomes—is represented by its *utility* for that object. One task of decision theory is to determine how people assign utilities to alternatives and use these utilities in making decisions.

Utility curves: Which shape best represents utilities? What is the psychological value of money? Consider this situation. A benefactor has just given you an unexpected gift of $50. How pleased does this gift make you? Now, consider how much the gift would have to be to make you twice as pleased, four times as pleased, and eight times as pleased. When this experiment was first done by Galanter (1962), it was found that people differed in the value they attached to money; clearly the wealth of individuals would be expected to influence their perceptions of the value of money. However, it was found that the utility of money appeared to increase roughly as the square root of the money value. That is, the monetary amount would have to quadruple to double the pleasure it produced. While this experiment is far from conclusive, it does indicate that the psychological value of an item tends to increase more slowly than its numerical value.

This point underlies the basic conceptualization of utility as considered in the eighteenth century by the Swiss mathematicians Cramer and Bernoulli. The central issue is that the utility of an additional amount of money is inversely related to the wealth of a person. For example, an additional dollar would be of greater value if one has only $50 compared to someone who has $5,000. Furthermore, it was proposed that all people were rational and would behave in the same manner.

This speculation formed the basis for a fundamental law which stated that the utility of money could be represented as a logarithm of the amount of money. Cramer specified that the square root of the amount of money should be used to measure utility, which produced a curve of utility for money plotted against money in the general shape shown in Exhibit 3.4. As amount of money is increased, less utility is produced by each additional increment of money.

Subsequently, it was pointed out that the shape of the utility curve suggested by Bernoulli and others failed to explain the behavior of some gamblers who exhibited more and more utility for money as the amounts increase (at least, up to some point). This type of gambling behavior can be described by a utility curve which is concave upward, as shown in Exhibit 3.5 on page 64. Clearly, this is a departure from the utility curve suggested by Bernoulli which specified that people had less and less utility for money as the amount increased (Vickrey, 1945). Another departure from the type of utility curve posited by Bernoulli has been shown in insurance-buying behavior. This type of behavior can be explained by a curve in the negative quadrant shaped as indicated in Exhibit 3.6. In this curve "disutility" (i.e., the opposite of utility) of each increment of loss is greater as the amount of loss increases.

EXHIBIT 3.4 Bernoullian Utility Curve

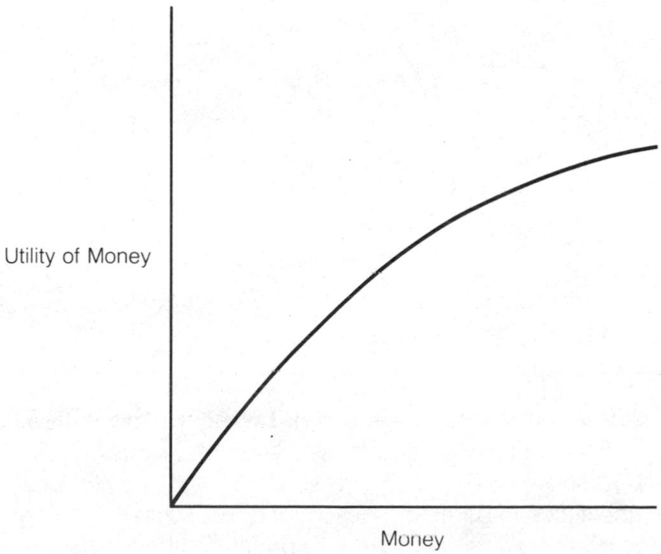

EXHIBIT 3.5 Utility Curve for Gambling Behavior

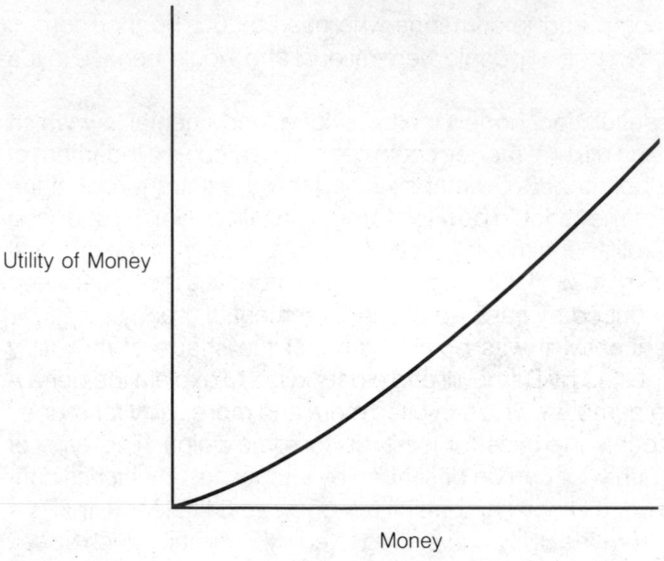

EXHIBIT 3.6 Disutility Curve for Buying Insurance

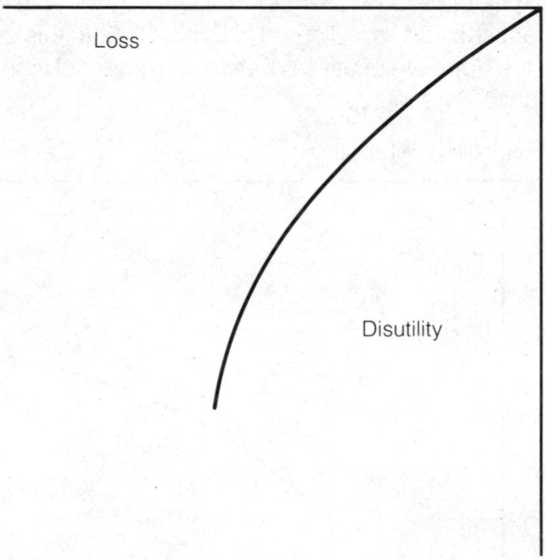

Using utility curves to assess risk-taking propensities. Friedman and Savage (1948) used these ideas to support a utility curve shaped as shown in Exhibit 3.7. They noted that one gives up a sure thing (the stake) in gambling to accept a risk, while in buying insurance one gives up a risk in favor of a sure thing (the loss represented by the premium). They said that the part of the curve in the negative quadrant explained insurance-buying and the part of the curve in the upper, right-hand (positive) quadrant explained utility in gambling situations. Both Bernoulli and Friedman-Savage curves are based on the assumption that the curves represent a rational assessment of the consequences expected to follow from taking actions involving risk. The assumption that individuals make decisions by evaluating expected value of an outcome has been questioned by some theorists (Radford, 1975).

More recently, Markowitz (1955) suggested that wealthy and poor individuals don't necessarily behave as utility curves based on their relative wealth would prescribe. For each person, the changes in behavior implied by the changes in the slope of the utility curve would take place at a different level of wealth. This is to say that the axes on the diagram in Exhibit 3.8 would intersect at different points on the absolute money scale for each individual. The individual's "customary wealth" (amount of money usually possessed by a person) would determine the point at which the intersection is placed. Another change in the Friedman-Savage utility function also was suggested by Markowitz. He reasoned that at great amounts of customary wealth an organization or person would become satiated with money and the utility of increments of money would decline. Similarly, very large levels of loss would be expected to reflect a leveling-off in the disutility of increments of loss. The utility curve proposed by Markowitz to reflect the criticisms of the Friedman-Savage

EXHIBIT 3.7 Utility Curve Suggested by Friedman and Savage

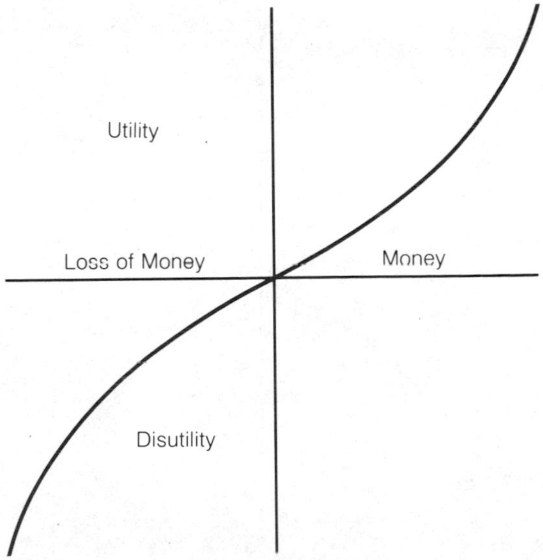

curve is shown in Figure 3.8. Here the axes intersect at a level reflecting the customary wealth of an individual or organization.

Swalm (1966) has summarized the literature on the interpretation of utility curves. He suggested on the basis of this literature review that utility theory can be used to derive curves describing risk-taking behaviors of decision makers, as well as serving as a prescriptive theory (indicating how decision makers should behave). The descriptive nature of utility theory is still being questioned, but MacCrimmon (1968) has found some evidence that managers behave roughly in accord with the axioms of utility theory. When they acted in a manner which is inconsistent with the axioms, they regarded these deviations as mistakes that they would like to correct. If utility theory can be regarded as descriptive, then its study can lead to understanding the behavior of decision makers.

Swalm described a study in which utility curves reflecting the decision-making behaviors of business executives were empirically derived. A "planning horizon" was established for each executive—defined as twice the maximum single amount the executive had authority to spend annually. Since Swalm was interested in describing decisions made by executives on behalf of their firms (rather than based on their personal customary wealth), the planning horizon was used instead of dollar amounts in drawing utility curves. This feature of the study was important because the decisions were taken by the executives for their organizations. The utility curve considered was that of the organization, or at least, the individual manager's per-

EXHIBIT 3.8 Utility Curve Suggested by Markowitz

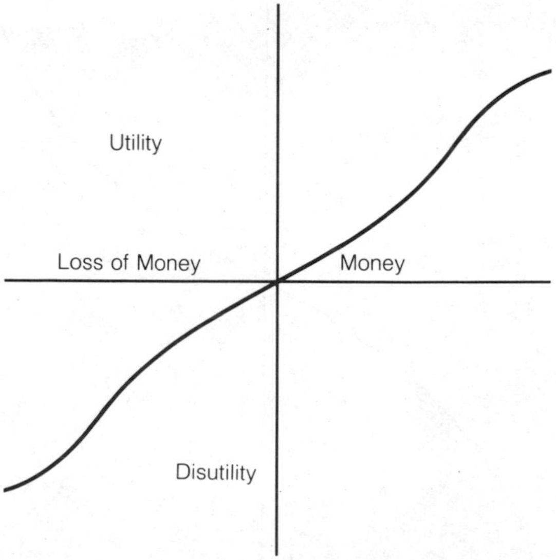

ception of the organizational utility curve. The use of the executive's personal utility curve in studying organizational decision making could be very misleading.

Executives in this study differed widely in their utility curves—even executives from the same company. The utility curves ranged from reflecting extreme risk-taking to extreme conservatism. These utility curves, shown in Exhibit 3.9, however, were similar in that the executives tended to be conservative in situations involving loss to the organization. This is reflected in the downward-sloping curves in the lower left-hand quadrant. Swalm pointed out that this attitude toward risk may indicate a bureaucratic tendency in organizational decision making. The executives may avoid risking losses because they believe rewards for taking risks are not enough to outweigh the penalties for losses.

Axioms of utility theory. Although we speculated above that utility theory may be used in a descriptive sense, it was originally a normative theory. For decision makers not to maximize expected utility would be contrary to their values and beliefs, since they are represented in expected utility. This is shown by the formal theories

EXHIBIT 3.9 Utility Curves Found by Swalm

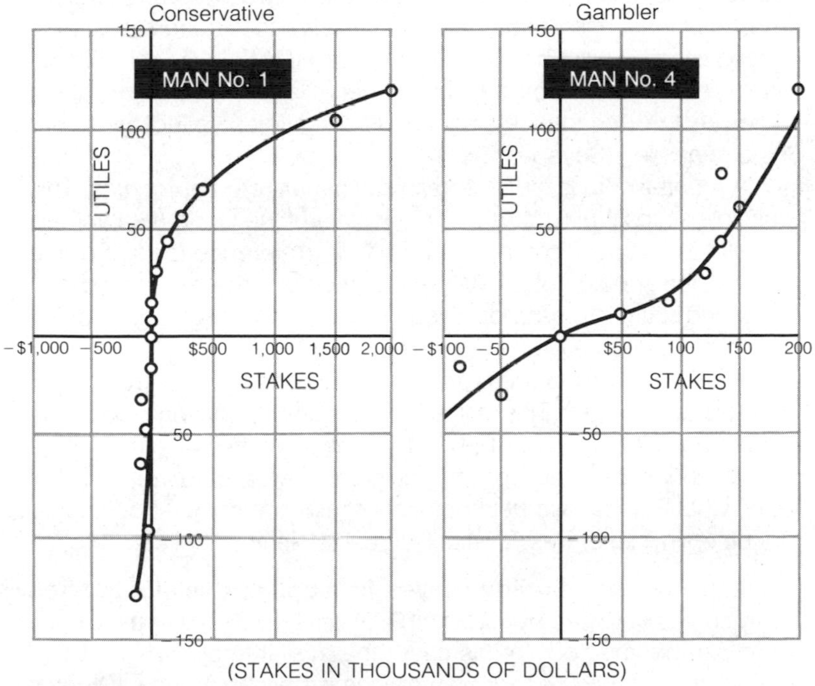

Source: Swalm, R.O. Utility theory — Insights into risk taking. *Harvard Business Review,* 1966, 132.

of utility that are derived from more simple axioms. These axioms prescribe decision making that is logically consistent. There are five major axioms, plus a few other conditions required to maximize expected utility (Luce & Suppes, 1965).

Transitivity specifies that if A is preferred to B, and B is preferred to C, then A must be preferred to C. As Edwards and his associates have observed, anyone failing to satisfy this requirement would be exploited as a "money pump." For example, if you prefer steak to lobster and lobster to pork chops, but pork chops to steak, this would violate transitivity. Then someone could trade you lobster for the pork chops you have, plus some money, then trade steak for the lobster, plus more money, then sell you back the original pork chops for the steak, plus more money. This could be repeated until you had run out of money, with no actual gain to you (the pump ran dry) or, hopefully, until you recognized the unreasonableness of being intransitive (Becker & McClintock, 1967).

The second axiom is *comparability.* This requires that individuals must always be willing to compare two outcomes and decide either that they prefer one to the other, or are indifferent between them. A third axiom is *dominance* or "sure thing." If, in every possible condition, one action (A) leads to an outcome that is at least as desirable as the outcome that results if a second action were taken—and, for at least one possible condition, A leads to a more desirable outcome than B—the dominance principle states that you should not prefer B to A. Since you are sure to get at least as much by taking action A, the dominance principle is sometimes called the "sure thing principle" (Savage, 1954).

A fourth axiom is the *irrelevance of nonaffected outcomes.* This principle states that if, for a particular state of the world, two actions result in the same outcome, your relative preference for one or the other action should not be affected by the outcome associated with that world state. In other words, only outcomes that actually discriminate among alternatives are considered.

A fifth axiom is *independence of beliefs and rewards* (no wishful thinking is permitted). This states that your desires for some outcome should not influence your beliefs that the outcome will occur. Your beliefs about the likelihood of rain tomorrow should not depend upon what you have to gain or lose if it rains tomorrow. You should not be optimistic or pessimistic, but realistic in your beliefs.

Implications of utility curves for applied decisions. The utility curves obtained by Swalm (1966) were derived using the standard gamble method. In this case, the available options had outcomes which could be represented completely by money. It seems reasonable to assume that executives involved in this study would express their preferences for different sums of money, that their preferences would obey transitivity, and that they would prefer the certainty of a larger sum of money to a gamble involving only the probability of a lesser amount. In addition, the implicit assumption that the executives were working toward a single objective (maximizing profit) appears reasonable in this experiment.

Yet, there is some question whether the assumptions required for deriving utility on an interval scale (i.e., a scale with equal distances between points) is met in day-to-day managerial decision making. Mosteller and Nogee (1951) have reported one attempt to investigate this experimentally. It appears doubtful, however, that laboratory experiments involving persons with little responsibility and sums of money much smaller than the amounts dealt with by executives provide a satisfactory test of managerial behavior (Marschak, 1964). The extreme difficulty of experimenting with actual executives in real-life situations has prohibited more conclusive research. Some researchers have tried to overcome some of the problems in applying the Von Newmann-Morgenstern treatment of utility to practical decision making, with inconclusive results. This is an area in which a great deal of research still is needed.

CRITERIA FOR CHOOSING

A decision maker's preferences are important in forming *criteria* for choosing among alternative courses of action. By criteria we mean the standards against which the possible actions we may take are evaluated. In deciding which career to enter, for example, it is likely that a person concerned with job security would consider criteria such as the availability of jobs in various fields, the time and expense involved in becoming qualified to enter the field, and the salary the job would be expected to pay. A person less concerned with job security may choose a job using very different criteria. The latter person may use such criteria as interesting work or the opportunity to help other people. The literature of economics, psychology, and management science have contributed useful methods for specifying attributes of decision alternatives which are likely to lead to desired outcomes.

Dealing with Multiple Criteria

Criteria are seldom, if ever, unidimensional. For example, in personnel selection decisions, "on the job success" contains many dimensions—except in the case of an abstraction such as the criterion of "ultimate worth" described by Thorndike (1950) to include everything that ultimately defines success on a job (e.g., total contribution of an employee to the organization). In dealing with immediate- and intermediate-level criteria (measurable outcomes related to the ultimate criterion), we are likely to find that they are quite diverse. The general low intercorrelations among criteria (e.g., output, quality, absences, tenure, rate of advancement, accidents, and ratings of success), coupled with an awareness that different combinations of criteria can result in selecting very different types of employees, make the frequent practice of ignoring all but one criterion, or forming an arbitrary composite criterion, seem ill-advised.

Guion (1965) suggested that the elements of a criterion should be combined if they can be shown to be related; otherwise, independent predictions should be made for each of the independent criteria. This operates to move the reliance on judgment to a point later in the selection process—the decision maker can predict several aspects of job success and, later, make judgments about their importance to the decision.

Synthetic validity. Synthetic validity (Balma, 1959) is another way to deal with the problem of multiple criteria. It requires the identification of the elements important in performing job duties and looks for attributes that have previously been shown to predict each element. Each element identified as important for performing this job in a company is judged for importance, and the tests are correspondingly weighted and combined. Although the method has obvious advantages for small firms that hire only a few workers for a given job and cannot carry out a statistical study of the usual type to determine predictor weights, it also has all the faults noted in combining criteria by judgment procedures. One reassuring feature of this technique is the recommendation that follow-up studies be made to check its accuracy. For more detailed discussions of synthetic validity see Dunnette (1966), Cronbach (1970), and Guion (1965) in addition to Balma (1959).

Suboptimization and criteria. McKeen (1964) has warned that selection of inappropriate criteria can contribute to "suboptimization." Since complex decision making is generally broken into component parts (each part being dealt with by a different decision-making unit), decision makers compare alternative courses of action that pertain to only a part of a problem. The resulting analyses may be intended to discover optimal solutions to subproblems; in the language of systems analysis, this is the process of suboptimization. Suboptimization presents the advantage of being able to take into account more detail in the analysis of problems. Yet, the danger of suboptimization in the selection of criteria is that lower-level criteria may be inconsistent with higher-level criteria. McKeen (1964) described the following example of suboptimization in a military situation:

> Suppose that we compare alternative machine guns and adopt as our test the lowest-cost gun that will fire a number of rounds the equivalent of three years' steady combat operation. Experience may indicate, however, that such durability is superfluous since guns are usually lost after, say, the equivalent of three months' combat. The criterion of the best machine gun should be related to the test of an effective ground force. Hence, it is always urgent at least to ponder higher level criteria in order to avoid serious inconsistencies. (pp. 84–85)

Compensatory and noncompensatory attributes. The attributes of decision alternatives may be treated as either compensatory or noncompensatory. With compensatory criteria, poor values on one attribute may be offset by high values on other attributes. Hence, one attribute can compensate for another. On the other hand, particularly good values on one attribute cannot offset poor values on another attribute when noncompensatory criteria are used. The operation of these rules can be observed in making hiring decisions on the basis of psychological test scores. Using multiple cutoff scores eliminates applicants who are low on any test; thus, the tests are used in a noncompensatory manner. The use of a composite score is compensatory in that it permits an applicant who is very low on one test to make up for this by a very high score on another.

The essential difference between multiple cutoff rules and a cutoff score for a single composite predictor is that the weighted composite acts on the assumption of compensation among abilities. A person weak in manual dexterity, for example, may be hired if that person has exceptional perceptual ability; strength in one is assumed to make up for weakness in the other. Noncompensatory use of attributes in decision making is shown by selecting a football player on the basis of his running, passing, or kicking ability, without permitting, for example, a potential quarterback's mediocre passing ability to be offset by some skill in kicking. In personnel selection, however, the use of compensation seems to be justified in most cases.

The multiple cutoff score has the advantage of simplicity both in calculation and in explaining the decision rules to psychological test users. Yet even when the doctrine of compensation is unsound, the multiple cutoff is not the most efficient rule. As Lord (1962) has shown, due to reduced measurement error, a cutting rule based on a properly positioned regression curve (a compensatory method) does the best job of prediction. When the line is properly drawn, all individuals along the line are expected to have equally good criterion scores. The United States Employment Service has recognized this issue by applying a confidence-interval technique—which warns that decisions are risky for any case that falls into a region close to an occupational cutoff line on the General Aptitude Test Battery.

More complex compensatory models have been developed in which some degree of interaction among attributes is considered. Slovic (1969) has used analysis of variance to study the interactions among attributes of stocks as judged by stockbrokers. Einhorn (1970) has explored weighting models represented by hyperbolic and parabolic functions.

Absolute vs. relative standards. The usual strategy for personnel selection decisions involves comparison of applicants against a standard (norm), and considers multiple attributes (predictors). Note that in this context the standard can be thought of as a surrogate alternative and is used to screen out unacceptable alternatives. The attributes are generally quite complex in terms of both the number of predictors that one must work with and the number of independent dimensions represented by these predictors. Systematic methods for analyzing the meaning of intercorrelations among predictors (dimensional analysis) have been developed; the most widely used is factor analysis. Basically, dimensional analysis attempts to develop clusters of tests that correlate well with each other and to logically infer the nature of the underlying dimension (factor) that may have caused such a pattern of correlations.

Dimensional analyses have been applied to many kinds of predictors (tests, ratings, checklists, interviews, etc.), but the intellect has received the most attention. Cattell (1953) proposed a universal index number to assign to a factor when its identification became accepted, but the suggestion has not received wide use. A well-organized taxonomy of intellectual factors has been presented by Guilford (1956) as a theory of the structure of the intellect. Although the theory has had critics, it demonstrates the nature of an organized classification of descriptive traits and its potential number of factors (120) indicates the complexity of human abilities. For useful treatments of factor analytic methods with psychologically oriented illustrations see Fructer (1954) and Harmon (1960).

The procedure described by Kepner and Tregoe (1965) for choosing among decision alternatives involves a combination of both absolute and relative criteria. They require the decision maker to decide which criteria "must" be met if the choice is to be successful; these are treated as absolute criteria, and no trade-offs are permitted to compensate for less than satisfactory values on these criteria. Other criteria, however, are described as "want" criteria. The want criteria reflect attributes that are desirable in decision alternatives, but are not absolutely necessary. Hence, these criteria are treated in a compensatory fashion. For example, in purchasing a house, a minimum of three bedrooms may be specified as a must criterion. No houses having fewer than three bedrooms will be considered, no matter how attractive their other features may be. The purchaser may also prefer a house with a family room, but not consider this an essential feature of a house. The family room would be treated in a compensatory manner, and a house without a family room may be purchased if it has other desirable features.

CHOOSING: MAXIMIZING, SATISFICING, AND INCREMENTALIZING

Three major approaches to making choices among decision alternatives (choice modes) are described in this section: maximizing, satisficing, and incrementalizing (MacCrimmon & Taylor, 1976). These approaches differ in conceptual frameworks, in assumptions they make about their decision makers, and procedures. A brief discussion of rationality in decision making precedes our discussion of the choice modes.

Rationality and the ''Economic Man''

The foundation for exploring ''reason'' as a basis for human choices has been provided by the notion of an ''economic man.'' Simon (1955) has described the economic man as:

> an ''economic man'' . . . is in the course of being ''economic'' is also ''rational.'' This man is assumed to have knowledge of the relevant aspects of his environment which, if not absolutely complete, is at least impressively clear and voluminous. He is assumed to have a well-organized and stable system of preferences, and a skill in computation that enables him to calculate for the alternative courses of action that are available to him, which of these will permit him to reach the highest attainable point on his preference scale. (Simon, 1955, p. 99)

The economic person, thus, knows what is best for one's own economic interests and acts accordingly. Actions are based upon a careful consideration of their possible consequences, and the course of action that can be expected to bring maximum gain is chosen. This notion of personal gain originated in the marketplace with the work of Adam Smith, but has been broadened by decision theory to include nonbusiness choices as well. Considered broadly, the *hedonistic calculus* developed by Jeremy Bentham posed a similar basis for choice. He viewed man as seeking pleasure and avoiding pain; actions which will give the greatest happiness should be chosen. Keep in mind that hedonistic calculus prescribed that happiness should be sought, but not that it would necessarily be attained.

The rational people of decision theory, then, make choices which are best for themselves. They may be best in terms of either a psychological or a material gain. Radford (1975) has stated, "If he carries out all the steps in the decision process . . . and arrives at the resolution stage with an evaluation of options and a criterion of choice between these options, he is regarded as rational if he chooses the option that is selected as best by his process" (p. 12). Rationality, then, has also been attributed to the procedures for making choices. Since procedures for making choices differ in the choice modes discussed below and yet each can be viewed as compatible with rational decision making, it appears unnecessary to limit rationality by specifying the procedures by which it may be attained. To be rational, a choice need not require extended deliberation or quantitative analysis; all that is necessary is that an objective exist and the decision maker select an alternative which that person believes will best meet the objective.

Difficulties in Specifying Rationality in Decision Making

Lee (1971) lists four characteristics of decision situations which make it difficult to specify the "rationality" of decision making.

1. All decision alternatives must be known before rationality of a choice can be specified. The rational decision is only one of many courses of action the decision maker can take. To say that one action is best requires that the other actions against which it is to be compared are known. In laboratory studies decisions are generally made from a specified set of actions, but outside the laboratory the need to seek other alternatives presents difficulties for specifying rational choices in decision theory. Consider the task of the committee responsible for selecting a site for a new sports stadium. While they may be provided with a list of proposed sites, the list is unlikely to contain all possible sites, and a better site may exist elsewhere. The committee may refuse to choose from the proposed list of sites and seek additional sites.
2. The investigator defines what is rational behavior. Rationality is determined by the decision principle used by an investigator. A decision principle is a rule for specifying which of a set of decision alternatives is rational. The decision principles used in investigations of decision making do not always agree upon the rational choice.

   When the objective probabilities for events are known (e.g., the probability of winning in roulette), they are an appropriate basis for specifying the rationality of choices. For most decisions, however, objective probabilities are not known; an individual's subjective probabilities are then used as a criterion for rationality. Two difficulties for specifying rationality are introduced when subjective probabilities are used: 1) individuals can choose different alternatives, yet each decision can be rational; and 2) people may be rational with respect to their subjective probabilities, but not rational with respect to objective probabilities.
3. Rationality is specific to the values of an individual. Decision makers may differ in evaluating the consequences of a decision. For example, in choosing a city in which to live we cannot require that the rational decision be the same for everyone. Individuals differ in the attractiveness they attribute to alternative cities.
4. Rationality depends upon the information available to a decision maker. In

most decisions, it is difficult to determine what information is relevant and its value for reaching a rational decision. Even the availability of information is difficult to specify in most decisions since information generally can be made available, but at a cost. The decision maker must determine how much time, effort, and money to spend in obtaining information.

It also is important to distinguish between rational decisions and rational people. A person's decision may be rational in one context and not rational in another. People cannot be classified as rational over all decisions. Even for a particular decision, it is better to recognize the degree of departure from rationality by describing people along a continuum of rationality.

Maximizing

Maximizing places great demands upon a decision maker's cognitive abilities. To maximize, the decision maker is required to develop a complete set of possible courses of action, to specify all possible outcomes resulting from taking any of these actions, and to judge the actions in the light of appropriate criteria. Therefore, the decision maker requires a well-specified set of alternatives and a clear basis for choosing the alternative that comes closest to the ideal level. Another way of stating the maximizing mode is to say that we are dealing with "economic man." Economic man is presumed to be perfectly informed, perfectly sensitive, and perfectly rational (Edwards, 1954). In classical theories of consumer demand and theories of the firm, consumers maximize their utility defined over commodity bundles and the firm maximizes its profits (Marshall, 1980).

Maximizing in decision making generally refers to maximizing expected utility. To maximize expected utility, a decision maker must list all relevant decision alternatives, the events that may result from choosing each alternative, and the payoffs for each event. Then personal probabilities are assigned to the events and utilities assigned to the payoffs. The expected utility for any action is found by multiplying the probability of an event leading to an outcome by the utility of the outcome, then adding the products for all events that would result from taking the action. Finally, the course of action yielding the largest expected utility is chosen (Savage, 1954; Fishburn, 1968).

Expected utility analysis is extremely difficult to apply. Ideally, all possible alternative courses of action should be listed. However, failure to do so does not seriously hamper the use of expected utility analysis if the major courses of action are included. Utility functions can be obtained for actions described by a single dimension without great difficulty. However, as is usually the case, there are typically many attributes to consider. Luce and Krantz (1971) have developed an approach to "conditional expected utility" which reduces the number of probability judgments required, but the number of judgments is still likely to be prohibitive in practical situations. Utility has been recognized as an important consideration in personnel selection decisions (Cronbach & Gleser, 1965); yet the extreme difficulties in estimating utilities have led Dunnette (1966) to suggest that it be viewed as a way of thinking about personnel decisions, rather than as a formal set of rules.

Satisficing

Although most decision makers would prefer to maximize, Simon (1955) pointed out that it is not feasible to do so. In most practical situations decision makers *satisfice,* since it is not feasible to meet the requirements of the maximizing choice mode. The limited capacity of the human mind for comprehending all alternatives in a given decision is implied in Simon's concept of bounded rationality. He suggested that, rather than a decision that maximizes utility or satisfaction, a more realistic choice is one that satisfices. By definition, satisficing consists of choosing a course of action that is good enough in view of the intended goal or current level of aspiration of the decision maker; a "satisfactory" course of action.

Simon (1957) and March and Simon (1958) have suggested that human decision makers behave rationally within their limited perception of decision problems. However, when confronted by the great complexity of most organizational problems, humans are forced to view the problems within sharply restricted "bounds" of rational decision making. It appears that decision makers try to compensate for their limited ability to cope with the informational demands of a complex of problems by developing simple models of the problems. Their behaviors can be considered rational, but only in terms of their simplified views of the problems. The idea of bounded rationality is generally accepted by theories of administrative decision making; it explains departures from rationality as specified by the maximizing choice mode. In a satisficing choice mode, a feasible aspiration level is set, and alternatives are sought until one that meets the aspiration level of the decision maker is located. When a satisfactory alternative is found, search is terminated and the alternative is chosen.

Satisficing behavior has been found in many studies (e.g., for department store buyers, Cyert and March, 1963; and for trust investment officers, Clarkson, 1962). Because it is derived from observations of decision makers' behavior, satisficing is primarily descriptive. Although it has been proposed that under some circumstances decision makers should satisfice, as a prescriptive strategy satisficing has serious shortcomings. It may be good enough for some administrative decisions, but it offers little in the way of assistance to decision makers attempting to improve their performance.

Incrementalizing

Lindblom (1959) has described a choice mode which is similar to satisficing in that it places relatively little cognitive demand on decision makers. This approach, which we mentioned in our previous discussion of problem formulation, is called "disjointed incrementalism." Using this choice mode, the decision makers attempt to take only small steps, or incremental moves, away from the existing state in the direction they desire (successive limited comparisons). In this approach, few objectives would be considered, and the alternatives would generally be ones that are familiar to the decision makers or that could be generated by local search. Important outcomes, values, and alternatives may be neglected in incrementalizing. Agreement among decision makers is sought instead of high goal attainment. Clearly, this is primarily a descriptive model of how decisions are made—particularly when decisions are made by groups which have conflicting preferences. However, when decision making can proceed by a series of small, sequential subdecisions and substantial adverse consequences of decision making are anticipated, this approach suggests that the subproblems may be treated more effectively as new and separate problems. Also, unanticipated adverse consequences may be handled more effectively by waiting for them to appear than by attempting to anticipate every contingency. Lindblom (1965) has described one application of the incrementalizing choice mode.

> A city traffic engineer, for example, might propose the allocation of certain streets to one-way traffic. In so doing, he might be quite unable to predict how many serious bottlenecks in traffic, if any, would develop and where they would arise. Nevertheless, he might confidently make his recommendations, assuming that if any bottlenecks arose, appropriate steps to solve the new problem could be taken at that time—new traffic lights, assignment of a traffic patrolman, or further revision of the one-way plan itself. (p. 150)

SUMMARY

Some of the central issues in developing alternative solutions were discussed in this chapter. Decision alternatives can be familiar solutions that are routinely applied to well-structured problems or the creative ability of decision makers may be severely challenged by the need to discover or invent solutions to ill-structured problems. Whereas many heuristics have been developed (e.g., SOPs or computer programs), even after devoting considerable research attention to studies of brainstorming, relatively little is known about how decision alternatives are created. Nevertheless, creativity stimulating techniques appear to be useful in some circumstances.

We examined the role played by goals and objectives in evaluating alternative courses of action. Strategic uses of objectives have been explored and suggestions made for formulating objectives more accurately. Little is known about the behavioral bases for setting or modifying objectives, although the theories and research on level of aspiration are relevant. Methods for assessing subjective preferences have attracted much research attention. The indirect methods have a more adequate theoretical basis, and, although the procedures are somewhat time-consuming and tedious, significant advances are being made in this area.

Ways in which the value of decision alternatives can be represented (costs-benefits and utilities) were briefly discussed and compensatory vs. noncompensatory uses of criteria were explored. Use of compensatory criteria in personnel selection and placement decisions was described. Choice has been the focus for decision theory, leading to well-developed theories of rational decision making. While the descriptive implications of maximizing expected utility for practical decision making are in question, the satisficing choice mode appears very useful in many decision contexts. Incrementalizing also has proved useful when agreement among decision makers is more important than decision quality.

Each of the next three chapters will examine a major difficulty in processing information for making choices—complexity, uncertainty, and organizational influences. Comparing several courses of action and choosing one is an extremely difficult task in most practical decision situations. Typically, each course of action is complex, and it strains the human information-processing capacity to understand a single alternative and its implications—let alone to carry in the mind several courses of action simultaneously in order to compare them with each other. Frequently, even if they could be laid out beside each other, there is no clear way to make comparisons among courses of action. In addition, there are generally a number of unknown factors that intrude on the decision. Some of the consequences of actions are uncertain, and no one knows what will actually happen. Finally, decisions frequently are made in an organizational context in which some of the consequences depend on how other people react to a decision, and often the other people don't even know how they will react.

CHOOSING IN COMPLEX DECISION PROBLEMS 4

A major challenge confronting managerial decision makers is their sharply limited ability to process the volume of information required in complex decision problems. The rational model which underlies traditional decision-making theories and techniques assumes that decision makers have extensive information regarding the features of the decision problem. Ideally, a complete set of possible courses of action will be known, all possible outcomes that may result from taking any of these actions will be specified, and courses of action will be judged in the light of appropriate criteria to determine the extent to which they attain the decision maker's objectives. Clearly, these requirements are impossible to meet in most practical decision problems.

Consider the following situation. You are a production unit supervisor in a farm tractor assembly plant. Your boss, the operations manager, has called you on the carpet about the declining output of your unit during the past month. After assuring your boss that you will correct the problem, what would you do? This problem contains many factors which may influence production. Is the machinery operating properly? Possibly, neglected maintenance has taken its toll. What about the skill and morale of the workers in your unit? Have product modifications led to unwieldy production procedures or to levels of precision which strain the capability of your production equipment? Somehow, you must keep track of all this information if a sound decision is to be made. And, of course, your boss is watching to see the results of the actions you take.

SOURCES OF COMPLEXITY IN DECISION PROBLEMS

Decisions of this complexity—and much greater complexity—are not unusual in applied decision making. For example, whether or not to seed hurricanes to reduce their destructiveness, what premiums to set for automobile insurance, what stock to purchase, or what new product to market are even more complex than the decision facing the production supervisor in the above situation. Studies of ongoing organizations and in the laboratory both demonstrate that decisional complexity is a serious block to effective decision making. In addition to the prohibitive cost of acquiring extensive information, complex decision problems can lead to information overload and the attendant consequences of cognitive strain and poor-quality decisions.

Major sources of complexity in practical decisions are the number of factors that must be taken into account and the highly interconnected nature of these factors. Two issues in complexity will be highlighted in this chapter—the difficulties produced by informational demands which exceed an individual's ability to process information and the very complex decision problems produced by the multiple attributes of decision alternatives and the multiple objectives of decision makers. Next, the behavioral aspects of information processing in complex decision problems will be discussed, including the major views regarding the nature of human information processing and the implications of these views for improved information-processing ability. Finally, strategies for overcoming the difficulties of complexity in decision making are suggested.

PROBLEM COMPLEXITY AND BOUNDED RATIONALITY

As was pointed out in the previous chapter, the concept of *bounded rationality* is central to managerial decision making in complex organizations. Simon (1978), in attempting to describe how managers actually make decisions, has contrasted the narrow economic definition of rationality with a more general meaning of being intelligent and reasonable. An important feature of bounded rationality is Simon's contention that administrative decision makers do not follow an exhaustive process of evaluating all options open to them and selecting the best option. Rather, the "satisficing" decision maker proceeds only until a course of action that is satisfactory or good enough is found. Satisficing involves setting a feasible aspiration level, seeking courses of action until one is located which is good enough to meet this aspiration level, and choosing this satisfactory course of action. The satisficing model implies that decision makers accommodate the excessive informational demands of complex decision problems by developing a simple model of the decision problem. Their decision-making behaviors are rational, but only within the bounds of this simple model of the problem.

Influence of Cognitive Strain on Bounded Rationality

Bounded rationality has been explained on the basis of cognitive strain. Cognitive strain is a breakdown of decision makers' cognitive processes when the informational demands of a decision problem exceed their information-processing capacity. Clearly, both unsystematic observations and research with actual organizations have shown that cognitive strain is a widespread condition, affecting administrative decisions in such diverse contexts as natural resource management, military tactics, governmental policy, and business.

The bounds on rational decision making imposed by cognitive strain can be viewed within the framework suggested by Reitman (1964) as psychological constraints on decision problems. Hence, decision makers' limited ability to handle the informational demands of a problem may force them to close many of the open constraints relevant to the problem and to formulate the problem in a restricted manner. This approach shields decision makers from cognitive strain by simplifying the problem, but it produces considerably less precision in decision making than many problems require. In coping with bounded rationality, a better approach would be to help decision makers to increase their information processing capacity and, thus, to expand the "bounds" within which decision making can occur.

Expanding the Bounds of Rational Decision Making

Decision-making performance depends upon both the behavioral characteristics of the decision maker and the features of the decision environment. Hence, the bounds of rational decision making can be expanded by either modifying the decision maker (e.g., through selecting "good" decision makers or training decision makers) or the decision situation (engineering the decision problem and environment). The reason for examining the behavioral aspects of making complex decisions is to draw upon our understanding of human information-processing and decision-making capabilities in suggesting strategies for coping with cognitive strain. While our discussion of cognitive limitations in decision making, in this section, focuses upon individual decision makers, similar phenomena exist in decision-making groups. These phenomena will be examined later in the context of decision making in organizations.

MAKING DECISIONS INVOLVING MULTIPLE ATTRIBUTES OR MULTIPLE OBJECTIVES

Major causes of complexity in practical decisions are the great many factors that should be taken into account, and the highly interconnected nature of these factors. It is frequently necessary to cope with a large number of desired objectives and many attributes of the decision alternatives. Although multiple-objective decision making and multiple-attribute decision making frequently are used interchangeably, it is useful to distinguish between them (MacCrimmon, 1973).

Multiple-Attribute Decisions

Multiple-attribute decision problems require that choices be made among alternatives described by their attributes (characteristics). Houses being considered for purchase can be described by price, number of bedrooms, location, appearance, etc. Generally, multiple-attribute decisions can be resolved in a rather straightforward manner by specifying both the decision makers' preferences among values of a given attribute (e.g., How much are three bedrooms preferred over two bedrooms?) and their preferences across attributes (e.g., How much more important is price than location?). Techniques for assisting in making multiple-attribute decisions either infer these preferences from the decision makers' past decisions or they directly assess them.

Multiple-Objective Decisions

Multiple-objective decision problems require that means-ends relationships be specified, since they deal explicitly with the relationship of attributes of alternatives to higher-level objectives of the decision maker. The two approaches will be the same only when there is a direct correspondence between attributes and objectives. In addition to the information needed for multiple-attribute decisions, in making multiple-objective decisions a decision maker's preferences regarding objectives must be stated and the relationships between objectives and attributes for each course of action must be identified. A decision maker's objectives in buying a house may include social status, financial security, comfort, minimum commuting time, etc. Making multiple-objective decisions requires that the relative values assigned to each of these objectives be given, and the extent to which the attributes (e.g., price, number of bedrooms, location) contribute to the attainment of the objectives be specified.

An Example

Let's return to the problem of developing a lighter-weight air cleaner for an automobile. Recall that the desired state included not only a reduction in weight, but also other objectives. These objectives included maintaining the same level of performance in filtering efficiency and capacity, in silencing capabilities, in temperature control, and in ease of adaptability to changing under-hood engine configurations. In addition, it was desired that the solution be found in time for use in the next year's model automobile and that it be done within the specified limits in money, manpower, and technology. These multiple objectives of the Air Cleaner Division of Apex Automobile Company are embedded within the corporate objective of increasing the profitability of the company by selling more automobiles. Sales may be increased by offering more functional automobiles (those with more trunk room, more leg room, improved styling, better handling, etc.) and automobiles with improved gas mileage. The gas mileage of automobiles can be improved by designing more efficient engines, streamlining the design of the automobiles, and by designing lighter automobiles. The air cleaner is only one feature of the automobile that can be made lighter.

In this problem, although the overall relationship of the automobile components to the rest of the automobile must be kept in mind, it is feasible to reduce the complexity of the overall problem—designing a lighter-weight automobile—by factoring the problem. Thus, each component of the car can be lightened with a minimum of coordination among the groups working on the various components. In highly interconnected decision problems, such factoring into simpler problems is not feasible.

A number of techniques have been developed to assist in making decisions plagued by multiple objectives and/or multiple attributes. Essentially, these strategies attempt to reduce the complexity of the decision problem by aggregating the decision maker's preferences regarding various features of a decision problem. Some of the more useful techniques for managerial decisions are described below.

RULES FOR USING INFORMATION IN SOLVING COMPLEX PROBLEMS

Managerial decision making can be improved by understanding the behavioral processes by which humans handle information and make choices. A considerable amount of research has been devoted to this end by researchers interested in cognitive processes, judgment, and problem solving, as well as research on information processing and decision making. In this section we will examine some of the mechanisms of information processing that underlie human thinking, summarize the major conclusions drawn from research on models of decision processes, and suggest the implications of these research conclusions for developing strategies to improve decisions in complex situations.

Information Processing Mechanisms and Human Thought

Drawing upon psychological research on thinking, reasoning, and concept attainment a simple model of human information-processing mechanisms can be developed. The implications of this model for aiding decision making in complex situations can then be examined. Two issues drawn from the model are particularly useful in developing decision aids—trade-offs between processing and memory which form the basis for "expert" judgment, and the features of a human information-processing system which improve its capacity to process information by permitting the system to do several things at a time. Readers who desire to go beyond the discussion presented here are referred to the classic books by Miller, Galanter, and Pribram (1960) and Bruner, Goodnow, and Austin (1956) and to more recent reviews by Neimark and Santa (1975) and Falmagne (1975). Raphael (1976) and Hunt (1975) provide useful reviews of the implications of artificial intelligence for problem solving, and Newell (1973) has proposed that analysis of production systems may yield insights into human cognition.

An Information-Processing Model

Consider a simple model of the human mind proposed by Lindsay and Norman (1972) containing four key elements: (1) processing units, (2) a supervisory processor, (3) a memory, and (4) an input-output mechanism. These components are shown in Exhibit 4.1.

EXHIBIT 4.1 An Information-Processing System for Thinking

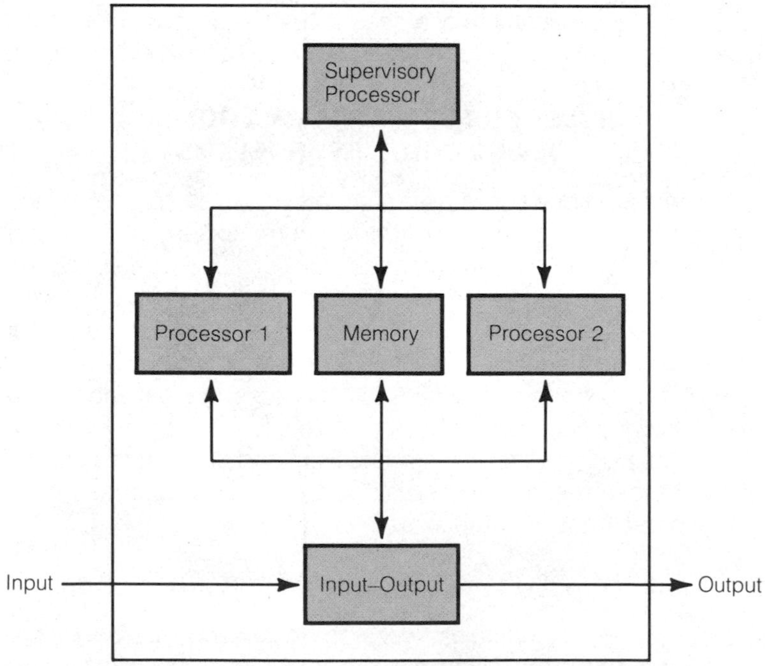

Source: Lindsay, P.H. and Norman, D.A. *An introduction to psychology.* New York: Academic Press, 1977, 603

In this model the mind is organized so that many separate information-processing units exist, each with the capability to perform predetermined (programmed) operations on the information contained in the memory, and with a single overseeing supervisory processor. Given the present state of knowledge concerning the organization of the human mind, this model is probably about as accurate as we can get. Whether or not the model corresponds to the structures of the human brain is immaterial to our analysis; what is important is that the model be useful in suggesting decision aids based on our understanding of its features.

The four key components of the model need to be defined before we explore the manner in which they operate. The *processors* actually carry out the operations of the system—examining information in memory, comparing the contents of memory units, and/or deciding what operation to perform next. Processors follow specific sequences of action prescribed in programs. The *supervisory processor* enables the information processing system to do more than one thing at a time. Its main function is to control the operations of the information-processing system to insure that the system attains a specified goal or goals. It monitors what each processor does, compares the performance of the processors, and resolves any conflicts which exist.

Memory is the place where two types of information—data and programs—are stored. Data are facts used by processors in performing their operations; programs are sequences of instructions to be followed. Perhaps the most familiar examples of programs are those described in our earlier discussion of responses to well-structured problems, but in the model discussed here all information processing is viewed as program-directed. An important feature of programs in information-processing systems is that they can be treated as data; thus, programs can be evaluated and modified. Also, information in memory takes on meaning only as a processor interprets it. Hence, the same information may be interpreted differently from one time to another. Finally, the *input-output* component is the mechanism by which information is received from the environment and transmitted back to the environment.

Rules for Information Use

Memory-processing trade-off. In complex problems ease of performance often can be traded off against the amount of material that must be learned *memory-processing trade-off.* In human information processing, the more the material learned (i.e., stored in short-term memory), the less the computations to perform (i.e., processor operations) and the easier the task becomes. If one works hard to learn a task, it is easy to perform the task. A simple illustration of this principle is seen in the difference between the amount of time (and processor activity) required to compute and report the product of two large numbers a first time and the time required to give the same answer shortly afterward from memory.

A trade-off between processing and memory can be seen in the nature of "expertise" in many areas of competence—in learning to play soccer, to read, to become a competent lawyer, and in becoming an expert chess player. During the long period of study or practice, large amounts of structured knowledge are placed in memory. Well-learned, meaningful patterns of information are easier to remember and to use in decision making than are patterns that make no sense to the processor. Many memory aids use this principle. Students, for example, who are required to remember a list of items may make up words using the first letter of each item in the list.

Can you remember a sequence of letters? Read the following letters, then look away from the page and try to repeat them.

TMNAENMAEG

Few people can recall this many unrelated items of information, so you are to be congratulated if you were successful. If you could not recall the items in the pattern above, arranging them in another pattern might help. Let's try the following arrangement and ask you to read the letters, then look away from the page and repeat them.

MANAGEMENT

This task was much easier, wasn't it? You probably did not even think of them as ten separate letters since they make up a word which has meaning for you. Hence, the word can be stored in your memory as one psychological unit. Songs, sentences, or even entire written passages can be remembered in this way.

The favorite example of processing-memory trade-off in the literature of psychology is the chess master. Experienced chess players can treat configurations of chess pieces much as most people treat the letters in the recall task above. Games contain logical sequences of moves, and the moves form systematic patterns on the chess board. In fact, an expert player knows the names given to many of the patterns. The great familiarity of the chess master enables the player to view configurations of pieces as easily as a less experienced player may view the position on the board of a single piece. Much as in the case of the word-recall exercise above, familiar configurations can be stored as a single psychological unit in the memory of the human information-processing system. The intent of this discussion is not to denigrate the ability of experienced chess players—differences in skills are evident even among experienced players—but to point out one mechanism that underlies expertise in many tasks. A learned meaningfulness of information is the basis for several strategies discussed below for making decisions in complex situations (e.g., chunking).

External aids to short-term memory. Another principle that can be developed from the model of information-processing systems described above is the use of external aids to short-term memory. Clearly, human short-term memory is very limited. In a classic study, Miller (1956) concluded that about seven chunks of information were as much as most people could retain in short-term memory. External aids are commonly used to overcome the limitations of short-term memory; consider how lost we would be without pencils and paper (or Xerox machines!). There is an important difference between a Xerox copy of an academic journal article, however, and notes on the article prepared by a student. The mind is viewed as an active information handler (Posner, 1963), which stores a personally meaningful abstracted interpretation of the data to which it is exposed, rather than a complete representation of the data. In trans-

EXHIBIT 4.2 The Gorky Street Algorithm

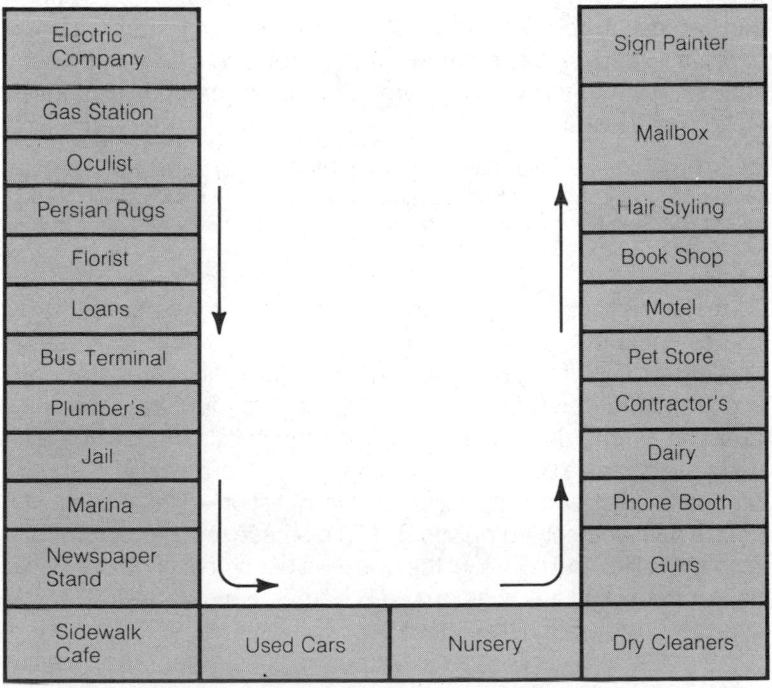

Source: Crovitz, H.F. *Galton's walk*. New York: Harper & Row, 1970, 38.

forming lecture comments into notes for study, the student generally writes down a highly abstracted and idiosyncratic version of the lecture content. The notes have greater meaning for the student than did the lecturer's remarks.

Familiar locations can provide a "mental map" for aiding memory by providing associations with new items one wishes to remember. This method has been called the *Gorky Street Algorithm* (Crovitz, 1970). It involves memorizing lists of items by associating each item with a location on Gorky Street, Exhibit 4.2 on page 87. Of course, you can substitute a street familiar to you. To remember a shopping list containing milk, eggs, oranges, etc., simply form vivid images of each item at successive locations. For example, the vivid image linking milk to the first location on Gorky Street, the electric company, could be that of a cow being milked by an electric milking machine. Next, at the gas station a car could be getting new springs so that the eggs being carried in it would not be broken. Such images are developed for all items in the list and, at the grocery store, one would think of the familiar locations on the map of Gorky Street to recall the grocery list. Much more complex maps have been used by famous mnemonists to astonish crowds with their feats of memory.

Symbols such as pictures, words, or numbers play an important role in overcoming the limits of short-term memory. Since symbols can represent complex concepts and relationships among concepts, a valuable aid to memory can be provided by symbolic notation. To illustrate the value of symbols in aiding memory, try to answer this question.

> If the puzzle you solved before you solved this one was harder than the puzzle you solved after you solved the puzzle you solved before you solved this one, was the puzzle you solved before you solved this one harder than this one? (Restle, 1969)

To make this complex question simple, just substitute the symbolic names "puzzle A" and "puzzle B." Then, "this one" is changed to "puzzle A" and "the puzzle you solved before you solved this one" is changed to "puzzle B." Making these substitutions clarifies the question. "If puzzle B was harder than the puzzle you solved after you solved puzzle B, was puzzle B harder than puzzle A?" Only one phrase is not clear in this form of the question—"the puzzle you solved after you solved puzzle B." This phrase must refer to puzzle A. With this final substitution, the question becomes "If puzzle B was harder than puzzle A, was puzzle B harder than puzzle A?" At this stage of simplification the question becomes trivial.

Pictures also can serve as symbols to aid memory. Apparently, not only is a picture worth a thousand words, it can also summarize a great many words. To illustrate the use of pictures to provide a meaningful context for written passages, imagine that you are a subject in an experiment conducted by Bransford & Johnson. First, read the following paragraph:

> If the balloons popped the sound wouldn't be able to carry since everything would be too far away from the correct floor. A closed window would also prevent the sound from carrying, since most buildings tend to be well insulated. Since the whole operation depends on the steady flow of electricity, a break in the middle of the wire would also cause problems. Of course, the fellow could shout, but the human voice is not loud enough to carry that far. An additional problem is that the string could break on the instrument. Then there would be no accompaniment to the message. It is clear that the best situation would involve less distance. Then there would be fewer potential problems. With face to face contact, the least number of things could go wrong" (Bransford & Johnson, 1972, p.719).

Now look away from the page and try to remember what you just read.

Most people find it difficult to remember this type of passage without knowing the situation that is being described. But when a picture was shown to the subjects in the Bransford and Johnson study, more than twice as many of the ideas from the passage were remembered. Look at Exhibit 4.3 on page 90. Does it help you remember ideas from the passage you read?

Simultaneous information processing. The model of human information processing also can be used to describe how the mind can perform simultaneous information processing—a principle that underlies many strategies for aiding decision making in complex situations. Many tasks can be performed simultaneously by one person. Typically, we can sing while we shower, chew gum while we talk, etc. Yet, there are limits to the things we can do at the same time, as students who attempt to do homework while engaged in other tasks may find. Similarly, we may have trouble listening to one person while talking to another person on an unrelated topic and conversing while driving through heavy traffic. Two ways to compensate for limited information-processing ability are to capitalize upon the ability to do things simultaneously by either *time sharing* or *multiple processing*.

Time sharing takes advantage of lulls in demands made on processors and permits time spent waiting for further information about one task to be used for other tasks. Suppose you have placed a telephone call to a business contact and that person's secretary has temporarily placed your call on hold. There may be a long silence before the person can talk to you. You cannot go ahead with the conversation until your party is available, so your "processor" is free to do another task during the interim. This type of situation has been called "input-output limited."

Time sharing is potentially useful in any task that involves idle time. Yet, if time sharing is to be used effectively, two features of the task are essential: (1) the status of the task must be monitored so you will know when to return to it, and (2) there must be some way to save the results of your prior work on the task so you will not have to start over each time you resume the task. Have you ever heard a lecture by a slow-moving speaker? If so, you probably used time sharing. Students, for example, have been known to time share during slow lectures by thinking about other things while the same point is mentioned several times. Typically, students in this situation learn to monitor the lecture, while thinking of other things, so that their attention can return when the next point is introduced.

Saving the information relevant to the problem when tasks are switched is essential if time sharing is to work. Two ways to accomplish this involve: (1) making a written note of the results of the work done, and (2) permitting breaks in attention devoted to the task to occur only at natural points (i.e., where results do not have to be saved). Have you ever been interrupted while adding a column

EXHIBIT 4.3 Picture Used to Aid in Remembering a Written Description

Source: Bransford, J.D. & Johnson, M.K. Contextual prerequisites for understanding: Some investigations of comprehension and recall. *Journal of Verbal Learning and Verbal Behavior,* 1972, 11, 718. (Courtesy of Academic Press, Inc.).

of figures? Unless you could either delay the interruption or make note of the sum reached at that point in the column, you may have had to start over. Busy executives sometimes set aside an hour or so at the end of each day for tasks which must be accomplished without interruptions. Similar processes are used with computers, and, as in the case of the student mentioned above, it is important that computer systems either be protected from interruption or designed so that temporary results can be stored.

Another way to increase human information processing capacity by simultaneous processing is by the use of multiple processors working in parallel. Processors can work simultaneously and independently of each other, and—when combined with the principle of factoring a problem into independent components—this approach is a widely used strategy for dealing with complex problems in organizations. When faced with a lengthy job assignment that would require staying after hours at the office and a party scheduled for the same night, an enterprising young employee may persuade someone else to do part of the task. When, as in the case of many highly complex problems, the elements of the task are highly interconnected (i.e., dependent), multiple processors may not operate effectively in parallel. Some problems involve interaction among the processors in that one processor is dependent upon other processors for information before it can proceed with the problem. An information-processing system with several processors working simultaneously has greater information-processing capacity, but conflict among the processors can be disruptive. The supervisory processor attempts to control and to resolve these conflicts.

COGNITIVE MODELS OF JUDGMENT AND CHOICE IN COMPLEX DECISIONS

An important skill for decision makers confronted with complex problems is to be able to combine information from a variety of sources into a single judgment. While everyone needs to deal with the challenges of assessing and combining information from many sources in making choices, this skill is particularly crucial in jobs such as stockbroker, personnel officer, medical diagnostician, and major league scout.

Early research by Meehl (1954) on clinical vs. statistical prediction in psychology has stimulated much of the subsequent research on the ability of humans to combine cues from multiple sources in making judgments. The startling finding of the early research was that simple actuarial combinations of cues could make judgments with accuracy as great or greater than those made by expert clinicians. More recently, Dawes and Corrigan (1974) pointed out that the superiority of actuarial methods did not necessarily imply that human clinical judgment was inept. Nevertheless, much research has been devoted to finding out why the clinicians' judgments generally were inferior to statistical predictions, and the conclusions regarding human ability to integrate information in making judgments are not encouraging. In deriving strategies for aiding decision making under conditions of complexity, it is instructive to draw upon the conclusions from this line of research which have implications for cognitive strain.

A number of cognitive models of information processing and choice have emerged from the research literature. The major approaches to investigating cognitive processes involve the use of the lens model, integration theory, policy capturing, conjoint measurement, and introspective methods. Examining these approaches, and some of the major research conclusions pertaining to each approach, provides insights into how information is processed and how choices are made. For example, if normative models can be constructed for decisions, individuals' decisions can be compared to the normative models to determine deviations from the optimal decision. Even when normative models are not available, insights into individuals' decision processes can be fed back to them to assist in learning how the people actually make decisions. Relatively little research attention has been devoted to identifying how decision makers differ in either decision-making behaviors or the psychological processes underlying these behaviors, but some implications for improving decision making can be derived from the available research.

The Lens Model

The multiple-cue lens model (Brunswick, 1956) has been widely used to describe how a person combines the available cues in arriving at a decision and compares the importance assigned to the various cues by the person to an "optimum" judgment of the value of the cues.

Exhibit 4.4 shows the relationships among cues, criteria, and the person's response depicted in the lens model. Two aspects of decision processes are observed using this approach: (1) the right-hand side of the model describes the idiosyncratic manner in which a person weighs and combines cues in reaching a decision, and (2) the left-hand side of the model describes which features of the decision problem have the greatest influence on the decision.

For example, an employment officer may use the lens model to make hiring decisions (Y_s) based on cues in the decision environ-

EXHIBIT 4.4 The Lens Model

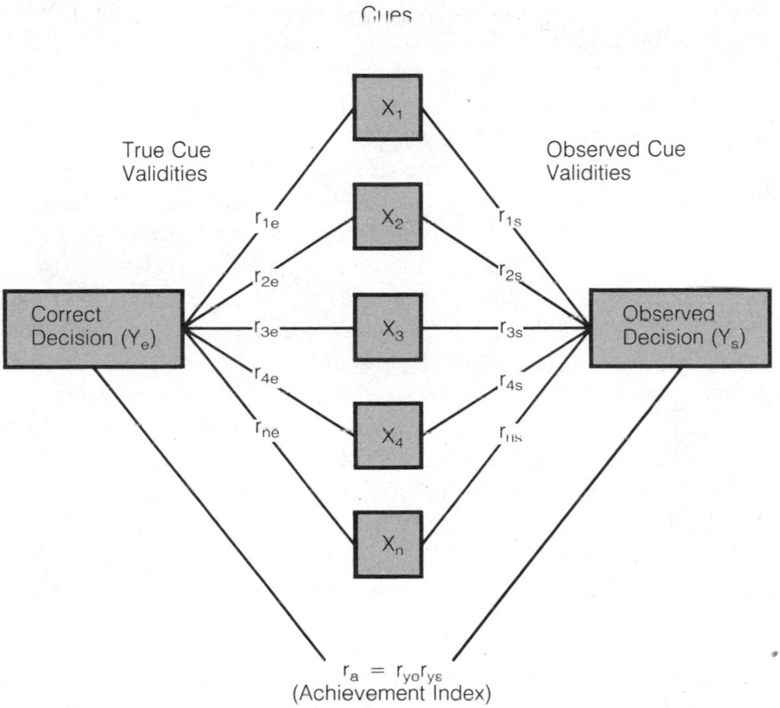

ment (X_1 to X_n). Typically, cues such as education, work experience, and employment tests are used to determine the suitability of the applicant for a job. Correlating cue values with how they are actually used yields "observed cue validities." The personnel officer's idiosyncratic decision processes are shown in the way cues are combined. To determine the features of the decision problem that have the greatest influence on the decision, an optimal hiring decision must be identified; perhaps (Y_e) based on the expert judgment of personnel selection specialists or from prior hiring experiences. The contributions of cues to accurate decisions are shown by the correlations between cue values and correct decisions. These are called "true cue validities." Finally, an "achievement index" (r_a) can be calculated to determine any inaccuracies (biases) in the actual hiring processes. The "achievement index" is the correlation between a personnel officer's actual decision and the optimal decision.

In many studies based on the lens model, the numerical cues are varied in importance and in the form of their relationship to the criterion being judged. For example, much research has dealt with the use of either linear or nonlinear methods for combining cues drawn from multiple sources (e.g., interviews, test results, etc.). Nonlinear combinations of cues would be expected to produce more precise judgments, since they take into account the configural relationships among the cues. Yet, one of the most striking conclusions from this line of research is that people typically settle for a simple, linear use of cues. This strategy appears to be less cognitively demanding since the cues are weighted individually and not in relation to other cues. In making judgments using a linear model, all that is necessary is that the decision maker add up the individual effects of the cues to get a total judgment value.

The influence of the form in which the cues are presented on whether the information is used in a simple linear fashion or used in more complex ways has been examined in the context of the lens model. Several features of the cues appear influential in making judgments. Cues which are highly interrelated tend to be combined and weighted equally (Slovic, 1966). When shown a list of cues, for example, judges tend to emphasize the importance of cues that vary across conditions. Slovic and Lichtenstein (1971) suggested that this tendency may occur because a cue that varies in value facilitates making judgments. But, in comparing multi-attribute alternatives, subjects tend to assign inappropriately high weights to cues that are common to both alternatives and to ignore cues that are unique to one alternative (Slovic & MacPhillamy, 1974). Even though they may have low predictive value, it appears that common cues provide information on all alternatives which is easy to compare. In many judgment tasks, the costs of various actions supply data that are directly comparable. But, restricting a comparison of alternatives to cost considerations can be misleading. Deciding where to spend a vacation only on the basis of relative costs of vacation sites, because the other attributes of the vacation plans are not directly comparable, would probably not lead to an enjoyable vacation.

There is some evidence to suggest that the *amount* of information provided will affect the judgment process, but perhaps not in the way one would expect. As more cues must be considered, accuracy of judgment declines. Additional cues can improve judgments only if they are of higher quality than the cues that were previously available. Information is important for decision making, but for judgments to be accurate, that information must have predictive value. Kahneman and Tversky (1973) found additional evidence that people tend to incorrectly perceive the value of a large amount of information. People tend to be more confident of their judgments when they believe that a set of cues is redundant than when they believe the cues are independent. This is incorrect, however, since redundant cues contain less information than would the independent cues and warrant less confidence in judgments based on them.

Integration Theory

Research on *integration theory* also has shown that simple linear models can be used to describe how judgments actually are made in situations such as stud poker and preferences for bus transportation (Anderson, 1973). The theory attempts to show how stimulus cues are combined by taking their algebraic average value as the judgment. Two weaknesses in the research on integration theory limit its usefulness. Making an algebraic model of a judgment does not necessarily show what was in the mind of the decision maker. It may accurately predict the judgment, but fail to describe the cognitive processes involved (Graesser & Anderson, 1974). A second limitation of research based on integration theory is that the quality of judgments is not considered.

Policy Capturing

Policy capturing research also uses the lens model in an attempt to describe how a judge uses cues. To *capture* the policy being used, a great many decisions must be obtained from the judge. For example, the voting records of United States senators have been analyzed to identify the values which underlie their judgments. The procedures for policy capturing have been demonstrated clearly, both in the laboratory and in complex real-world judgments. Among the real-world examples are attempts to describe the policies used in assessing the merits of various accounting procedures, in selecting graduate students, and in predicting business failures and performance of the stock market. Even in highly dynamic and complex tasks, such as production planning, it has been possible to identify policies concerning the use of cues. As we noted above in discussing the lens model, the policy capturing research typically has found that simple, linear regression equations can accurately describe how cues are weighted by judges.

Conjoint-Measurement Analysis

Conjoint-measurement analysis of human judgment (Luce & Tukey, 1964; Krantz & Tversky, 1971) supplements the use of numerical approaches, such as those based on the lens model. This approach also attempts to describe how attributes are combined in making a choice, but it is a qualitative method that is useful when the attributes are difficult to measure on an interval scale. Axioms are used to derive the independent effect of each attribute on the ordering of the alternatives when judges are consistent and follow transitivity (i.e., if X>Y, and Y>Z, then X>Z). In addition, the axiom of ordinal independence requires that the ordering of the choices must be used to order the attributes independently of each other.

Conjoint-measurement analysis of human judgment can be illustrated by examining a study by Ullrich and Painter (1974). Profiles describing hypothetical applicants for managerial jobs were developed, in which the attributes of intelligence, years of work experience, and achievement motivation were varied across the set of profiles. Judges were shown ten applicant profiles at a time and asked to rank order each applicant from most to least desirable. The rankings were then analyzed to determine how each judge combined the attributes to arrive at preferences. Other rules were found to be used, but one-third of the subjects used an additive composition rule, in which the overall evaluation of the managers was the algebraic sum of the separate contributions of each attribute level. A conclusion similar to that observed in research with the lens model—the widespread use of simple rules for combining cues in judgment tasks—also has been noted in research using conjoint measurement.

Introspective Methods

Introspective methods for investigating decision-making processes have begun to be used more frequently. One introspective method is "process tracing." In this approach subjects are asked to "think aloud" as they process information and make choices. Their verbal protocols, then, are represented graphically as a tree or network of successive decisions (Swinth, et al., 1975). In contrast to the lens model research which infers values from behaviors (e.g., choices of rankings), the introspective approach assumes that subjects are well aware of the factors affecting their decisions. This assumption may not be completely warranted, but introspective reports are useful as supplements to the more objective methods of observation.

Introspective studies of decision processes have found that many decision rules are used sequentially in making a decision. In initial decision-making attempts, courses of action may be contrasted on the same attribute. At this stage a conjunctive rule—that requires the alternatives to meet every criterion—may be used to eliminate some alternatives from further consideration (as described in the elimination by aspects strategy below). A conjunctive rule for selecting university professors could require that they meet at least a minimum standard in all aspects of the job: teaching, research, university administration, etc. The reduced set of alternatives may, then, be compared using a compensatory rule to weigh their strengths and weaknesses. The compensatory rule could consider trade-offs among the criteria, such as an outstanding researcher may be preferred over an outstanding teacher because of the prestige the researcher would bring the university. People generally seem to prefer simple strategies (e.g., strategies without rigorous use of numerical computations, trade-offs, or relative weighting) that are easy to understand and to explain to other people. For example, when faced with two alternatives of equal value, subjects tended to choose the alternative that was better in the most important dimension—a strategy that is easy to use and to justify to other people (Slovic, 1975). Decision strategies that can be justified to others are important in organizations; even if the decision is unsuccessful, no blame will accrue to a decision maker if the method of reaching the decision is in line with standard practices in the organization.

The cognitive strain-reducing strategies are frequently used when making decisions in complex situations (e.g., problems characterized by many alternatives, many attributes for each alternative, information overload, or time pressures). In complex decision situations, research has shown that subjects may attempt to simplify the decisions by such strategies as ignoring small differences among alternatives, simply counting the number of attributes in which each alternative is superior, and comparing two alternatives at a time and retaining only the better alternative for later comparisons (Svenson, 1974). These strategies, of course, seldom would be expected to lead to optimal decisions.

ROLE OF PSYCHOLOGICAL CHARACTERISTICS IN MAKING COMPLEX DECISIONS

A central theme that runs through this brief analysis of research on models of judgment is the notion of "cognitive strain." In complex tasks, judges are confronted with more information than they are able to process, and they attempt to cope with this overload by developing simple heuristics (i.e., general rules of thumb) for information processing. At times, these heuristics are biased, incomplete, or incorrect.

A growing body of research evidence on the psychological characteristics of decision makers shows considerable individual differences in their susceptibility to cognitive strain (MacCrimmon & Taylor, 1976). Although human information-processing ability is sharply limited, some decision makers have a much greater capacity to process information than do others. Among the psychological characteristics of decision makers that have been shown to underlie cognitive strain are dogmatism and cognitive styles.

Dogmatism

One of the most thoroughly documented research conclusions is that dogmatism tends to inhibit information seeking. Dogmatic decision makers (identified by the Rokeach Dogmatism Scale as having closed belief systems) have been found to make rapid decisions on the basis of relatively little information. Moreover, once these decisions have been made, the dogmatic person would be expected to hold those decisions confidently and inflexibly (Block & Petersen, 1955; Brengelmann, 1959). These early research conclusions have led to interpreting dogmatism as a defense mechanism that tends to restrict information processing (Long & Ziller, 1965). In this view, limiting the information search serves to close the mind to new information and eliminates any need for decision makers to reevaluate their self-concepts, a prospect that may be seen as threatening. A dogmatic decision maker, therefore, would be likely to unduly curtail information input, especially in decision problems which appear to threaten self-concepts. The resulting reduction in information-processing activity could severely hamper performance in complex decision tasks.

Cognitive Styles

Susceptibility to cognitive strain also has been shown to be influenced by a decision maker's cognitive styles. Two cognitive styles—*cognitive complexity* and *field independence-dependence*—have revealed the strongest evidence of an impact on information-processing behaviors.

Cognitive complexity. An extensive program of research on cognitive complexity has shown that, when information-processing capacity is measured under various levels of stress, the amount of information processed plotted against level of stress reveals the inverted U-shaped relationship (Schroeder, et al., 1967) shown in Exhibit 4.5. Stress in these experiments was a combination of environmental complexity and uncertainty. The U-shaped function indicates that there is an optimal level of information load; information-processing performance will first improve, then deteriorate as the information load increases. Decision makers, then, would be expected to perform best under intermediate levels of stress. At high levels of stress, relative to individual information-processing capacity, the dysfunctions of cognitive strain would occur.

This line of research has also differentiated individuals as to their comparative capacity to process information. For example, *abstract* and *concrete* information processors have been contrasted (Schroeder & Suedfeld, 1971). Abstractness refers to a tendency to process many dimensions of information and to use a complex approach to integration; concreteness is characterized by use of a few dimensions of information and a simple integrating approach. Abstract decision makers have been found to be more information oriented and to be able to process more information in complex decision environments. Concrete decision makers, however, tend to experience cognitive strain at lower levels of environmental complexity. Hence, they must restrict the amount of information they can process. Due to their greater ability to handle the cognitive demands of information search and integration, abstract decision makers appear better prepared to cope with heavy informational demands. Also, their more efficient use of information, deriving from an observed tendency for them to "rescue" information for complex integrations, enables the abstract decision maker to reach effective decisions based upon limited information.

Research on management information systems has investigated the impact of cognitive complexity on information systems' acceptance and use. The Decision Style Model of Driver and Mock (1975) segregates decision makers in terms of the amount of information they tend to use and the degree of focus they exhibit. The Decision Style

EXHIBIT 4.5 Relationship Between Information-Processing Capacity and Level of Stress

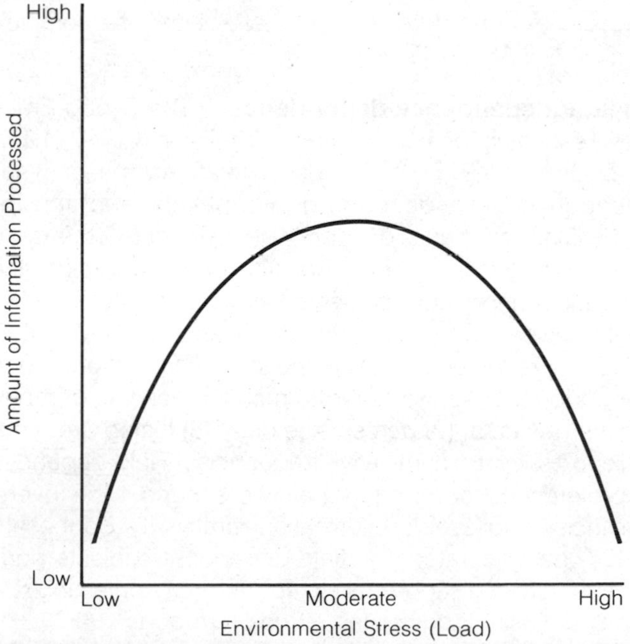

Source: Schroeder, H.M., Driver, M.J. & Streufert, S. *Human Information Processing.* New York: Holt, Rinehart & Winston, 1967

EXHIBIT 4.6 The Decision Style Model

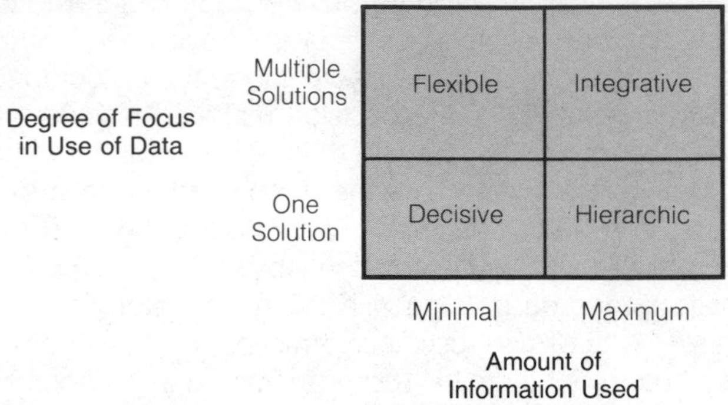

Source: Driver, M. and Mock, T. Human information processing, decision style theory, and accounting information systems, *The Accounting Review,* 1975, L, 497.

Model is shown in Exhibit 4.6. Two psychometric measures are used in assessing the cognitive style of information users—the Integration Style Test (a business problem to solve) and a questionnaire that reveals a person's view of how information is used. In a complex experimental task that gave subjects the option of buying various amounts of information, the major conclusion concerning cognitive strain was that " 'decisive' decision makers become rapidly overloaded in complex structured tasks and, hence, cannot effectively use complex feedback" (Driver & Mock, 1975, p. 507).

Field independence-dependence. The Group Embedded Figures Test has been used (Lusk, 1973; Bariff & Lusk, 1977; Benbasat & Dexter, 1977) in studies of relationships between field independence-dependence and information reporting formats. Lusk (1973) found that field-independent subjects were more likely to invest in a company described by a report with high analytical content. Field-dependent subjects were more likely to invest in a company described by a report with low analytical content. Bariff & Lusk (1977) presented users with the same information in four different report formats—classified in terms of increasing complexity as (1) tabular raw data, (2) percentage data, (3) histogram, and (4) an ogive report showing cumulative frequencies. Field-dependent subjects' preferences for report formats were found to be inversely related to increasing levels of information complexity. Benbasat & Dexter (1977) demonstrated that field-dependent subjects performed better when given disaggregated reports, (i.e., containing raw data) than they did using aggregated, structure reports.

Hence, field-dependent decision makers have been shown to both prefer information that is presented in a relatively raw form and to make better decisions using data of this type. In addition, when asked their perception of the decision approach used in the experimental task, field dependents were more likely to indicate that they used flexible, changing strategies. Field independents, on the other hand, said they used stable, fixed strategies. These research conclusions lend support to the interpretation of field independents as individuals who use more structured and analytical approaches in making decisions.

Relative Influence of Psychological Characteristics

Taylor and Dunnette (1974) investigated the individual and joint effects on information processing and decision making of a number of the psychological characteristics that had been examined by other researchers. They found that, for a sample of industrial managers, cognitive characteristics (e.g., intellectual efficiency, intelligence) and personality, interests and motivations (e.g., risk-taking tendency, cognitive complexity, and dogmatism) appeared to influence decision-making performance in very different ways.

Cognitive attributes were related to the judgments that lead to cognitive strain. They appear to contribute to effectiveness in aggregating preferences and information, judging the diagnosticity of information, and retaining information in short-term memory during decision making. Cognitive attributes also were found to influence information-processing ability. For example, intelligence was found to affect the information-processing rate and the length of time required to reach decisions. More intelligent decision makers tended to process information more quickly and make faster decisions. The cognitive characteristics of decision makers influence information handling and choice behaviors, and have little effect on postdecisional processes.

The interests, personality, and motivations of decision makers were found to exert a major influence on idiosyncratic decision-making behaviors (e.g., amount of information sought and processing rate). Post decisional processes, such as decision confidence and flexibility in the face of adverse consequences of a choice, were strongly related to the personality trait of dogmatism (i.e., a closed belief system). The influence of motivation on decision making may reflect a shift in aspiration levels over a series of decisions, producing corresponding changes in decision criteria or otherwise affecting the evaluative aspects of decision making.

Conclusions from Research on Judgment and Choice

The central role of bounded rationality and cognitive strain in decision making is the focus of this chapter. A wealth of literature related to the causes of cognitive strain, the dynamics of its operation, and ways to overcome its adverse consequences has been developed. Hopefully, highlighting some of the major issues and conclusions in this literature will demonstrate both the pervasiveness of cognitive strain in administrative decision making, and the severe limitations it imposes upon the computational and aggregative processes required in complex decision problems.

Research based on models of judgment can be used by decision makers to understand their own decision processes and to build upon this understanding. Some researchers have suggested that since people don't appear capable of using configural combinations of cues effectively, training problems in decision making should teach people to use linear combinations of cues appropriately (Hammond, 1971). Simply providing feedback about decision outcomes does not appear to be a very effective way to improve decisions; such feedback fails to identify why the decisions were successful or unsuccessful. It also appears that simply informing people about the known biases that hinder judgment is not likely to alert them to avoid the biases.

One approach that has been proposed for reducing distortions in perception and memory is to have people set up record-keeping systems to carefully record the considerations that led to their decisions. A current example of such a documentation system is seen in the elaborate records maintained by football coaches in which each play is analyzed and its consequences are recorded (Goodman, et al., 1978). Such a record also could serve as a data file from which actuarial models might eventually be developed. When decisions can be programmed (i.e., each decision is complex and many similar decisions are to be made), judgment can be aided by substituting a linear regression model—describing the way a decision maker evaluates cues in the initial set of decisions—for making subsequent decisions. This "boot-strapping" strategy, which is derived from the policy capturing research described earlier, is one aid for making decisions in complex situations.

AIDS FOR IMPROVING DECISION MAKING IN COMPLEX SITUATIONS

Complex decision problems tend to place extreme demands on the information-processing capabilities of decision makers. The great many factors to identify and consider in making decisions in complex situations, and the extent of interconnectedness among these factors, cause difficulties in decision making. The difficulty is that, in attempting to acquire information relevant to a decision, the complexity of the problem may require that information be processed at a level which exceeds a decision maker's cognitive abilities. Hence, a state of "overload" and the accompanying decline in the efficiency of information processing results.

Bounds placed on effective decision making by cognitive strain can be expanded by operating upon the decision maker, the decision environment, or both, to achieve a correspondence between the amount of information required for making an effective decision and the processing capacity of the decision maker. Such a correspondence can be produced in three basic ways: (1) decision makers with high information-processing capacities can be selected; (2) decision makers can be trained to overcome the informational limitations and biases that lead to cognitive strain; or (3) the informational demands of a decision problem can be reduced by applying appropriate decision aids.

Selection and placement of decision makers capable of processing information rapidly and accurately is useful in dealing with complex decision problems; consider the value of this strategy in selecting air traffic controllers. However, the intent of this book is to suggest strategies to improve the effectiveness of all decision makers. Accordingly, aids for making decisions in complex situations discussed in this section are those which can be used without drastic structural changes in either the decision maker's job or the organization (i.e., aids that the decision maker may personally use to compensate for cognitive strain). Training decision makers to overcome the limitations of cognitive strain and to use decision aids for reducing the information demands of problems are of this type. Five classes of strategies have proven useful in dealing with complex problems: (1) representations for depicting the complex features of a problem; (2) decomposition for simplifying the problem structure; (3) techniques for acquiring information about alternatives; (4) techniques for choosing in multiple-attribute and multiple-objective decisions; and (5) Multiattribute Utility Analysis (MAU). Decision aids of each class are discussed in turn.

Representing the Complex Features of Problems

The complex aspects of decision problems can be simplified by models or diagrams of the problem. Representations reveal the relationships among the various elements of a problem. In representing complex decision problems it is important to include all essential elements. Failing to include all important elements of the problem may seriously alter the nature of the problem; such a representation would have limited value for solving the original problem.

Many ways to model decision problems have been presented in the literature. The types of representations described here are: *deci-*

sion matrix, flow chart, decision tree, and *decision table.* Choosing a type of representation to use in a given situation depends upon the nature of the problem you wish to solve.

A decision matrix is best for comparing complex sets of alternatives containing many common attributes. Flow charts or decision trees are useful in representing complex sequences of actions and events. Decision tables reveal relationships between conditions and outcomes (i.e., the consequences of decisions are contingent upon certain conditions). Note that both the decision matrix and the decision tree can be extended by assigning probabilities to uncertain events. The use of representations to aid decision making under conditions of uncertainty is discussed in the next chapter.

Decision matrix. In a decision matrix the multiple attributes of decision alternatives are described. Typically, the attributes are presented in columns and the courses of action available to a decision maker are listed in rows of a decision matrix. An example may help to clarify the nature of the decision matrix representation. In deciding which salesman to promote to sales manager it may be helpful to list the candidates in the rows of a decision matrix and the characteristics relevant to the sales managerial job in the columns. Relevant characteristics may include seniority in the sales department, job performance ratings, scores on a supervisory knowledge test, performance in an assessment center, educational qualifications, etc. Direct comparisons then can be made for candidates on their job-related qualifications. If certain minimum qualifications are believed to be necessary for successful performance as sales manager, these could be listed for a hypothetical candidate. This step would alert the decision maker if none of the candidates matched up to the job requirements. The major benefit of using decision matrices is to clearly describe the relative merits of alternative courses of action.

Flow chart and decision tree. Flow charts and decision trees can reduce problem complexity when sequences of actions are involved. By use of shapes depicting operations, questions, etc., connected by arrows indicating precedence relationships, flow charts can represent sequences of operations diagrammatically. Flow charts have been used to diagram complex sequential processes in a great many contexts (e.g., in production management, evaluating stocks, and human thinking).

An advantage of decision trees over decision matrices in representing a complex set of alternatives is that decision trees make explicit the hierarchical levels of alternatives. A decision tree displays the levels that exist in alternatives by a series of nodes and branches. Alternative courses of action are shown by the main branches, which in turn have subsidiary branches for further refinements of these al-

EXHIBIT 4.7 A Decision Tree Showing Diversification Alternatives for an Automobile Manufacturing Firm

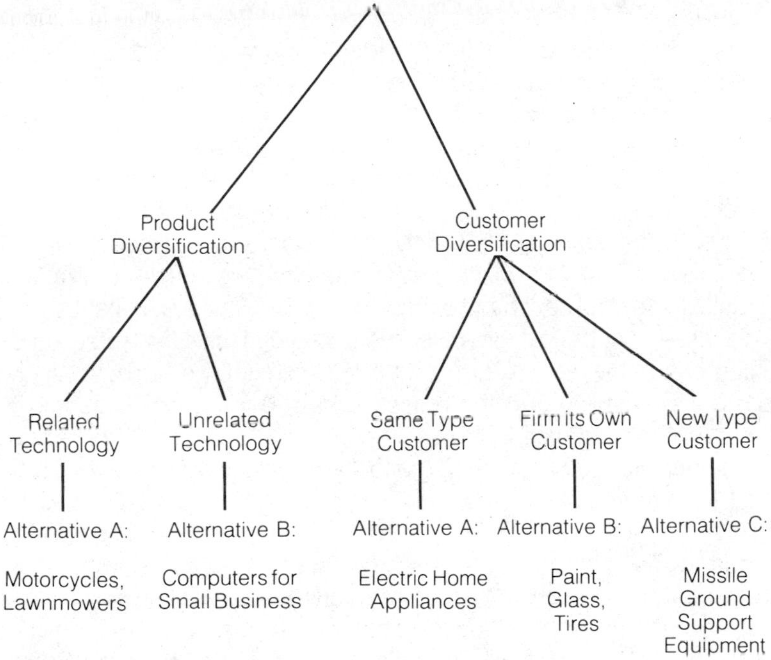

Source: Ansoff, H.I. *Corporate strategy* New York: McGraw Hill, 1965, 133.

ternatives. Frequently, it is useful to begin with a very general description of the alternatives, then to make the description progressively more specific. Ansoff (1965), for example, has discussed the alternative strategies available to an automobile manufacturing firm with regard to product and market diversification. As can be seen in Exhibit 4.7, the initial options can be refined into at least five diversification strategies, and these alternatives can then be further specified. Examples of the types of markets or products included in each strategy are given. When uncertainty is present, as is discussed in Chapter 5, the decision tree offers the additional benefits of representing the risks related to various courses of action and their possible consequences.

Decision table. A decision table is useful in showing what combination of problem conditions will lead to choosing a particular course of action. Hence, it is superior to the other types of representations discussed here in describing the basis on which actions should be taken. Conditions of the problem situation are listed in the top rows of the table, and possible actions are listed in the bottom rows. A column represents a decision rule that specifies the combination of conditions under which certain actions should be taken. In using a decision table, the conditions that exist in a decision situation would be listed. The list, then, would be compared with the columns to find the column containing the identical conditions; this column gives the decision rule. The action given in the row which intersects the selected column would be taken.

In deciding which customers should be granted credit, a department store may follow a set of rules such as: If the applicant has an American Easycredit Card, grant credit to applicant to a limit of $3,000. If the applicant has only oil company credit cards, grant credit to a limit of $1,500 if a credit check reveals no delinquent accounts. If the applicant has no credit cards, but has held a steady job for a three-year period, give credit to a $1,500 limit if the applicant's income is below $15,000, or to a $3,000 limit if the applicant's income is at least $15,000. In all cases, a $1,500 limit can be doubled if the applicant has lived in the same residence for at least five years. These decision rules are depicted in the decision table shown in Exhibit 4.8. Either a yes or a no can be entered in the brackets shown in Exhibit 4.8; it will have no effect on the action you take. A decision regarding whether or not to extend credit to a customer would require matching the customer's characteristics against the conditions shown in the columns to find the appropriate decision rule, then applying the rule by taking the action shown at the bottom of that column.

EXHIBIT 4.8. A Decision Table Showing Decision Rules for Granting Credit

	Decision Rules						
Conditions	**1**	**2**	**3**	**4**	**5**	**6**	**7**
Has American Easycredit Card	yes	no	no	no	no	no	no
Has only oil company credit cards and no past delinquencies	( )	yes	yes	no	no	no	no
Steady job for three years	( )	( )	( )	yes	yes	yes	no
Income is below $15,000	( )	( )	( )	yes	yes	no	( )
Lived in same residence for 5 years	( )	no	yes	yes	no	( )	( )
Actions							
Grant credit to $0							X
Grant credit to $15,000		X			X		
Grant credit to $3,000	X		X	X		X	

Simplifying complex problems by decomposition. The most widely used decision aid for overcoming bounded rationality involves decomposing a complex problem to bring it within the bounds of a decision maker's cognitive ability. As Raiffa (1968) has stated, the intent of decomposition is to divide and conquer. Decomposing a complex problem into its elements and dealing with each element separately reduces the cognitive demands imposed on a decision maker. Thus, a complex problem is decomposed into simpler problems, the simpler problems are analyzed, and the analyses of the simpler problems are pasted together with logical glue to reconstruct the complex problem.

Decomposition of problems allows division of labor and specialization to be brought into play when the parties involved in decision making have differing capabilities, and it permits decision-making activities to be performed by individuals or groups working in parallel. Delegation of decision-making activities is a salient example of problem decomposition in organizations. Of course, breaking up a problem into subproblems is useful only when few interrelationships exist among the subproblems. When many interrelationships exist, the advantages of decomposing clearly are outweighed by the difficulties of coordinating. The principle of decomposition has proven to be an extremely useful response to the difficulties of information overload in complex managerial decisions. Simon (1973) has proposed that broad organizational decisions can also be improved by using the principle of decomposition of decision-making activities in designing organizational structures. Issues in decomposing organizational decision-making structures are covered in our discussion of organizations in Chapter 6.

Decomposing a problem does not require that every element of a problem be assigned to a subproblem. Decision makers can simplify complex problems by modeling only important aspects. The challenge is to build a model that can be more easily manipulated than the complex system, yet which includes the aspects of the system that have the greatest implications for the decision. Simon (1969) suggested that complex management problems should be decomposed into semi-independent components corresponding to their functional parts. The use of *decomposable matrices* is based on his view of complex systems as containing a hierarchy of levels, in which the operation of the system at each level can be specified by describing its component functions. Most practical problems meet the conditions for *nearly decomposable* systems in that interactions among subsystems exist, but tend to be weak. Hence, decomposable matrices can be used to analyze problems by viewing them as complex systems.

When done appropriately, the use of decomposable matrices can simplify the decision-making task with little loss of relevant information. The informational requirements of the decision can be brought closer to the cognitive capabilities of the decision maker by ignoring weak interactions among subparts belonging to different components of the system for which the decision is to be made. Strong interactions, however, should be taken into account in the decision. For example, while it is not necessary to observe the interaction of each member of one organization with each member of another organization to understand the interface between the two organizations, it may be necessary to observe the relationships between top executives of the two organizations.

Techniques for Acquiring Information About Alternatives

Cognitive demands of complex decision problems can be reduced by appropriately organizing information input. In discussing the cognitive limitations of decision makers we suggested some insights as to mechanisms for helping decision makers to deal with the dysfunctions of cognitive strain. In this section, we will discuss five aids which capitalize upon our understanding of the cognitive processes underlying information handling—(1) chunking, (2) matching information format to a decision maker's cognitive style, (3) using an appropriate aggregation level, (4) searching locally and (5) focusing.

Chunking. Information which is meaningful to a decision maker can be more easily stored in short-term memory. Hence, helping a decision maker to organize information in a way that the individual finds personally meaningful can reduce cognitive strain. One technique for effectively organizing the information contained in a complex array of stimuli is *chunking* (Simon, 1969). Grouping the information into meaningful categories (chunks), and then ordering the categories in terms of importance may increase information-processing capacity. As a manager receives reports from operating units, the information they contain may be cognitively sorted into actual or anticipated decision problems (e.g., inventory levels, wage rates). This process reflects the view of "active" information processing by humans reported in the literature; that is, rather than attempting to remember facts, people arrange information in a way that they find personally meaningful.

Fitting the information format to the cognitive style of the decision maker. Another approach for reducing cognitive strain is suggested by the research linking cognitive styles of users with information formats used in management information systems. Since research evidence indicates that "abstract" information processors are better able to process information in complex decision problems than are "concrete" information processors, it may prove advisable to assign more complex problems to organizational members identified as abstract information processors. Or, information users can be differentiated according to their field independence-dependence scores and provided with reports which use a format that is compatible with their cognitive style. That is, field-dependent information users would be expected to perform better in processing information presented in relatively simple formats containing raw data (i.e., tabular raw data and percentages) and field independents would better utilize more complex information formats (i.e., histograms and cumulative frequencies). Hence, each decision maker would be better served by receiving information in a form that is compatible with the individual's cognitive style.

There has been some debate in the literature regarding the best way to carry out this recommendation. Bariff and Lusk (1977) suggested that report formats should be assigned to information users on the basis of their scores on cognitive styles tests. An alternate approach is to make available a variety of report formats, and permit information users to request the format that they prefer and feel they can use most effectively. In view of the measurement error in the psychological tests used to assess cognitive styles—and the accompanying inaccuracy in predicting an individual's cognitive style—the latter approach seems advisable.

Arranging information by optimal level of aggregation. Presenting information to decision makers in an appropriately aggregated form has been discussed by Marschak (1959). This is a widely used method for improving the efficiency of information processing. While detailed information (e.g., unemployment for each age group) may be needed for some decisions, information load can be reduced by reporting aggregated information (e.g., overall unemployment). It is important that information be given at a level of aggregation suitable for the decision. It may be very difficult to disaggregate information, so aggregated information should be used only when it is necessary to reduce information load.

Using local search for information. Problem solving in organizations typically attempts to find immediate solutions to specific problems, so local search is probably a feasible way to initiate information seeking (Cyert & March, 1963). In using local search, a decision maker should look for similar policies or practices to replace inadequate ones, and try to determine reasons for failure to meet goals by examining local activities. If an adequate solution cannot be found by local search, then more extensive and cognitively demanding search strategies can be undertaken. The major benefit of using local information search is that, if successful, cost of the search will be relatively low. However, limiting information seeking to local search seems inappropriately simple for complex problems and is unlikely to succeed (MacCrimmon & Taylor, 1976). For example, choosing production techniques on the basis of techniques already known to an organization may overlook a superior technique based on the use of industrial robots. The implications for an organization of failing to solve problems could be very costly.

Using conservative focusing or focus gambling. Information-seeking strategies which differ sharply in the level of cognitive strain they entail can be derived from research on concept formation (Bruner, et al., 1956). In a typical experiment, an array of wooden blocks is placed on the table in front of the subject. These blocks may differ along three dimensions—size, form, and color—each with three values. One block that represents a positive example of the concept (e.g., the concept of Large Square) is shown to the subject, and the subject is asked to guess what the concept is. Before making the guess about the concept the subject can point to another block and ask the experimenter if it contains the concept. The experiment continues until the concept has been identified.

Two strategies identified in these experiments hold special interest for our discussion of ways to reduce cognitive strain in making complex decisions. *Conservative focusing* involves finding one positive instance of the correct concept and, then, varying one attribute at a time to identify the concept; *focus gambling* proceeds by varying more than one attribute at a time. Focus gambling requires relatively little information to be sought in determining the correct concept, whereas conservative focusing requires a good deal of information seeking. If a decision maker has a hunch about the correct decision alternative, the more risky strategy of focus gambling can be adopted to reach the solution quickly with less information processing. However, if not guided by the correct hunch, the decision maker may fail to reach a solution altogether. In the absence of sound hunches, adopting the safer, and more demanding, strategy of conservative focusing would be advisable.

An illustration of these information-seeking strategies can be seen in marketing new products. Products being considered for marketing may be described by their attributes. Market researchers typically regard "ideal levels" for these attributes as the levels most desired by consumers. Frequently, these ideal levels are found by test marketing. In testing a range of products sequentially to find the ideal levels, a market researcher may choose either to test products which differ from prior partially successful ones by only one attribute or to test products which differ from previously tested products in several attributes. If, in testing several products, clear insights into consumer preferences emerge, the focus gambling strategy could quickly lead to a successful product. Otherwise, the information seeking strategy of conservative focusing would be more likely to lead to development of a successful product.

Choosing in Multiple-Attribute and Multiple-Objective Decision Situations

Problems that are complex due to the sheer number of objectives held by a decision maker and/or the multitude of attributes by which the decision alternatives are described can severely strain a decision maker's cognitive ability. Fortunately, a great many techniques have been developed to assist decision makers in solving such problems. Problems of the first type—which involve many objectives—have been called multiple-objective decisions; problems of the second type—in which the courses of action among which a decision maker must choose are described by many attributes—are called multiple-attribute decisions.

Practical managerial decision problems typically require that both multiple objectives and multiple attributes be considered in solving them. Neglecting one or more of the crucial factors in the problem can be disastrous. An example of the serious consequences of inappropriately specifying the factors relevant to a problem can be seen in the aftereffects of the "Zero Defects" program (Birkin & Ford, 1973). This widely used program was intended to solve the problem of defective workmanship by motivating employees to do the job right the first time. The consequences of high scrap rates and product failure are extremely costly to firms, and the Zero Defects program was eagerly adopted by managers. Yet, once the program was implemented, many firms discovered that increasing quality had highly undesirable side effects—productivity declined, production deadlines were missed, and amounts of spoiled and scrapped goods increased. Many firms, finding that they simply could not live with the consequences of making quality the primary objective, abandoned the program.

It is clear that specifying the great many objectives which need to be considered in most decision problems, and weighting the relative importance of these objectives, places severe demands on the sharply limited ability of decision makers to process information and make choices. Research on human limitations in cognitive abilities indicates that, faced with complex choices, decision makers typically resort to simple methods for judging cues and making comparisons among alternative courses of action. In many instances, few cues are examined, these cues are weighted with little differentiation (e.g., only + or − is used), and the cues describing a decision alternative are combined in a simple, linear manner to form a judgment of the overall quality of the alternative. In comparing decision alternatives to determine which is superior, decision makers have been found to use inappropriately simplistic, or outright misleading, strategies. In this section, methods for dealing more appropriately with complex objectives and/or attributes will be discussed. Two classes of methods are covered—weighting methods and sequential elimination methods.

Weighting vs. direct trade-off methods. The weighting methods have been very widely used in applied decision making. Three factors common to all weighting methods are: 1) a means for comparing attributes by numerically scaling attribute values (intraattribute preferences) and assigning numerical weights across attributes (interattribute preferences), 2) a method for aggregating the preferences into a single number representing the decision maker's preference for each alternative, and 3) a rule for choosing the one alternative that receives the highest weight (or for rating the entire set of alternatives). A decision maker's preferences can be assessed either by direct questioning of the decision maker or, indirectly, by inferring them from past choices. Techniques of each type that have proven useful in managerial decision making are discussed below.

Two of the major methods for making multiple-attribute decisions, in which decision makers' preferences for attributes are assessed by direct questioning, are by making trade-offs and by additive weighting. While these methods do not require knowledge of the decision makers' preferences, as revealed in a prior series of similar decisions, they do assume that the decision makers are capable of accurately verbalizing their true preferences. A major advantage of these direct assessment methods is that they are relatively easy to understand and use.

The direct trade-off method involves determining, by direct questioning, the marginal rates at which decision makers are willing to trade one attribute for another. After all relevant trade-offs have been made (i.e., canceled out), the choice can be reached on the basis of the small set of attributes which remain. MacCrimmon (1973) reports a simple form of the trade-off method which Benjamin Franklin (1772) called "moral algebra"; it was described in a letter to Joseph Priestley. Since it illustrates the nature of the direct trade-off method so well, the entire letter is quoted here.

London, Sept. 19, 1772

Dear Sir,

In the affair of so much importance to you, wherein you ask my advice, I cannot, for want of sufficient premises, advise you what to determine, but if you please I will tell you how. When those difficult cases occur, they are difficult, chiefly because while we have them under consideration, all the reasons pro and con are not present to the mind at the same time; but sometimes one set present themselves, and at other times another, the first being out of sight. Hence the various purposes or inclinations that alternately prevail, and the uncertainty that perplexes us. To get over this, my way is to divide half a sheet of paper by a line into two columns; writing over the one Pro, and over the other Con. Then, during three or four days consideration, I put down under the different heads short hints of the different motives, that at different times occur to me, for or against the measure. When I have thus got them all together in one view, I endeavor to estimate their respective weights; and where I find two, one on each side, that seem equal, I strike them both out. If I find a reason Pro equal to some two reasons Con, I strike out the three. If I judge some two reasons Con, equal to some three reasons Pro, I strike out the five; and thus proceeding I find at length where the balance lies; and if, after a day or two of further consideration, nothing new that is of importance occurs on either side, I come to a determination accordingly. And, though the weight of reasons cannot be taken with the precision of algebraic quantities, yet when each is thus considered, separately and comparatively, and the whole lies before me, I think I can judge better, and am less liable to make a rash step, and in fact I have found great advantage from this kind of equation, in what may be called moral or prudential algebra.

Wishing sincerely that you may determine for the best, I am ever, my dear friend, yours most affectionately.

B. Franklin

Simple additive weighting. The simple additive weighting method is widely used for making multiple-attribute decisions. An early example of its use was in the mustering out system in the United States army at the end of World War II (Stouffer, 1949). In this method, a decision maker assigns importance weights to each attribute and numerically scales the alternative on each attribute. The decision maker can then get a total score for each alternative simply by: (1) multiplying the importance weight assigned for each attribute by the scale value given to the alternative on that attribute, and (2) summing the products over all attributes. When the overall scores are calculated for all of the alternatives, the alternative with the highest overall score is chosen. One danger in using the simple additive weighting method is that it does not consider interactions among the attributes. Churchman and Ackoff (1954) provide a detailed discussion of this method and the circumstances under which it should be used.

Hierarchical additive weighting. A more sophisticated form of additive weighting—hierarchical additive weighting—acknowledges that attributes may serve as means to attaining higher-level objectives. In using this method, values or preferences are assigned to higher-level objectives and, then, the instrumentality of each attribute for attaining the higher-level objectives is assessed. Hence, the interattribute weightings can be inferred from a decision maker's direct assessment of the higher-level objectives. Use of this method in choosing a job is described by Miller (1970). He specified four factors which exerted major influence on the choice—(1) salary, (2) the nature of the work, (3) the geographical location of the job, and (4) the travel requirements. These factors were decomposed to identify more specific attributes describing each of the potential jobs. When weights were indirectly assigned to the attributes, and combined with values indicating the worth of attributes, a total worth score was derived for each job.

Linear weighting. Instead of asking decision makers directly about their preferences, linear weighting methods can be used to infer the preferences from a prior set of decisions. This approach is derived from the research on the lens model and policy capturing discussed above and helps decision makers to improve future decisions by eliminating the random errors that might be made without such aid. Using decision makers' inferred values to improve subsequent decisions has been called "bootstrapping," since the decision makers can be viewed as lifting themselves up by the bootstraps. The method can be used when many similar decisions are to be made (e.g., judges deciding on workers' compensation awards, production scheduling, or admission of graduate students).

Dawes (1971) was able to identify the importance of three attributes of applicants for admission to graduate school—(1) Graduate Record Examination score, (2) grade point average, and (3) quality of undergraduate school—and to develop a linear model for making future admissions decisions. The admissions committee was found to place highest value upon grade point average ($r = .54$), and lesser values upon quality of undergraduate school ($r = .19$) and Graduate Record Examination scores ($r = .05$).

In making employment decisions, it is common practice to use attributes of job candidates (e.g., employment history, psychological test scores) to predict success on the job. If the fit of the linear equation is good, then this equation can be used routinely in future hiring decisions to screen job applicants. Reducing the number of job applicants that have to be considered by weeding out clearly unsuitable applicants would lower the informational demands of the decision.

An intriguing feature of the bootstrapping method is that, when simple linear models of decision-maker behavior are substituted in future decisions of the same type, the linear regression models have been shown to perform as well as the original decision maker, or even better. Linear weighting procedures have been very popular in managerial decision making. Kunreuther (1976) has specified the conditions under which the model should be relied on in production planning and when it should be contravened. This issue has also been examined by Meehl (1954) in the context of psychiatric diagnosis. He concluded that, in the absence of strong additional evidence which would invalidate the linear regression prediction, a decision maker can reach better decisions by relying on the model rather than on "clinical" judgment. More recently, advances have been made in the ability of the model to handle poorly defined and/or hard to measure variables (Einhorn, 1974). Linear weighting models have been used to infer the values of decision makers in many contexts, such as production scheduling (Kunreuther, 1969), medical diagnosis (Hoffman, Slovic, & Rorer, 1968), and judicial cases (Kort, 1968). Its most frequent application, however, is in personnel selection decisions.

Sequential elimination. Sequential elimination methods are less demanding of a decision maker's cognitive abilities than are weighting methods. Rather than attempting to evaluate all information relevant to the quality of various courses of action before making choices, the sequential elimination methods permit decision makers to focus upon subsets of alternatives and to make a series of choices among these smaller sets of alternatives. In a sense, then, the complex choices are composed into simpler and more limited choices. None of the sequential elimination methods discussed here involves either compensatory judgments or consideration of higher-level objectives pertaining to the attributes by which alternatives are described.

The essential features of sequential elimination methods are: (1) attribute values (intraattribute preferences) are scaled in at least an ordinal manner and, in some cases, preferences are ordered across attributes; (2) standards are specified across attributes; and (3) a process is given for comparing the value of attributes so that alternatives may be either eliminated or retained. Alternatives can be judged by comparing them to some standard, or alternatives can be compared to other alternatives to determine their relative merits. One method discussed here, the use of disjunctive or conjunctive standards, involves comparing alternatives to standards. The other two methods we discuss, lexicography and elimination by aspects, operate by direct comparison of alternatives.

Setting preferences as standards. Possibly the least demanding approach for multiple-attribute decision making is for decision makers simply to specify their preferences as standards that must be met by the chosen course of action. One standard could be the stipulation that a job applicant must have a high-school diploma. Then, decision makers compare the attributes which describe decision alternatives against standards which have been specified. Standards can be applied either disjunctively (i.e., only one standard must be met) or conjunctively (i.e., all must be met). Typically, conjunctive standards are applied in a satisficing manner; that is, alternatives are sought until one is found that meets the standards, without trying to determine if an even better alternative exists. Examples of the use of standards have been reported in consumer choice decisions (Bettman, 1971), in portfolio decisions made by trust investment officers (Clarkson, 1962), and in judging MMPI profiles (Kleinmuntz, 1968).

Lexicography. Both lexicography and elimination by aspects reduce the cognitive demands of choosing by comparing alternatives on one attribute at a time. Also, when using these methods a choice can be made before all attributes have been considered if one alternative emerges as clearly superior on the most important attributes.

The term *lexicography* refers to the similarity between this method of making choices in multiple attribute situations and the manner in which words are ordered in a dictionary. In the lexicographic method (Aumann, 1964; MacCrimmon, 1968), a decision maker would order attributes in terms of their importance, then focus on the most important attribute (e.g., salary may override all other factors in job choice). If one alternative (job) has a higher value than any other alternative on this attribute, it would be chosen. In the event of ties, the tied alternatives are examined on the second most important attribute (e.g., hours of work), and so forth, until only one alternative is left. Since only one attribute is considered at a time with this method, poor values on one attribute cannot be directly compensated by good values on another.

One danger in using this method is that the alternative chosen may be only slightly better on one attribute. To guard against this, using bands of discrimination to insure that the rating scales against which alternatives are judged reflect important differences in each attribute has been suggested (Luce, 1956). Bettman (1971) and Alexis, et al., (1968) have described examples of the use of lexicography in consumer choices.

Elimination by aspects. Elimination by aspects (Tversky, 1972) involves viewing alternatives as sets of aspects (i.e., attributes). Aspects relevant to the purchase of a car, for example, may include price, number of passengers accommodated, and color. Rather than considering aspects in the order of a decision maker's preferences for them, aspects are ordered in terms of the extent to which they permit a decision maker to *differentiate among alternatives.* Although it is important to the purchaser that a car have an engine, this aspect would not serve to differentiate among cars since all cars being considered for purchase would be quite likely to have an engine. As in lexicography, elimination by aspects proceeds by comparing alternatives on one aspect at a time. In elimination by aspects, however, alternatives which fail to meet a specified standard are eliminated from further consideration. The elimination by aspects approach can also be used by eliminating undesirable aspects, when none of the possible courses of action appear attractive. In this case, choice involves discarding the most undesirable alternatives and choosing the best of the remaining unattractive options.

When using sequential elimination, standards may be loosely set during the initial stages of decision making, then gradually tightened by emphasizing the attributes that the decision maker considers most important. By sequentially tightening standards a decision maker can narrow down the set of acceptable alternatives, possibly to the point of having only one remaining alternative. This procedure would be useful when little is known initially about the available decision alternatives. In hiring someone for a job when little information about the pool of potential applicants is available, the initial screening may use very broad criteria. If this screening yields a great many qualified applicants, then the standards could be tightened for subsequent screenings until only the "short list" remains. Applicants on the "short list" could then be interviewed for a final selection.

A decision regarding the purchase of a house may also take the form of elimination by aspects. In order to cope with the overwhelming number of houses typically listed for sale, purchasers may begin by specifying the attributes which are both important to them and which will serve to differentiate among the available houses. Among the aspects typically used are price, proximity to work, and number of bedrooms. Price is likely to emerge as one of the top aspects and may be considered early in the elimination process, followed by number of bedrooms, and proximity to work. If the purchaser sets a ceiling price of $75,000, all houses that are listed above this price—and those with prices not sufficiently negotiable to bring them below this price—would be eliminated from further consideration. The remaining houses would then be compared on the next aspect, and so on, until only one house is left.

The sequential elimination methods are attractive because they are easy to use and easy to justify to other people. In fact, they follow closely the procedure typically used in satisficing decisions, and, as such, they appear to represent a common response to bounded rationality. However, these methods do not insure that the alternative which is actually selected is better than the rejected alternatives. The weighting methods, while cognitively more demanding, have the advantage of greater assurance that the chosen alternative actually is superior. The reader interested in a more thorough discussion of methods for making multiple-attribute and multiple-objective decisions is referred to an excellent treatment by MacCrimmon (1973).

Using multi-attribute utility analysis (MAU). One of the most promising techniques for assisting managers in making complex decisions is multi-attribute decision analysis (MAU). Applications of MAU have increased greatly in recent years. Moreover, the accumulating evidence indicating the robustness of the technique in the face of minor violations of its underlying assumptions suggests that it can be applied to many practical problems. MAU has been extensively used in making decisions regarding budgets, plant locations, student admissions, land use, and personnel assignments.

MAU provides a single measure of overall utility for a course of action that has more than one important attribute to consider in evaluating its quality. The theory underlying MAU specifies that the weighted utilities for an object be computed and summed across all attributes:

$$MAU_j = \sum_i w_i u_{ij}$$

where w_i is the relative importance of the ith attribute and u^{ij} is the utility of the jth object on the ith attribute. For example, in using MAU to help teachers find jobs, jobs can be described by the attributes of location, type of position, type of school, community size, and salary. Here, w_i could be the importance of job location, and u_{ij} would indicate how appealing the location of job j is. Weights and utilities can be assessed either directly or indirectly. Direct assessment methods (e.g., asking the assessor for the numbers) are much simpler, but are not justified by the theory. Indirect methods are consistent with the theory, but can be very complex, lengthy, and tedious.

Einhorn and Hogarth (reported in Goodman, et al., 1978) have developed a simple method for teaching the essential features of MAU to managers, in which a set of simple rules are provided to permit the managers to perform their own MAU's.

The steps recommended for conducting the analyses are:

1. Begin by listing all important attributes of the alternatives under consideration.
2. Scale all attributes to indicate their value to the decision maker.
3. Since precise differentiations among values assigned to attributes doesn't seem to matter, weight all attributes equally. If you must differentiate the attributes, then rank order them by importance.
4. Form a matrix with the alternatives in the rows and the attributes in the columns. Fill the cell entries with ratings; where possible, use dollar values or other objective measures.
5. Find the mean and standard deviation for each attribute.
6. Standardize each cell entry by subtracting the column mean and dividing by the standard deviation.
7. Multiply each standardized cell entry by the weight assigned to the attribute.

8. Add the weighted standardized scores for each alternative.
9. Choose either the alternative with the highest score or the alternative with the highest benefit-to-cost ratio.

While these steps are relatively easy to use, they are based on extensive research evidence. For example, the advantages of linear regression rules for combing attributes and the demonstrated effectiveness of equal weights in additive models have been observed in research studies. A thorough review of methods for assessing utilities has been written by Kneppreth et al. (1974).

MAU is based on a theory in which the models, the methods for measuring utilities, and tests for determining which model is applicable are specified by the axioms of utility theory (Slovic, et al., 1977). In practice, however, there has been some dispute regarding the manner in which MAU is carried out. Disagreement about methods for generating lists of attributes and assessing weights and utilities have been particularly heated. Two approaches for listing attributes are interviewing (at times extensive interviews with a number of decision makers) (Beach, et al., 1976) and use of the Nominal Group Technique. The Nominal Group Technique is a structured procedure for guiding a decision-making group through its deliberations that is discussed in Chapter 6. MAU has been found to be very robust when minor attributes are omitted, but omitting important attributes can seriously alter the results (Aschenbrenner & Kasubek, 1976).

The issue of the validity of MAU has raised some controversy, and the early attempts to determine its validity by correlating the results of MAU with overall judgments made by subjects in the same situation clearly were inadequate. Although one study showed that three different decomposition procedures were more in agreement than were three overall judgment procedures (Fischer, 1972), generally empirical research evidence is not considered in determining the validity of MAU. Rather, the validity of MAU is determined by acceptance of the theory. The theory specifies the models, the assessment procedures, and the tests for choosing the appropriate model. If the decision maker accepts the axioms of utility theory (e.g., transitivity of choices) and the tests are met, then MAU is considered to be valid.

SUMMARY

Choosing in complex situations presents major challenges to the cognitive abilities of decision makers. This chapter has examined the difficulties arising from the sheer multiplicity of factors that need to be considered in making decisions—in the form of multiple-attributes and multiple-objectives and/or the interconnections among the factors.

To derive strategies for coping with complexity in decision making, the nature of bounded rationality and cognitive strain were analyzed. A simple model of cognitive information processing was described, and its implications for overcoming cognitive strain explored. To provide insights into the cognitive processes underlying cognitive strain, some of the research approaches taken in investigating cognitive processes and the major conclusions they have yielded were highlighted.

Finally, aids were suggested for improving decision making in highly complex situations. Among the decision aids discussed were ways to see clearly the relationships among the elements of a problem or to decompose a complex problem into simpler subproblems. Next, techniques were examined for efficiently gathering information about the problem and for choosing among alternatives when they are described by many attributes, or when a decision maker wants to choose a course of action which will attain many objectives. The last decision aid discussed was multiattribute utility analysis and the promise of this technique for applied decision making was pointed out.

Chapter 5 will discuss the nature of uncertainty in decision contexts. Seldom can decisions be made with certainty; most practical decisions must be reached on the basis of very incomplete information about the important features of the decision problem, the courses of action that are available to the decision maker, and the consequences of taking any given course of action. Many theories and techniques relevant to making decisions under conditions of uncertainty have been advanced over the past several decades. We attempt to signal a few of the major developments in this field.

CHOOSING IN UNCERTAIN DECISION PROBLEMS 5

Suppose that you are a buyer for a large chain of shoe stores and have an option to buy five thousand pairs of shoes from a factory in a foreign country at four dollars a pair. You know that they can be resold at an average price of ten dollars a pair in your own country, but you must be granted an import license before you can do so. Other buyers are interested in buying the shoes, so you cannot wait until the import license has been granted to make the purchase. Yet, if the import license is not granted, the contract will be cancelled with a penalty of one dollar a pair. It is clear that the probability of being awarded the import license figures very importantly in your decision. What would you do?

The probability of receiving the import license introduces uncertainty into your decision. Uncertainty is one of the most troublesome aspects of making decisions in organizations, and refers to problems in which a decision maker does not have sufficient information to make a sound decision. While a decision maker may have some information about what courses of action are available and believes that choosing a given course of action may lead to a particular outcome, it is almost always necessary to choose a course of action without complete knowledge of the consequences that will follow from implementing it.

Decision problems may be uncertain for many reasons. There may be insufficient knowledge of the events in the decision environment that will influence the decision outcome and the causal relationships that exist among the aspects of the decision problem. Or some elements of the decision problem and its environment may be beyond the decision maker's control. Moreover, decisions are made in organizational environments that are highly unstable due to the introduction of new technology, rapidly changing markets, or a host of other uncertain features. Uncertainties also may arise from the social and political aspects of organizational processes, but discussion of these features will be reserved until the next chapter.

ANALYTICAL FRAMEWORKS FOR REDUCING UNCERTAINTY

When a decision maker has only partial information about a problem, analytical frameworks are needed to reduce the uncertainty surrounding the choice and to improve the decision. The analytical frameworks typically used for dealing with uncertainty are discussed in this section.

In addition to assessing the utilities of the various possible outcomes, as we discussed earlier, the decision maker must gamble on what is actually going to happen. For example, the value of insurance depends on the chances of living for some specified length of time. Similarly, the value of a decision to carry an umbrella depends on the likelihood of rain. In considering decision behavior, one needs to consider both utilities of courses of action and the odds of various consequences resulting from taking the courses of action. Thus, when outcomes are uncertain, both utility and chance need to be considered.

To provide a basis for our discussion of behavioral aspects of decision making under uncertainty, the concepts of risk, probability, expected value, and subjective expected utility are introduced in this chapter. When appropriately used, these concepts offer considerable assistance in reducing uncertainty with regard to analyzing alternatives and evaluating potential outcomes. Behavioral research conclusions which have implications for these topics are used to suggest ways to improve decisions made in uncertain situations.

Uncertainty and Risk

Dividing uncertainty into *measurable* and *unmeasurable* uncertainty is a common way to deal with a degree of knowledge in a decision (Knight, 1920). According to this approach, measurable uncertainty refers to situations in which the probability of an event is objectively known on the basis of historical data or *a priori* calculations. This type of uncertainty is called *risk* and figures prominently in gambling. Unmeasurable uncertainty involves situations in which probabilities are not known—which includes most decisions in organizations.

Since probabilities based on relative frequencies, in this view, would be appropriate only for dealing with measurable uncertainty, probabilities would be of little use to many decision makers. Instead, decision makers would have to resort to techniques which assume that they have no information about the probabilities of occurrence of possible outcomes for a given course of action—such as the *maximin* or *maximax rules* (Baumol, 1972). Maximin represents a pessimistic view of decision outcomes. A decision maker using the maximin rule would determine the worst that can happen if any given course of action is taken and select the course of action for which the worst outcome is most advantageous for the decision maker. An optimistic decision maker, on the other hand, may wish to use the maximax decision rule. This involves selecting the course of action which yields the maximum payoff.

Although these decision rules are widely used, the distinction made in this view of uncertainty has been shown to be false on the basis of both logical and empirical evidence. There are two major logical flaws in the distinction between measurable and unmeasurable uncertainty: (1) even when the distribution of outcomes is unknown, decisions frequently are made on the basis of subjective judgments about the likelihood of an event (e.g., people do insure against the unique occurrences of natural disasters), and (2) the poles of complete knowledge and complete ignorance are unrealizable (MacCrimmon 1968).

While the decision rules for dealing with unmeasurable uncertainty specify that courses of action must be identified and payoffs estimated, they assume that a decision maker is completely ignorant regarding the probabilities of the occurrence of the payoffs. If the decision maker knows about the courses of action and payoffs, however, it is reasonable to expect that judgments about the chances of outcomes occurring would be made. In addition, to specify the two poles of the measurable vs. unmeasurable uncertainty dimension and not to permit intermediate levels of knowledge is unrealistic. Seldom, if ever, would complete ignorance or complete knowledge exist. Moreover, it is misleading to use the term *risk* in this manner—no resources may have been committed, and this is a central feature of risk.

In conducting empirical research to investigate the distinction between risk and uncertainty, Ellsberg (1961) found that subjects preferred bets involving drawing balls from an urn in which the proportion of red and black balls were known over an urn in which the distribution of red balls and black balls was unknown. He interpreted these findings as evidence that bets on draws from the urn with known distributions of balls was preferred because it is a case of risk, whereas the urn with the unknown distribution of balls involved uncertainty. Yet, MacCrimmon (1968) found that this distinction failed to hold when business executives were used as subjects. Instead, few business executives made the distinction between risk and uncertainty, and very few of them said that the distinction seemed reasonable.

A better analytical framework for measuring uncertainty would result from abandoning the complete ignorance assumption underlying uncertainty and considering uncertain aspects of decision problems in terms of the actions available to a decision maker who must deal with incomplete knowledge of the decision environment. Most decisions made in organizations involve partial knowledge of the relevant factors. Hence, in suggesting techniques for coping with uncertainty, a better approach would be to ask the decision maker to use experience, judgment, and available information to assign subjective probabilities when objective probabilities of events are not available. The approach taken for understanding decision making in this chapter is appropriate for such decisions, since it recognizes that a decision maker must gamble in uncertain situations and gives strategies for making choices which represent the best bet.

Probability Theory

Probability theory attempts to draw conclusions about the occurrence of random events (i.e., events whose outcomes are affected by chance). Random events generally are caused by the joint contribution of a great many influences and probability theory focuses on events which occur as an outcome of these influences (Miller & Starr, 1967). Probabilities, ranging from zero through one, are used to indicate the relative frequency with which an event is expected to occur over an extended time period. Assigning a probability of 1.0 to an event suggests that the event is always expected to occur. The probability of death is 1.0, since everyone is expected to die. On the other hand, assigning a probability of .0 to an event indicates that it is never expected to happen. It is conceivable that an event with a probability of .0 will actually happen, but we never expect it to occur. Assigning a probability value between 1 and 0 to an event shows the frequency with which it is expected to happen. When a coin is flipped repeatedly, tails would be expected to turn up half of the time. Hence, getting tails has a probability of .5. While no one can know future events with absolute certainty, the statistical probability of getting tails can be stated.

Objective vs. Subjective Probabilities

There are two major interpretations of probability theory—the frequency school (i.e., using objective probabilities) and the personalistic school (i.e., using subjective probabilities). While these schools agree on the mathematical properties of probabilities, they disagree in interpreting probability and in determining the probabilities of actual events. The relative frequency interpretation holds that probabilities must relate to the long run frequencies with which events occur. Hence, in this view, probabilities properly apply only to events which can be repeated over many trials; and in which an uncontrolled variation exists (i.e., haphazard or random) such that prediction of individual observations are impossible. Therefore, we can speak of the relative frequency of events and the associated probability of occurrence only after repeated observations (Halter & Dean, 1971).

Subjective probability, on the other hand, pertains to events which can be thought of in probabilistic terms, but not in terms of relative frequency. For example, a firm introducing a new product cannot observe the process of launching the product twenty times, or even twice; nor can it assume that previously introduced new product lines will yield precise data about future new product introductions. Yet, while the firm's marketing managers cannot determine objectively the probability that the new product will be successful, they may have opinions regarding the likelihood that the new product will succeed. Subjective probabilities permit these personal feelings and judgments to be quantified as degrees of belief. Subjective probabilities can be based on all information available to the decision maker; including experience, judgment, and intuition. Since subjective probabilities are widely used in managerial decision making, in this chapter we focus primarily on the assessment and use of subjective probabilities.

Objective probability. The objective, or relative frequency, concept of probability can be traced to ancient times, but the first well-developed discussion of frequency theory was presented by Venn (1888). In this treatment, probability was defined as the limiting value of a relative frequency as the number of cases increased indefinitely. The relative frequency concept of probability was developed originally to deal with situations such as games of chance in which plays are repeated a number of times (e.g., spinning a roulette wheel or tossing dice). In these situations, the various events of interest (e.g., getting a two or a three on a throw of a die) can be assumed to be equally likely.

Measuring objective probabilities. Often, as in the games of chance mentioned above, objective probabilities can be assigned by analyzing the physical characteristics of the device producing the events. The fact that a die is six-sided and evenly balanced produces an expected probability that any number of the die will show up on the average of one-sixth of the time. When the nature of the physical mechanisms underlying the occurrence of an event is not understood, objective probability can be estimated by observing the relative frequency of the event in the past.

For example, if oil wildcatters have found 25 dry wells (no oil present) in the 50 places where they have drilled which had a geological structure of a given type, the objective probability of striking oil in future explorations in geological structures of this type would be .5. Or the data may be more detailed. Drake and Keeney (1978) reported the use of fire department response times to previous fires as a basis for estimating the probabilities of response times to future fire alarms. They developed a histogram, shown in Figure 5.1 reporting the percent of alarms that were answered in 1 to 8 minutes (reported for each minute). Given this type of data, objective probabilities can be generated to guide estimates of future response times to fire alarms.

EXHIBIT 5.1 Fire Department Response Times to Prior Fires

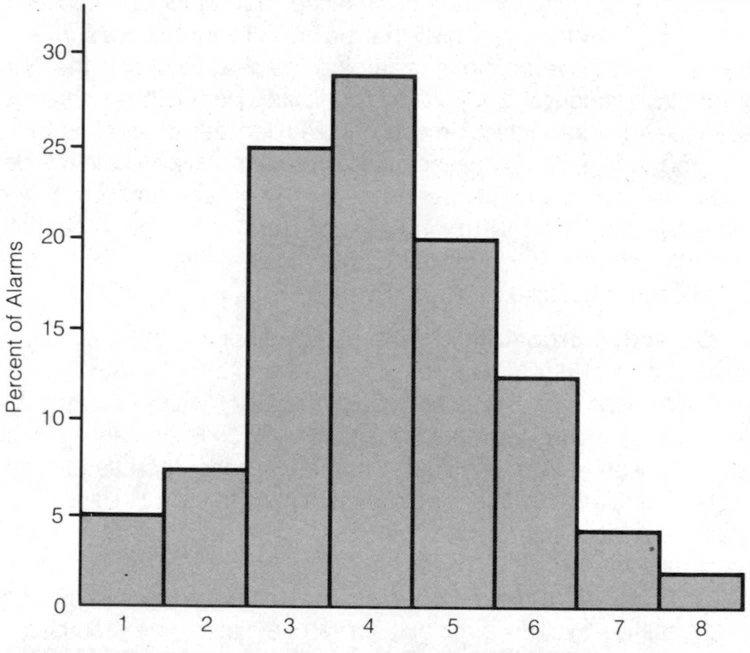

Source: Drake, A.W. and Keeney, R.L. *Decision Analysis*. Cambridge, Mass.: Center for Advanced Engineering Study, Massachusetts Institute of Technology, 1978, 10.6.

Two major objections to the relative frequency view of probability can be raised. First, while this school of thought views itself as empirically based, statements about the limits of an infinite series cannot be empirically confirmed by actual observation. For example, in 100 coin tosses one may get a number of heads ranging from 1 to 100, although the probability of heads would be held to be .5. No finite series of any length can prove the proposition "probability of heads is .5" to be true, or false. Similarly, statistical techniques of estimation and hypothesis testing can be seen as giving reasonable conclusiveness based on the evidence, but do not guarantee certainty.

A second limitation of the relative frequency interpretation of probability is that it cannot deal with unique events. For example, the probability of rain tomorrow in Vancouver may be taken as .5. This statement refers to a particular place and day. Therefore, we cannot count the relative number of rainy to total days in estimating the probability of rain—only one day is of interest. Although one may examine the frequency of rain on this date for prior years in Vancouver, it is necessary to show that these days and conditions are sufficiently similar to those of today before we can justify their being included in the historical data. Or consider the statement that there will be a manned landing on Mars prior to the year 2000. No historical data pertaining to manned landings on Mars will help us in determining the probability of this statement.

Despite these limitations in the relative frequency view of probabilities, there are many situations in which repeated measures can be made and in which the relative frequency approach can be used to estimate the probability that events will occur. For example, production managers carry out quality control procedures to monitor output from their factories in order to estimate, through appropriate sampling, the proportion of defective items being produced. Also, actuarial statisticians regularly record claims in relation to life, property, and car insurance so that estimates of the frequencies of various types of claims can be made.

Subjective probabilities. The application of subjective probabilities to decision making has occurred during the past forty years (Hamburg, 1970). This view interprets the probability of an event in terms of the degree of belief or confidence that a decision maker places in the occurrence of the event. While the data upon which the belief is based may include relative frequency data (e.g., historical information, trends), they are not limited to this type of data. Subjective probabilities also may be based on a decision maker's own judgments and/or the judgments of other people. Subjective probabilities, then, are applicable to events which have not been, or may not be, tested by the performance of a large number of trials. In the example of the oil wildcatters, knowledge that oil had been found in the immediate vicinity may lead the wildcatters to alter the probability of striking oil to a subjective probability which is greater than the .5 indicated by the historical data.

Savage (1954) has provided one of the major discussions of personalistic or subjective probability. Although the terms *personal probability* and *subjective probability* have been used interchangeably, it is more accurate to speak of the personal probabilities of "ideal people" and the subjective probabilities of "real people." Personal probability, then, pertains to the degree of beliefs of an ideal person who has perfectly consistent beliefs. In contrast, the behavioral research treated in this chapter has investigated the subjective probabilities of actual people and this will be the focus of our discussion.

Subjective probabilities are generally different for each person, since they are based on an individual's knowledge, beliefs, and opinions about an event. And, being based on the amount of information a person has, subjective probabilities would be expected to change as additional information is obtained. If, for example, a commuter typically has a half-hour drive to work, it is possible to attribute a subjective probability to the event of "arriving at work on time" if the commuter leaves home at the usual time. This is a prior probability, since it is reached on the basis of prior information. While driving to work, the commuter hears a traffic report on the car radio stating that a tunnel on the commuter's route has been blocked by a traffic accident; necessitating a long delay or detour. On the basis of this new information, the commuter can make a new estimate of the probability of arriving at work on time (i.e., a posterior probability).

Many applied decisions involve weighing the available imperfect information and determining the subjective probabilities of future events. Subjective probabilities are central to the analysis of many decision problems in business and government, particularly those problems that are unique; or at least nonroutine, in the sense that the decision situations cannot be duplicated. For example, subjective probability, but not relative frequency, interpretations can be given to an event such as the price of silver moving by more than 20 percent either way in the next six months. While a decision maker may be able to make an assessment of the probability of this event, it is likely that experts on the topic would be consulted to reach appropriate objective probabilities.

The value of subjective probability is that it permits decision makers to describe their feelings about the effects of uncertainty in defined and understood terms—and to incorporate these judgments into the decision process. The resulting subjective probabilities do not imply authority, they are simply a way to put subjective views into more precise form and to provide a basis for comparing courses of action.

A decision maker typically uses subjective probabilities just as objective probabilities are used. Judgments can be quantified by specifying probabilities based on all the information that a decision maker has, and these probabilities can be used in analyzing a decision problem. Subjective probabilities, however, may differ from one decision maker to another since people differ in the data they have, their experiences, and their hunches. For this reason, subjective probabilities may say more about the individual's belief in the occurrence of an event than about the facts of the event. A great deal of research has investigated the way in which people form subjective probabilities. This research is central to our discussion of the behavioral aspects of making decisions in highly uncertain situations.

The objective and subjective views of probability have much in common. Both accept the basic properties of mathematical probability theory, both attempt to present logical and consistent theories of probability, and both realize that a probability value can be largely determined by sufficient amounts of frequency data. There are, however, important differences in the implications of these schools of thought for decision making. Savage (1954) reversed his original belief that probability theory did not suggest changes in statistical practices. One implication of the acceptance of the theory of personal probability is that measured subjective probabilities, even when not objectively justified, could be given more credibility. Yet, if subjective probabilities are not found to be consistent, then personal probability theory could not justify the use of such measures in decision making. One solution to this difficulty would be to attempt to improve the consistency of subjective probabilities by pointing out inconsistent judgments to assessors (Savage 1954).

In addition to these normative uses of personal probability theory, it has provided useful descriptive applications. Much research has investigated whether the subjective expected utility (SEU) model, or some variation of it, can describe actual human behavior. The SEU model prescribes that a decision maker will choose the course of action which maximizes expected gains. Of course, a person's interpretation of probability will influence the way in which the results of these research studies are viewed. If one believes that there are objective probabilities which, ideally, should apply to decision making, then one would be less inclined to view SEU-consistent behavior as rational than would someone who accepted personal probability theory.

Measuring subjective probabilities. One of the major challenges to decision making is the accurate assessment of subjective probabilities. A number of methods for measuring subjective probabilities exist, generally falling into one of two classifications—direct or indirect methods. Using the direct methods, the strength of a decision maker's beliefs concerning various events may be determined by more or less direct questioning. Alternatively, in using the indirect methods the decision maker's preferences among various decisions are observed and, then, an attempt is made to infer the subjective probabilities that appear to correspond with the indicated preferences. Savage (1954) has referred to the indirect methods as *behavioral methods* of interrogation.

Direct methods. A number of direct methods for assessing subjective probability have been advanced. For example, the assessor can be asked to give probabilities for a series of events in numbers ranging from 0 to 1. Or, rather than requiring a direct statement of probabilities, a decision maker may be asked to divide a line into two parts reflecting the relative probabilities of two exclusive (and exhaustive) events, and probabilities may be calculated on the basis of the two lengths. Similarly, subjects may be asked to pile poker chips into stacks proportional to the probabilities of events.

Another direct method of assessing subjective probabilities involves stating odds favoring one event over another event. Rather than asking for the probability of an event (e.g., "rain tomorrow"), the decision maker may be asked for the odds favoring rain. In this formulation, the odds for an event "rain" (E_1) over the event "no rain" (E_2) is determined by the ratio of the probabilities $p(E_1)/p(E_2)$. Since these events are exclusive and exhaustive, if the decision maker states the odds of "rain tomorrow" as 4 to 1, then the probability of rain tomorrow can be determined as follows:

$$p(E\ ) = \frac{\text{odds }(E\ /E\ )}{\text{odds }(E\ /E\ ) + 1}$$

or in the example given above:

$$p(E\ ) = \frac{-4/1}{4/1 + 1} = \frac{4}{5} = .80$$

A *quantitative probability* does not have to be explicitly stated to measure subjective probability. Rather, a *qualitative probability* can be determined by asking the subject to order the probabilities in terms of relative magnitudes. Relative ordering of probabilities have been obtained using a number of experimental approaches. For example, a decision maker may be asked to report the relative subjective probabilities for a pair of events, or may be asked simply to rank subjective probabilities for a set of events.

Yet another direct method of obtaining subjective probabilities is by use of *confidence ratings* (i.e., subjects are asked to say how confident they are that an event will occur). Confidence ratings generally involve the use of quantitative probabilities, but it also is possible to indicate confidence of judgments on an ordinal verbal scaling ranging from the highest level of confidence (i.e., I am certain I was correct) to the lowest level of confidence (i.e., I am certain I was incorrect). When this method is used, identical subjective probabilities are attributed to responses with identical confidence ratings. Use of direct methods of subjective probability assessment has a long history, originating with the early work of Bentham (Keynes, 1921). He suggested that jury witnesses should be asked to indicate on a scale their degree of certainty concerning the innocence or guilt of the accused. This method has been widely used by researchers but, as is also true of other direct methods of assessing probabilities, the demands it places on the cognitive ability of probability assessors tend to be extreme.

Indirect methods. Indirect methods for assessing subjective probability, on the other hand, involve inferring the decision maker's degree of belief from behavior in choosing between two or more bets or alternatives. Rather than asking a decision maker directly for an assessment, degrees of belief are inferred from behavior in making choices among betting odds, lotteries, insurance premiums, etc. *The equivalent urn* is a very simple indirect method for assessing subjective probabilities. This urn is used as a standard reference device for determining the probability of success of a project a decision maker is considering. For example, the decision maker may consider two bets—bet A states that if the project is successful, $5,000 will be won, but if the project fails nothing will be won. Bet B is represented by the equivalence urn. The urn has been filled with 5,000 balls which are identical in size and shape; each assigned a number from 1 through 5,000. Initially, half of the balls in the urn are white and half are black. The decision maker is blindfolded and randomly draws one ball from the urn. Bet B, therefore, can be stated as follows: "If a black ball is drawn you will win $5,000; if a white ball is drawn you win nothing."

The choice confronting the decision maker in this method of indirectly assessing subjective probability concerning the success of the project is to decide whether bet A or bet B is preferred. Let's say bet B is chosen, in which the probability of drawing a black ball is .5. We would conclude that the probability of success of the project was less than .5. By changing the proportion of black balls in the urn, eventually a mix of black and white balls would be attained for which the decision maker is indifferent between bet A and bet B. The proportion of black balls in the urn at that point would be considered to also represent the decision maker's subjective probability of the success of the project in question. Therefore, from answers to simple questions such as, "Do you prefer this bet to that bet, or are you indifferent between them?" a decision maker's degree of belief can be inferred.

Another approach to eliciting subjective probability has been developed by Spetzler and Stael von Holstein (1975)—involving use of a probability wheel. A probability wheel, shown in Exhibit 5.2 is a disk with two differently colored sectors which can be adjusted to vary the area of each color shown. In using the probability wheel, the decision makers are asked to bet either on a fixed event such as "the project will be a success," or that the rotating spinner will stop in the blue sector of the wheel. The relative sizes of the two sectors are varied until the decision makers report that they are indifferent between the two bets. At that point, the proportion of the wheel which is blue is considered to represent the decision maker's subjective probability of the success of the project.

EXHIBIT 5.2 Probability Wheel

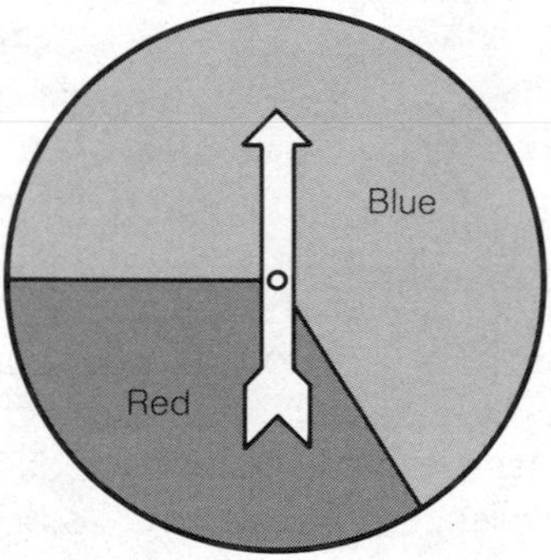

Source: Speltzer, C.S. and Stäel von Holstein, C.-A.S. Probability encoding in decision analysis. *Management Science*, 1975, 22, 349.

One more indirect method will be described here. The decision maker's subjective probabilities may be determined from a lottery or choice among bets. In the bet concerning the probability of success of the project mentioned above, what amount of money would make the decision makers indifferent between playing the bet or accepting the money? That is, what is their minimum selling price for the bet? This method assumes that the expected monetary value of the bet has been specified, and the amount of money for which the bet would be sold is equivalent to the expected monetary value of the bet.

One criticism of methods based on gambling frameworks is the possibility that producing a gambling context for the probability assessment task might evoke a special gambling behavior involving not only degree of belief about the occurrence of the event to be considered, but also risk attitudes and propensity to gamble (Moore & Thomas, 1976). Generally, however, the indirect methods for assessing subjective probabilities are superior to the direct methods in that they are less demanding of the decision makers' judgment capabilities and are better justified by the theoretical framework of personal probability.

Use of scoring rules. Scoring rules—deriving a score to indicate the accuracy of a decision maker's assignment of probabilities—have been developed to assist decision makers in providing accurate measures of their true beliefs. Such scores can be set up so as to provide financial rewards for good estimates in an effort to improve the quality of subjective probability assessments. Typically, scoring rules are derived as a function of both the true outcome of the event being assessed and the size of the probability associated with the true outcomes of this event. Slovic, et al., (1977) describe three purposes for scoring rules: (1) to indirectly assess probabilities, (2) to improve probability assessment by feedback of accuracy scores, and (3) to evaluate probability assessors.

Scores reflecting the accuracy of subjective probabilities can take the form of generating a list of bets, each bet represented by two numbers—the amount a decision maker wins if the event occurs and the amount lost if the event does not occur. The decision maker chooses the preferred bet from the list, and this bet indicates belief regarding the probability of the event. However, some research evidence indicates that subjects do not attempt to maximize winnings when this method is used (Jensen & Peterson, 1973; Seghers, Fryback, & Goodman, 1973). The method assumes that providing scores would motivate subjects to try to maximize the amount of money they win; failing in this, the method is of questionable validity.

Scoring rules also attempt to improve probability estimates through providing feedback concerning the results of using various scoring rules. For example, weather forecasters frequently use scoring rules to improve their subjective probability estimates. The evidence concerning improvements in subjective probability judgments resulting from the use of scoring rules in this context is mixed. While some studies have found that scores on a subsequent probability-assessment task were improved when feedback regarding scores was provided (e.g., Hoffman & Peterson, 1972), others found no improvement from feedback (e.g., Vlek, 1973). Also, weather forecasters have reported that thinking in probabilistic terms made them uncomfortable and that they doubted that feedback involving a single quantitative measure in the form of a scoring rule would be helpful in improving their forecasts (Slovic, et al., 1977).

Finally, scoring rules have been used to evaluate the probability assessors. When probability assessments are made under equal conditions, the best probability assessor would be the person with the highest score. Since all assessment situations are not identical, assessments involving greater uncertainty will tend to yield higher scores compared to assessment situations involving low uncertainty. To compensate for this, Murphy (1974) has demonstrated that scoring rules used in meteorology can be improved by partitioning it into three components representing 1) uncertainty inherent to the task, 2) the degree to which the assessor can successfully assign probabilities which differ from the overall hit rate, and 3) the assessor's calibration. Using this approach, assessors in different situations can be compared on the basis of the difference between the total score and the inherent uncertainty component.

BEHAVIORAL BIASES IN JUDGING PROBABILITIES

Empirical research on the assessment of subjective probabilities has shown that decision makers tend to be highly inaccurate in making such judgments. Researchers interested in judgment have focused on two major topics: 1) how subjective probability estimates are made, and 2) how probability estimates are updated sequentially as additional information is received. In this section we examine these topics and suggest interpretations for the research evidence related to behavioral biases.

Behavioral Biases in Estimating Probabilities

Accuracy in estimating probabilities has been investigated by many empirical studies using simple probability-learning experiments in which true probabilities are known. The general conclusion of experiments examining the ability of humans to function as *intuitive statisticians* (i.e., performing statistical calculations intuitively) is that they tend to ignore basic laws of probability theory when estimating subjective probabilities. Specifically, they tend to misjudge randomness, ignore base rates and sample sizes, and overestimate the likelihood of two events simultaneously occurring.

Misjudging randomness of events. In predicting the color of a series of balls drawn from an urn containing an unspecified mixture of white and black balls, it has been found that subjects are reasonably accurate in estimating the proportion of balls of each color. But they tend not to do well in making predictions regarding the color of the next ball to be drawn (Vlek, 1970; Peterson & Beach, 1967). Since they accurately estimate the proportion of balls of each color in the urn, they could increase their accuracy in estimating the color of the next ball to be drawn by consistently predicting the color of ball which is more numerous in the urn. Yet, subjects frequently predict that the less numerous color of ball will be drawn. Even when they are rewarded for accurate predictions, the bias toward balls of the less frequent color still occurs (Messick & Rapoport, 1965). These results suggest that subjects have difficulty in judging the randomness of sequences of events.

Misperceptions regarding how random sequences should look is shown in the *gambler's fallacy.* If you are given a pair of fair dice, how likely do you think it is that you would roll an eleven? If an eleven has not come up in the last fifty rolls of the dice, is an eleven more likely to occur on the next roll? Gamblers have been found to bet that an eleven will come up next, believing that the law of averages indicate that it is due to appear. In fact, the probability of an eleven in both of the situations described above is the same. Dice and coins have no memory of the outcomes of prior trials, so the probabilities of events are always the same on every try.

Ignoring base rates. A finding of the early psychological studies by Meehl and Rosen (1955) was that people tend to ignore the rate at which phenomena have occurred in the past (the base rate) in estimating the likelihood of a phenomenon occurring in the future. In judging the traits of individuals, for example, people did not appear to consider the extent to which certain traits occur in the population in general. In fact, intelligence in the genius range should seldom be attributed to a person, since this level of intelligence is rare in society. If the subject is in doubt about a trait possessed by another person, guessing that the most commonly occurring trait is true of this person is most likely to be correct (e.g., intelligence in the normal range).

Law of belief in small numbers. In estimating probabilities people tend to ignore the implications of sample size and to attribute greater stability to results obtained from small samples than is warranted. Tversky and Kahneman (1971) have called this the "law of a belief in small numbers." To illustrate this bias, consider the following situation. Your job is to judge the quality of a large quantity of grain being shipped by railroad. Would you be more confident that your analysis was correct if you took a single sample from one rail car, or if you took many samples from each rail car? Statistically, your sampling is more likely to be representative of the entire shipment of grain if multiple samples are taken. In fact, as more samples are taken you should become more confident that your analysis is accurate. Yet, in psychological experiments subjects tend not to report a degree of confidence in their judgments commensurate with the sample size observed.

Overestimating the likelihood of a conjunction of two events. If you know how likely each of two events is to occur, what does this information tell you about the likelihood of both events simultaneously occurring? Let's say that in commuting to work you can use either of two bridges. Does knowing the probability of each bridge being blocked by a traffic accident, permit you to estimate the likelihood that you will be unable to get to work because both bridges are blocked? The answer is yes, but subjects in psychological experiments have been found to overestimate the likelihood of the conjunction of two such events (e.g., Wyer & Goldberg, 1970).

Probability theory requires that the sum of the probabilities of members of a set of mutually exclusive and collectively exhaustive events (e.g., arrive at work early, on time, or late) must be equal to 1. Yet, this law frequently is ignored in estimating subjective probabilities, which violates the internal consistency of intuitive judgments (Peterson & Beach, 1967). It has been shown that the judged probability of compound events may actually be larger than the probability of the constituent events (e.g., Slovic, et al., 1976). Also, in experiments with groups of individuals, the average subjective probabilities for the lower probability events have been shown to be larger than the corresponding objective probabilities; whereas, the average subjective probabilities for the higher probability events generally are smaller than the corresponding objective probabilities (Lee, 1971).

Behavioral Biases in Revising Opinions

When making decisions in uncertain situations, as additional information is acquired, decision makers must update their beliefs about the probabilistic aspects of the decision environment. The Bayes theorem provides a normative model to guide opinion revision in such situations.

The Bayes theorem. To revise probabilities of independent events as additional information is acquired, the Bayes theorem can be used in the following manner. The probability of event X, given the occurrence of event Y—$P(X|Y)$—can be found by dividing the probability of the joint occurrence of the two events—$P(X \cap Y)$—by the independent probability of event Y—$P(Y)$.

Therefore:

$$P(X|Y) = \frac{P(X \cap Y)}{P(Y)}$$

And:

$$P(X|Y) = \frac{P(X) \bullet P(Y)}{P(Y)}$$

If:

$$P(X) = 0.2 \text{ and } P(Y) = 0.8$$

Then:

$$P(X|Y) = \frac{0.2 \bullet 0.8}{0.8}$$

And:

$$P(X|Y) = \frac{0.16}{0.8} = 0.2$$

When making decisions, generally one has some hunches regarding what is likely to happen (e.g., an item being purchased for a specified price, a stock price going down). Yet, before making a decision a person may gather additional information to be more certain of reaching a high quality decision. The Bayes theorem, given above in a simple form, represents one approach to prescribing the optimal influence that additional information would be expected to have on a decision maker's judgment about the decision outcome. The Bayes theorem is described in the Appendix in greater detail.

Research using the Bayes theorem. Most experiments on opinion revision require subjects to provide prior probabilities (estimates based on initial information) regarding a set of hypotheses concerning the state of the world. For example, in forming an opinion regarding changes in the price of a stock, one hypothesis may be, "it will rise by one dollar." An additional evidence is presented, subjects are asked to revise—on the basis of the additional evidence—their prior probabilities regarding the likelihood of the various hypotheses which may have generated the data. A comparison of prior probabilities with those prescribed by the Bayes theorem, shows how well subjects revise their opinions in the face of the new evidence.

In most studies it is assumed that the data are conditionally independent. When this is assumed, the essential information necessary for revising opinions is the probability of each hypothesis, $P(H_i)$, and the probability of the data given the hypothesis P(D/H) values. These values have been obtained in several ways, but the usual way is for the researcher to develop values to represent the experimental task and to give them to the subjects.

An interesting departure from experiments using balls and urns may serve to illustrate the research on consistency of opinion revision. Summers and Oncken (1968) conducted an experiment on the logical consistency with which probabilistic judgments are made concerning the attributes of other people. In this study, black and white university students made unconditional estimates about the occurrence of human attributes, and the number of blacks and whites in the population. The attributes examined included traits such as calm, moral, and unique. For example, subjects were asked to estimate how many people in a sample of one hundred would be moral, calm, unique, black, and white; then, they were asked to make conditional estimates regarding all possible pairs of attributes and racial types. They were given a sample of one hundred whites and asked to estimate how many would be calm.

The results indicated that internal consistency of judgment varied as a function of the stimuli—for white stimulus persons, internal consistency was greater than for black stimulus persons. The results suggest that subjects tend to be logically consistent in making probabilistic judgments about persons and their attributes, but that consistency was affected by the characteristics of both the stimulus and the subject. Possibly, this may represent the influence on degree of consistency of learned beliefs or stereotypes.

Conservativism bias. One conclusion from the research on opinion revision is that, although subjects generally estimate probability values which are proportional to the values obtained using the Bayes theorem, their revisions tend to be insufficient in amount. That is, a tendency toward *conservatism.* Although conservatism has been observed in a great many studies, there is little agreement regarding its explanation. Edwards (1968) has summarized three explanations that have received some support—misperception, misaggregation, and artifact.

1. **Misperception.** Misperception occurs when information is combined appropriately, but the diagnostic impact of each item of data is misperceived. According to this explanation, people are inaccurate in judging the importance of various data types and sources.
2. **Misaggregation.** Misaggregation means that individuals perceive each item of data correctly and are aware of its individual diagnostic meaning but they cannot combine its diagnostic meaning well with that of other data. Hence, people have difficulty in combining information to arrive at a single response—a difficulty in judgment discussed in Chapter 4.
3. **Artifact.** The artifactual explanation maintains that the complexity of experiments has produced the tendency toward conservativism (Peterson & Beach, 1967). Typically, experiments that describe the judgment process on the basis of the Bayes theorem have used highly complex tasks. To illustrate this point, consider the difficulty in estimating from which of two urns a sample of eight red and four blue balls comes—one urn containing seven hundred red and three hundred blue balls, the other urn containing seven hundred blue and three hundred red balls. Inability to process this complex information can produce conservativism, thus supporting the artifactual explanation. Ducharme (1970) has called this phenomenon *response bias* and has maintained that the Bayes theorem is a good descriptive model of judgment only for simple tasks.

Overcoming the Conservativism Bias

Attempts have been made to deal with conservativism by using payoffs to improve the motivation of subjects to perform well (Phillips &

Edwards, 1966). While providing payoffs was found to have a motivating effect and to reduce conservativism, payoffs did not eliminate conservativism. In fact, the human motivations involved in revising probabilities may not be motives that can be easily manipulated by rewards. It has been demonstrated that when diagnostic value of the data is increased by manipulating the data source or varying the sample size, an increase in conservativism results. Moreover, subjects become resistant to change as available information accumulates (Slovic & Lichtenstein, 1971). Further support for this position is provided by the finding that individuals are loath to change decisions once made (Taylor & Dunnette, 1974), and that a great deal more information is required to change a decision already made than to make a new decision (Pruitt, 1961). Subjects may become committed to a hypothesis and more than rewards will be required to overcome their reluctance to change their minds.

In addition, perception of skill and luck may influence subjective probabilities. Successful people may be viewed as being lucky, and attributing success to luck appears to be a highly subjective tendency. Also, an application of skill to what appears to be a game of chance may, in fact, change the situation and improve the performance of the player. Since all of these factors frequently exist in organizational decision situations, one must be careful in converting opinions to subjective probabilities. However, if such a conversion can be justified, it becomes possible to use subjective probabilities in organizational decisions and, thus, to treat uncertainty in a more quantitative manner.

Cognitive Processes in Biased Probability Estimates and Opinion Revision

McGuire (1968) concluded on the basis of the research evidence discussed above, that people's beliefs do not have the internal coherence which is required to satisfy the laws of probability. This concern has led to considerable attention being devoted to identifying and explaining the cognitive processes involved in biased probabilistic judgments. Four cognitive processes which appear to account for many of the inaccuracies in making these judgments—(1) representativeness, (2) availability, (3) anchoring and adjustment, and (4) overconfidence—have been observed in laboratory experiments. These processes may have a heuristic purpose in some judgment situations (i.e., providing rules of thumb that facilitate judgments), but in most instances these processes would lower the accuracy of judged probabilities. While some evidence regarding the occurrence of these processes outside the laboratory has been obtained, the question of their relevance for real world probability assessments is still open.

Representativeness. The representativeness heuristic appears to reflect the operation of a person's judgment abut how likely it is that an object being judged belongs to a given set of objects (Kahneman & Tversky, 1972). The cognitive processes underlying this phenomenon apparently involve examining the essential features of an object, then comparing these features to the features of a class of objects to see if the object is representative of the class. As a geologist working in oil exploration, you may have the job of determining the probability of certain geological formations yielding deposits of oil. The representativeness heuristic would suggest that your training and experience have taught you the features essential to geological structures that yield oil. In judging the probability of finding oil at a new site, you would simply compare the features of the new site to those of the class of oil-yielding geological structures.

Availability. The availability heuristic attempts to explain judgmental biases in which an event is viewed as likely or frequent if it is easy to imagine or to recall relevant instances (Tversky & Kahneman, 1973). Frequent events are given a higher probability of occurring since they are easier to recall than infrequent events. What is the probability of a postal strike in the next year? If the post office has a history of labor unrest leading to work stoppages, one would be more inclined to recall these events and to attribute a high probability to another strike. Yet, this cognitive process may mislead the decision maker, since many other factors should be taken into account in forecasting a strike. For example, the situations which prevailed at the time of prior strikes may not exist today. It is important to be sure that the instances which are recalled or imagined are the same as the event for which a probability is being assessed.

Anchoring and adjustment. Anchoring and adjustment involves setting a natural starting point (anchor), and this first approximation to the judgment provides a base for adjusting the judgment. In our discussion of the opinion revision literature it was pointed out that the initial probability assigned by a subject served as a starting point, and that this probability was shifted by the subject as additional information became available.

The cognitive processes described by anchoring and adjustment may operate in the following manner. An employment interviewer must judge the probability of success in performing a job on the basis of information that may be acquired about each applicant. An initial impression may be formed based on an applicant's physical appearance when the applicant enters the personnel office. This impression would, then, be modified as information about the applicant's abilities and experiences is obtained. Yet, both in hiring and in other decision contexts, adjustment in the face of additional information typically has been found to be imprecise and insufficient (Tversky & Kahneman, 1974).

Overconfidence. Research also has shown that people tend to be more confident of their ability to assess probabilities than their actual performance warrants. In fact, they tend to ignore both data reliability and the amount of data upon which judgments are based. This is mentioned above as an example of the belief in the law of small numbers. In addition, they tend to be inconsistent and inaccurate in making judgments regarding the probabilities of events (Slovic, 1972a). Despite the inaccuracies summarized in this section, research subjects generally report that they believe their probability judgments are accurate.

IMPLICATIONS OF BIASES IN JUDGING PROBABILITIES FOR APPLIED DECISIONS

Laboratory studies have shown that limited ability to handle information and neglect of the principles of probability theory lead to many systematic biases in judging subjective probabilities. Yet, the implications of this line of research on behavioral aspects of decision making for applied decisions should be interpreted with caution. Biases typically have been observed in specific types of probability assessment problems and no general theory to explain the underlying cognitive processes has been developed. Nor can the conditions under which any given bias will occur, or whether it will serve to facilitate or inhibit judgment, be specified.

One also should be cautious in generalizing the laboratory results to real-world decision making. Many researchers have pointed out difficulties in generalizing these laboratory results to the real world. Edwards (1975) has claimed that, by failing to give laboratory subjects the tools, time, and guidance needed for making accurate judgments, the laboratory studies have exaggerated the subject's limitations in probability assessment. Winkler and Murphy (1973) have criticized the laboratory experiments for being much more highly structured and simplistic than real-world decision situations. Since people have had more experience with real-world probability assessment situations in their everyday lives, they tend to behave in the laboratory as they would in the real world—treating information as unreliable and redundant. Hence, they may devaluate the reliable information provided in the laboratory and appear conservative. Finally, since the rewards for accurate judgments offered in the laboratory are very small compared to the rewards the subjects are accustomed to in the real world, laboratory subjects may not be highly motivated.

In support of generalizing these biases to decision making outside the laboratory, it should be pointed out that similar biases have been observed in real-world situations. It has been found that residents of flood plains tend to misperceive the probability of floods in a way that is consistent with the biases of representativeness and availability (Slovic, Kunreuther & White, 1974). Also, Tversky and Kahneman (1971) reported that research published in educational and psychological journals often involves experiments designed with inadequate provisions for statistical power; a behavior that appears to be consistent with the belief in a law of small numbers. Finally, biases in probability estimates in laboratory-like experiments have been found when "expert judges" are used—for example, bankers and stock market experts (Stael von Holstein, 1972), gambling casino patrons (Lichtenstein & Slovic, 1973), and statistically knowledgeable psychologists (Tversky & Kahneman, 1971).

BEHAVIORAL BIASES IN ATTRIBUTING CAUSES OF EVENTS

While research on probability assessment deals with judging the *likelihood* of events, a related concern is judging the *causes* of events. The latter issue is addressed by attribution theory. In contrast with the intent of research on probabilistic judgment, which is to determine how humans predict the probability of an event occurring, attribution theory is concerned with how people specify the reasons for the occurrence of events (i.e., attribute causes for events). Attribution theory derived from the early work of Heider (1958) and has been further developed by researchers such as Kelley (1967; 1973) and Weiner (1974).

What is Attribution Theory?

Attribution theory distinguishes between situations in which historical data concerning the behavior being investigated are available and situations in which such historical data are unavailable. When historical data are available, a matrix is used to derive attributions; in the absence of historical data, causal schemata (i.e., general laws) are used. Using historical data, three characteristics of the behavior to be explained form the basis for attributing causality. These are: 1) the degree to which the behaviors are consistent over time, 2) whether the behaviors are distinctive to the situation in question, or if they can occur in other situations, and 3) whether the behaviors demonstrate consensus, in that other actors respond to the situation in a similar way. These characteristics are organized in a three-dimensional matrix from which attributions can be derived by examining the manner in which acts and causes covary.

An illustration of research based on attribution theory in which historical data are available can be seen in a study by MacArthur (1972). In this study, information regarding the dimensions of consensus, consistency, and distinctiveness was systematically varied for the behavioral act—"John laughs at the comedian." On the basis of the information they were given, subjects were asked to determine what probably caused the event to occur. Four alternative causes were provided, and they were asked to choose the most likely cause. The causes from which they made a choice were: 1) pertaining to the person (John), 2) pertaining to the stimulus (the comedian), 3) pertaining to the circumstances, and 4) pertaining to some combination of these four causes. The major conclusion from this line of research was that, while each type of information has some effect on attribution, the "person" attributes tend to have the greatest effect. Considerable research has been devoted to investigating the extent to which attributions made for oneself correspond with attributions made for other people (e.g., Weiner & Seirad, 1975).

When historical data are not available, causal schemata are used in investigation of causal attributions. An example of causal schemata is the principle of behavior which prescribes that, in order to succeed in a difficult task, one must both have ability and try hard (Kun & Weiner, 1973). In research investigating how underlying dispositions can be inferred from behaviors, the subject's (actor) behaviors are analyzed in the following manner:

1. the observer lists the choices facing the actor
2. the actor's possible reasons for selecting each choice are listed
3. reasons which could have led to selecting acts other than the one chosen are eliminated, and
4. the importance for the actor of each of the remaining reasons is examined

A causal attribution can be made with confidence if a reason can be found that could only motivate the chosen act and that is not highly valued by people other than the actor. For example, according to this line of reasoning, one would have some confidence that politicians who advocated raising university tuition to contribute to lower taxes really mean what they say—if the politicians were talking to university students when the statement was made.

Attribution theory has been used in research on achievement motivation (Weiner, 1974), effectiveness of therapy (e.g., Bowers, 1975), sex role stereotypes (e.g., Kiesler, 1978), and order effects in impression formation (e.g., Jones & Goethals, 1972). Most of the research on causal attributions has investigated social perception; a topic with direct implications for decisions made in organizations.

Behavioral Biases in Attributing Causes

Behavioral biases in attributing causes for events have received limited research attention. In marked contrast to the pessimistic view of human ability to make probabilistic judgments that has emerged from the judgment literature, humans seem to be very effective in making causal attributions. Some evidence of behavioral biases in making causal attributions, however, has been found. Among the biases that have been identified are: distortion of information, inferring unjustified personal traits, and primacy effects.

Distortion of information. Subjects have been found to distort incoming data to better serve their own ego defense purposes or to enhance their sense of control over the world (e.g., Kelley, 1967; Luginbuhl, Crow, & Kahan, 1975). Similarly, research has shown that people may exaggerate both the predictability of accidents that may threaten them, and their ability to avoid the danger (Walster, 1967).

Inferring unjustified personal traits. Research has shown that behavioral acts are sometimes attributed to the actor by observers, but to stimulus circumstances by the actor. This has been interpreted as evidence of a bias toward inferring personal traits where none exist (e.g., Jones & Nisbett, 1972).

Primacy effects. People also show a tendency to rely upon the first sufficient explanation that comes to mind in making attributions of causes; thus demonstrating a primacy effect (Kanouse, 1972).

Implications of Biases in Attributing Causes for Applied Decisions.

Relatively little research attention has been given to investigating biases in attribution research. Even when biases are found, the researchers tend to question the information used by the subject and not the ability of the subject. As Fischhoff (1976) pointed out, attributional biases are viewed as proper conclusions derived from improper premises. Premises are not improper because of difficulties in handling or combining information; rather, they are improper because of inefficient information gathering, or distortion of events resulting from values or motives of the people making causal attributions. Essentially, the research based on attribution theory assumes that the attributions made in laboratory situations involve proper use of the techniques employed to assess causal attributions, and that these techniques provide adequate guides for making attributions. Moreover, it is assumed that laboratory research conclusions can be confidently generalized to causal attributions made outside the laboratory.

DETERMINING EXPECTED VALUE OF DECISION ALTERNATIVES

Decision theory specifies that, faced with outcomes that are probabilistic, a decision maker should attempt to maximize the long run expected gains. To choose an optimal course of action in such situations, it is necessary to consider both the probabilities of events and their values. Before discussing the behavioral research on subjective expected utility (SEU) it may be useful to briefly describe the concept of expected value. Recall that in Chapter 3 the notion of utility was described, and in the previous section of this chapter we discussed subjective probabilities. These three concepts—utility, subjective probability, and expected value—provide the basis for understanding subjective expected utility.

What is Expected Value?

The major principle for combining the probabilities of events and their values can be illustrated by a simple gambling situation. You are invited to bet on the outcome of a coin toss. A coin is flipped. If heads appears, you will win $20. If a tails appears you lose $10. You must decide if you should play the game. The expected winnings or losses over the long run is the "expected value" of the game. The calculations are simple. Two possible events can occur in this situation (heads or tails) and they are equally probable. Hence, you have an equal chance to win or lose. The probability of heads is .5, and if heads occurs you will win $20 (i.e., the value of heads is $20). The probability of tails is also .5, and the value of tails is -$10. The overall expected value (EV) for the game is the combination of these probabilities and values.

$$EV = [V(\text{head}) \times p(\text{head})] + [V(\text{tail}) \times p(\text{tail})]$$
$$EV = \$20 \times .5 + (-\$10) \times .5.$$
$$EV = \$5$$

Each time the coin is tossed you would expect to win an average of $5; after 100 tosses, you should be $500 richer.

Whenever probability values can be assigned for each outcome, it is possible to calculate overall expected value. While the optimal decision would be the course of action with the highest expected value, this does not mean that you will win on each try. It simply means that, if you repeatedly choose the course of action with the highest expected value every time, you would expect to be further ahead than if you used any other decision strategy.

An Example of Expected Value

Expected value analysis also can be used in more complex decision situations, and with subjective probabilities. Consider again the decision facing the buyer for the shoe stores mentioned above. The analysis of this problem uses subjective probabilities based on executive judgments, experience, and attitudes—along with "hard data" in the form of historical records.

Let's review the buyer's situation:

> The buyer for a chain of shoe stores has an option to buy 50,000 pairs of shoes from a foreign manufacturer at $4 a pair. Other buyers have received the same offer so our buyer must decide immediately. The buyer knows how to resell the shoes for $10 a pair, but the buyer believes there is a 50-50 chance that the government will refuse to grant an import license. If this happens, the contract will be annulled and the buyer must pay a penalty of $1 a pair.

The choice between alternative facts (i.e., whether or not to buy the shoes) is presented to the decision maker; yet the occurrence of a particular event (i.e., the approval or refusal of the import license) is beyond the decision maker's control. The uncertainty about the license (the 50-50-chance of approval) makes it impossible to determine in advance what would be the best decision. For example, if the buyer decides to buy the shoes but the license application is rejected, the loss will be, assuming a penalty of one dollar a pair, $50,000.

To reach a good decision, the probability of each of the two events, approval or refusal of the import license, as perceived by the buyer must be considered. Clearly, if the buyer assigns a high probability of approval the shoes should be purchased. Since the buyer actually believes that there is only a 50-50 chance of approval, there is a 50 percent chance of obtaining $300,000 (the estimated potential profit) against an equal chance of losing $50,000. The expected value analysis involves computing an expected consequence for all events. If the shoes are not purchased, nothing is gained or lost. If the shoes are bought, the expected gain would be $125,000; that is, .5 ($300,000) + .5 (−$50,000). According to this analysis, then, the shoes should be purchased. Although this simple problem is useful in illustrating the principle of expected value, actual business problems are considerably more complex and may involve delaying a decision until more information is obtained.

BEHAVIORAL BIASES IN SUBJECTIVE EXPECTED UTILITIES (SEU) AND RISK TAKING

Even when a decision maker is confronted with the uncertainty typically found in organizations—involving subjective probabilities and utilities— it is still desirable to make choices which seek to maximize long run expected gains. Selecting a choice that maximizes expected outcome in this situation requires combining the subjective probability of an event with the utility of the event to estimate its subjective expected utility (SEU).

What is SEU?

Subjective probabilities and utilities are combined in a manner analogous to the way in which expected values are calculated. In the SEU equation, however, subjective probabilities (sp) replace objective ones (p) and utilities (U) are substituted for values (V). If an event X consists of either outcome Y with subjective probability sp(Y) or some outcome Z, with subjective probability sp(Z), then

$$SEU(X) = [U(Y) \times sp(Y)] + [U(Z) \times sp(Z)]$$

An Example of SEU

An illustration may be useful to clarify the use of SEU in organizations. A supervisor wants to purchase one of two metal lathes for a machine shop. While both lathes meet production specifications, they also have potential flaws. Our supervisor could compare the SEU for lathe A with the SEU for lathe B, and purchase the lathe with the greater value. In making this comparison, our supervisor may talk to other supervisors about their experiences with the lathes. One supervisor may recall that lathe A was difficult for the operator to learn to use, but no other complaints were mentioned by the many supervisors who had used it in their shops. Lathe B, on the other hand, was bitterly criticized by another supervisor because maintenance people found it difficult to learn to service.

In fact, the "many" supervisors who recalled using lathe A may have been only 15 and 4 other operators may have had trouble learning to operate the machine, but did not mention their difficulties to the shop supervisor. The only weakness of lathe B among the 25 supervisors who had used it seems to have been the maintenance difficulty reported by the vocal supervisor, but it is likely that the vivid report may lead our supervisor to purchase lathe A. A proper calculation of SEU for this decision, with MPS representing "meets production specifications," TD representing "training difficulties," and MD representing "maintenance difficulties," would be:

$$SEU\ (\text{lathe A}) = U(MPS) \times sp(MPS) + U(TD) \times sp(TD)$$
$$SEU\ (\text{lathe B}) = U(MPS) \times sp(MPS) + U(MD) \times sp(MD)$$

Since both machines meet production specifications, their SEU on this aspect would be identical. For lathe A, the actual probability of presenting training difficulties is 5/15 or 1/3. For lathe B, the actual probability of maintenance difficulties is 1/25. If we assume that the utilities of being hard "to learn to operate" and "to learn to maintain" the lathes are the same, then lathe B would have the largest SEU and should be purchased.

SEU and Risk-Taking Propensity

A tremendous amount of research has been directed toward the study of decision making under conditions of risk. Two major lines of research have been used: (1) studies comparing behaviors against the SEU model, and (2) studies using psychological tests of risk-taking propensity for individuals and groups.

Comparing behaviors with the SEU model. The SEU model specifies that humans should behave as though the sum of the products of utility and probability were being maximized. Many challenges to the SEU model involve developing counter examples to demonstrate that people, in fact, do not behave this way.

One of the most thoroughly developed theories for explaining the correspondence between SEU and human behaviors is prospect theory. Prospect theory (Kahneman & Tversky, 1975) was developed to deal with two research findings that were inconsistent with the basic tenents of SEU theory. First, people tended to underweigh outcomes that were merely probable in comparison with outcomes that are obtained with certainty. This tendency, the *certainty effect,* contributes to risk aversion in choices involving sure gains and to risk seeking in choices involving sure losses. A stockbroker faced with a choice of purchasing either a stock with a small, but certain, gain or a stock with a large, but somewhat uncertain, gain would be likely to buy the former stock. This is despite the fact that SEU theory may suggest that the value of the latter stock is greater.

A second effect—the *isolation* or *reference effect*—involves a tendency to discard components that are shared by all alternatives being considered. This effect can lead to inconsistent preferences when the same choice is presented in different forms. Since, by altering the reference point, formally equivalent versions of the same decisions may elicit different preferences, this effect presents a serious difficulty to SEU theory. In prospect theory, value is assigned to gains and losses instead of being assigned to final assets, and probabilities are replaced by decision weights. It has been found that the value curve is normally concave for gains, convex for losses, and tends to be steeper for loses than for gains. Also, decision weights are generally found to be lower than the corresponding probabilities, except for low probabilities.

Assessing risk-taking propensity. Another line of research has attempted to measure the risk-taking propensities of individual decision makers, typically on the basis of psychological tests or utility functions. An increasing number of research studies have attempted to relate risk-taking propensity to problem-solving ability (Bruner, Goodnow, & Austin, 1956), creativity (McClelland, 1956), and vocational choices (McClelland, 1961; Ziller, 1957).

One of the most widely used psychological tests of risk-taking is the *choice dilemma test* developed by Kogan and Wallach (1960). This test presents the subjects with a series of problems in which they advise another person regarding what actions to take in a variety of situations (e.g., whether or not to recommend that a middle-aged man quit his present, secure job to move to another company). Higher risk-taking propensities are attributed to subjects who give this advice with minimum probability of success on the new job. A number of research studies have found that high scores on the choice dilemma test were positively correlated with processing less information and reaching faster decisions. However, Taylor and Dunnette (1974) observed that risk-prone decision makers do not correspond to the popular stereotype of cavalier disregard for the information base in a willingness to expose themselves to risk. Rather, risk-prone decision makers were found to make relatively rapid decisions based on little information, but to process each item of information more slowly and judge its value for the decision more accurately than did risk-averse decision makers.

In an attempt to determine the dimensionality of psychological measures of risk-taking propensity, Slovic (1962, 1972b) has investigated response set measures, questionnaires, and measures based on gambling experiments. The response sets measured were tendencies to guess on a doubtful test item, to include many responses as members of a given category, and to answer rapidly on a timed bet. Questionnaires measured experiences in risky activities (financial risks, risks in sports, etc.), and risks indicated in preferences for jobs. Gambling experimental tasks included preferences for bets and setting aspiration levels. The correlations among these measures of risk-taking propensity were very low, suggesting that willingness to take risks may not be a general trait at all. Instead, risk-taking propensity may vary from situation to situation (e.g., a person who may sky dive may not take financial risks).

Other research has examined the risk-taking propensity of groups, frequently contrasting the risk-taking of groups with the risk-taking of its constituent members. The answer to whether groups or individuals tend to be more risk-prone has important implications for use of committees, participation of subordinates in managerial decisions, etc. In many of these studies, individuals completed the choice dilemma test, then discussed the problems included in this test as a group and reached a group consensus on the answers. Generally, the group responses reflected greater risk-taking propensity than did the responses for individual group members—suggesting a shift toward greater risk for groups (i.e., the *risky shift*). The evidence seems to clearly indicate that groups tend to be more risk-prone. Reasons that have been suggested for the risky shift are: (1) leaders are more risk-prone and they exercise control over the group, (2) responsibility for the decision is diffused among the members of the group, and (3) being viewed as a risk-taker has high social value. Each of these explanations has received some research support (e.g., Kogan & Wallach, 1967; Vinokur, 1971). The question of why groups tend to be more risk-prone than individuals has not been resolved.

IMPROVING PROBABILITY ASSESSMENT IN APPLIED DECISIONS

Although most of the research on biases and distortions in assessing subjective probabilities has been based on studies performed in the laboratory, the implications for real-world contexts have been suggested for accounting, financial analysis, and geography. Some evidence regarding the ability to generalize these biases to the world outside the laboratory has been reviewed above, but more recent evidence (e.g, Carroll, 1980) has indicated major differences between laboratory and real-world contexts in the manner in which subjective probabilities are assessed. In view of these concerns, the implications of these biases for judging the probabilistic nature of features of decision problems and their environments should be developed cautiously. Nevertheless, two processes involved in assessment of subjective probabilities in organizational contexts can be profitably analyzed: 1) deriving an approach to probability assessment that is appropriate for use in organizational contexts, and 2) issues in motivating decision makers to make accurate probability assessments.

Assessing Probabilities for Applied Decisions

While no one method for assessing subjective probabilities has proven to be superior to all others, a promising approach for having applied decision makers judge probabilities has been recommended by the decision analysts at Stanford Research Institute (Spetzler & Stael von Holstein, 1975). In this approach to probability assessment:

1. problems are carefully structured with the decision maker to reduce the mental demands of the task

2. efforts are made to minimize judgmental biases which might affect the assessment
3. personal interviews rather than computer-interactive techniques are used, and
4. a combination of methods—both direct and indirect—are used to elicit subjective probabilities.

Such an approach has been widely used to determine probabilities in applied decisions. It has been found useful both in assisting decision makers to quantify degrees of belief about uncertain events, and in stimulating the assessor to give careful thought to the probability assessment task. Although there is some evidence that training improves performance in probability assessment, little is known about the cognitive processes underlying probability assessment (Pitz, 1974). This is an important area for further research into the behavioral aspects of decision making in organizational contexts. As Brown (1970) has pointed out, it is important to use methods that are seen by managers to be helpful and practical. In addition, methods for assessing the probabilistic aspects of decision problems must be consistent with the underlying theories of subjective probability assessment.

Motivating People to Improve Probability Assessments

Another important behavioral issue in judging probabilities for applied decisions concerns motivating people to make accurate estimates. Some attention has been given in the research literature to training subjective probability assessors in the laboratory by use of feedback concerning performance against scoring rules (e.g., Alpert & Raiffa, 1969; Shuford & Brown, 1975; Stael von Holstein, 1971; Goodman, et al., 1978). Yet, relatively little concern has been shown for motivating decision makers outside the laboratory to make more accurate judgments. In fact, much of the concern regarding the observed lack of motivation to maximize winnings discussed in laboratory tasks may not be as severe a difficulty in applied decisions where the rewards for good judgments would be expected to be much higher. It appears likely, however, that the literature on probability assessment could benefit from attention to the motivational aspects of such judgments. For example, while the scoring rules are carefully constructed to accurately measure performance in making these judgments, further attention could be devoted to motivating people to attain the prescribed levels of performance.

Expectancy theory and probability assessment. The literature of psychology offers a rich source of theory and research on motivation; theories with the potential to suggest ways to understand

and, perhaps, improve human performance in judgment tasks. For example, drive theory (e.g., Hull, 1943) with its emphasis on rewards which underlie motivation and, more recently, expectancy theory of motivation (e.g., Vroom, 1964; Porter & Lawler, 1968) present useful ways to motivate behaviors in this context. Both deal with understanding the outcomes that a person will try to attain and determining the behaviors a person will be motivated to perform in order to obtain the desired outcomes.

Expectancy theory of motivation is based on three points which have received general confirmation in the research literature: (1) decision makers prefer certain outcomes over others, (2) decision makers hold expectancies (probabilities) regarding the likelihood that, if they make certain assessments, then they will be able to meet the decision criteria (i.e., perform well against the scoring rules), and (3) decision makers also have expectancies about the likelihood that desired rewards will result from attaining high-quality judgments (Lawler, 1973). Finally, the theory specifies that the courses of action chosen depend upon the expectancies and preferences that the decision maker holds at the time of the choice, and may shift over time.

Improving assessment of probabilities in applied decisions. The most important determinant of expectancies is the objective situation. Generally, people's assessments of the situation are reasonably accurate, and learning plays an important role in determining these expectancies. With additional experience in a situation, assessors will generally develop more accurate expectancies that their assessments will lead to high scores. This occurs because, after doing a number of assessments, the ratio of successful to unsuccessful efforts is learned from experience. Although it is possible that personality factors (e.g., self-esteem) may influence these expectancies, the major determinant is likely to be the aptitude of the assessors in making such judgments and specific training to improve judgment skills. Training in probability assessment, as mentioned above, has a well developed literature, yet the psychological characteristics of probability assessors which may impact on the quality of their assessments have been virtually ignored.

More relevant to the issue of rewards for motivating performance in probability assessment is the expectancy that desired rewards will follow accurate assessments. This type of expectancy is also strongly influenced by past experiences in similar situations. Since many subjects (e.g., managers) are accustomed to rewards that are different and generally more valuable to them than the rewards offered in the laboratory, the difficulties observed in motivating them to try to maximize winnings may be attributed in part to the nature of the rewards. It appears useful to consider the use of rewards of both the extrinsic (e.g., money) and intrinsic (i.e., interest in the task) variety, rather than only monetary rewards. While probability assessments in organizational contexts may not suffer from the effects of unfamiliar monetary rewards, there is sufficient evidence that decision makers resist the use of many of the probability assessment techniques to suggest that more attention should be given to the intrinsic rewards of the assessment tasks (Brown, 1970; Murphy & Winkler, 1971). For example, one may use goal setting (Locke, 1978), positive reinforcement (e.g., Tharp & Wetzel, 1969), or simply make the assessment task more interesting.

STRATEGIES FOR IMPROVING CHOICES IN UNCERTAIN DECISION PROBLEMS

Understanding the nature of uncertainty in applied decisions and dealing effectively with it can be aided by a number of strategies derived from our analysis of behavioral aspects of uncertain decision problems. Integrating probabilities into models for representing decision problems—such as decision matrices, decision trees, and fault trees—is a useful method for identifying the uncertain aspects of decision problems. Forecasting methods (e.g., segmented or amalgamated forecasts) can be used to improve the judgment of probabilities. Finally, the costs of uncertainty can be estimated. Each of these strategies is discussed below.

Representing Uncertainty in Decision Problems.

Probabilities reflecting the uncertain aspects of decisions can be included in models for representing decision problems. Three methods for representing uncertainty in decision problems are discussed here. Although other methods are available, these three appear to be among the most widely used and the most helpful for making complex applied decisions.

Decision tree. Earlier we discussed the use of decision trees to generate lists of alternative courses of action. By indicating the uncertain elements of a decision problem, we can get a clearer picture of the nature of the problem to assist in analyzing alternatives and evaluating potential outcomes prior to choice. To illustrate how a decision tree can be used to represent uncertainty consider the following simple management problem. A manager is faced with two possible events: (1) there is a 70 percent chance that a 15 percent sales increase will occur, or (2) there is a 40 percent chance that a 10 percent sales decrease will occur. The manager can take either or both of two actions to deal with the consequences of these events: (1) new equipment can be purchased, and/or (2) employees can work overtime. The net cash flow corresponding to each combination of events and actions are:

	ACTION	
Event	**Work Overtime**	**Purchase New Equipment**
15% increase in sales	+$400,000	+$500,000
10% decrease in sales	+$300,000	+$250,000

If sales should increase, then purchasing new equipment would be the best course of action (payoff of $500,000). However, if sales decrease the best course of action would be to have employees work overtime ($300,000) rather than to invest in additional equipment ($250,000). Uncertainty about the possible future events concerning sales levels can be built into the decision tree as shown in Exhibit 5.3. To determine the expected value for each alternative, multiply the probability of sales either increasing (.7) or decreasing (.3) by the estimated payoff under each combination of events and actions. The expected value for having employees work overtime is

EXHIBIT 5.3 Decision Tree Showing Expected Value of Actions for Two Levels of Sales

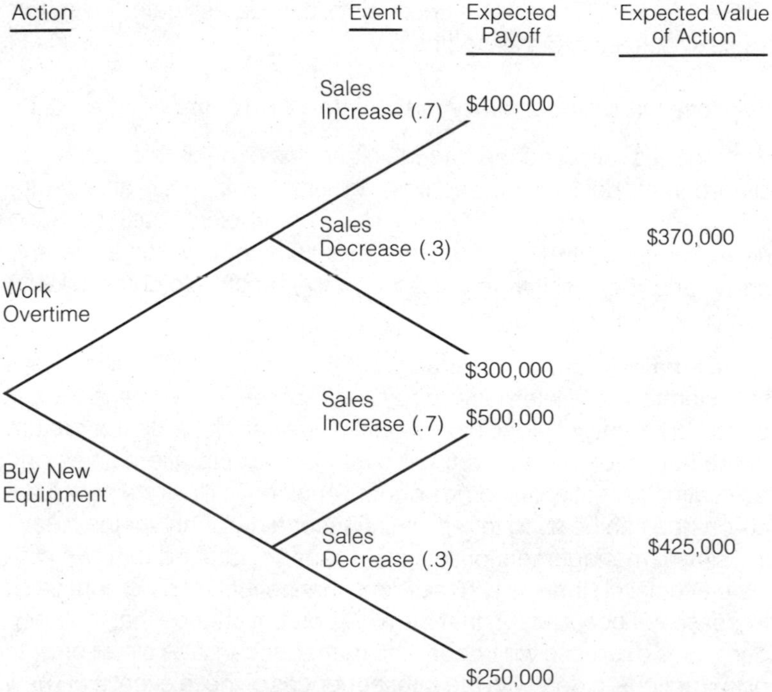

\$400,000 • .7 + \$300,000 • .3 = \$370,000. The expected value for purchasing additional equipment is \$500,000 • .7 + \$250,000 • .3 = \$425,000. Hence, the analysis indicates that new equipment should be purchased.

Decision matrix. A decision matrix represents a mapping of consequences to the uncertain aspects of the decision problem. As a general rule, a decision matrix is used most appropriately when only a few courses of action are available to the decision maker and these actions are clearly specified. When the actions that may be taken by a decision maker are sequential, with later actions contingent upon the outcomes of earlier actions, then a decision tree is most appropriate. Exhibit 5.4 shows a decision matrix depicting a decision to drill for oil (Grayson, 1960). The range of actions available in this situation and the payoffs resulting from each event are clearly represented.

EXHIBIT 5.4. A Decision Matrix for Oil Exploration

	POSSIBLE ACTS				
POSSIBLE EVENTS	Don't Drill	Drill with 100% Interest	Drill with 50% Partner	Farm-Out, Keep 1/8 Override	Farm-Out, Come Back in for 50% Interest After Payout
Dry Hole	\$0	\$ −50,000	\$ −25,000	\$0	\$0
50,000 bbls.	0	−20,000	−10,000	6,250	0
100,000 bbls.	0	30,000	15,000	12,500	15,000
500,000 bbls.	0	430,000	215,000	62,500	215,000
1,000,000 bbls.	0	930,000	465,000	125,000	465,000

Source: Grayson, C. J., Jr. *Decisions under uncertainty*, Boston: Harvard University Press, 1960, 249.

Fault tree. Slovic, et al., (1976) have described the use of a psychological analysis involving a *fault tree.* When one does not have objective probabilities regarding failure rates in a complex system (e.g., in assessing the probability of loss-of-coolant in a nuclear power reactor) (Rasmussen, 1974), the fault tree can be used to obtain estimates of the probabilities. The tree is constructed by listing all significant ways in which failure can occur, then listing all possible pathways to these ways, and so on. Next, probabilities can be assigned to each of the pathways in the fault tree. To illustrate this method, the main pathways in a fault tree designed to determine the probability of a car failing to start may include defects in the ignition system, the fuel system, etc. Deficiency in the ignition system could then be traced to loose battery terminals or a dead battery. These pathways could then be traced further to an analysis of the causes—a broken generator belt, lights left on, etc. The likelihood of these separate events then could be combined to yield an estimate of the overall probability of failure to start.

The use of the fault tree analysis could be improved by taking into account the psychological biases that may hamper performance in using the technique. For example, since a decision maker seldom has complete empirical evidence about failure rates on all parts of a complex system, these rates typically are estimated from slightly different parts, or from parts that were developed for a different purpose. It seems likely that anchoring and adjustment may bias these estimates; possibly, leading to estimates that are more appropriate for the original part or context than for the one in which we are currently interested. Another possible bias in fault tree analysis could result from omission of relevant pathways to failure. In the fault tree analysis illustration of the failure of an automobile to start, for example, the analysis would be seriously deficient if it left out the possibility of vandalism—at least in some cities. This approach to modeling the uncertain aspects of decision problems is very likely to be subject to omission of important pathways due to lapse of memory, perceptual distortions, ignorance, or lack of creative imagination.

Forecasting Uncertain Events

One widely used method for improving forecasting involves decomposing each uncertain aspect into current state and changes—then judging the probability of each component separately. This approach is similar to the base rate problem that we discussed earlier in the context of the representativeness bias. The impact of this bias should be reduced by making the decision maker aware of the importance of base rates. Another benefit of this approach is that any serious difficulties in measuring current state should be made evident. Little attention has been given to measuring current states in making judgments regarding uncertainty. However, Thompson (1961) has demonstrated the importance of considering current states in weather forecasting, Hedlund, et al., (1973) have shown the value of considering base rates in predicting which mental patients are dangerous, and Morgenstern (1963) has shown the importance of measuring current states in economics. The value of carefully considering base rates is indicated by the estimation that 40 percent of the errors in one year forecasts of the U.S. Gross National Product can be attributed to errors in measuring current GNP (Zarnowitz, 1967). Many types of forecasting in organizations can benefit from this method (e.g., market forecasts, manpower forecasts, etc.).

Amalgamated estimates. Using more than one judge for assessing the uncertain features of decision problems, then amalgamating their assessments has been shown to improve the reliability and validity of forecasts. The evidence favoring the superiority of amalgamated estimates is impressive. Research has indicated that amalgamated judgments are generally much better than the average quality of the individual forecasts which were amalgamated. In forecasting football scores, for example, amalgamated forecasts were nearly as accurate as the best judge (Winkler, 1968). Also, when forecasts of the U.S. GNP were made by "experts," the group amalgamation was better than the estimates of 62 percent of the individual judgments (Zarnowitz, 1967). The manner in which probabilistic judgments are amalgamated seems to have little effect on the accuracy of the amalgamated judgment. In a study which examined different weighing schemes for amalgamating football scores, Winkler (1968) found that the ways in which the judgments were amalgamated made little difference in the accuracy of the resulting forecasts. The important feature was the use of multiple judges in making the forecasts. Amalgamated forecasts can be used in any organizational unit that has several people who can serve as judges.

Segmented forecasts. Segmenting the estimates of the uncertain aspects of a decision problem also has proved to be helpful in complex, or highly diversified, organizations. In this approach, segmented estimates are made independently for each organizational unit and, then, combined for an overall organizational estimate regarding the uncertain feature. This approach is appropriate where the segments are independent, equally important, and the information for each segment is good. Even if the segments are not completely independent, the method can be used when the relationships among the segments can be accurately measured (Armstrong, et al., 1975).

Estimating Uncertainty Costs

Shackle (1952) has suggested that people do not usually model uncertainty through probabilities. Instead, when they assign a probability value to the outcome of a project that they are considering, they are using it as a measure of credibility or plausibility. The possible outcomes of a project are considered in terms of a small number of dominant hypotheses (focus values). The notion that these few potential outcomes are evaluated by considering their relative desirability and "potential surprise" is an interesting departure from previous formulations. Yet, no attempt has been made thus far to empirically validate this concept of "domain and value focusing."

Ways to analyze the *cost* of uncertainty have been proposed by Mack (1971). The costs of uncertainty that he has identified are: (1) costs resulting from attempts to implement actions for reducing uncertainty, (2) costs resulting from the deterioration of behavior in the face of uncertainty due to the limitations of the decision maker, and (3) *uncertainty discounting.* Uncertainty discounting can be illustrated by considering the difference in cost for a person-to-person and a station-to-station telephone call. The former type of call will cost more, but it may be worth the cost if it reduces uncertainty regarding being able to talk to the person of interest to the caller; and, if the caller is unable to reach this person, there is no charge for the call. Mack also provided a useful checklist of ways to reduce the cost of uncertainty (e.g., modify the decision problem so as to reduce the uncertainty discount, improve information concerning outcomes or their utilities, etc.).

SUMMARY

This chapter has examined the behavioral aspects of judgment and choice in uncertain decision situations. To provide a framework for this discussion, some of the central issues regarding uncertainty were briefly described—including the concepts of objective and subjective probability, expected value, and subjective expected utility. The behavioral science research regarding each of these issues is then highlighted in order to draw relevant conclusions regarding the psychological and cognitive processes which may advance our understanding of the implications of these issues for human behavior in applied decisions. A number of biases or distortions were identified in judgment of subjective probabilities, attributing causes to events, the use of scoring rules to improve assessment of subjective probabilities, opinion revision, and risk-taking behavior. Finally, the implications of these biases for advancing theory, research, and practice of decision making in uncertain situations were developed.

MAKING DECISIONS IN ORGANIZATIONS 6

Organizations have become important entities in our society, some with operating budgets that exceed the expenditures of states and even entire nations. And the influence of organizations on economic, social, and political life is commensurate with their pervasiveness and size. To be effective, organizations must judiciously manage their resources of time, material, capital, and people. Decisions made by those representing organizations significantly affect everyone's daily life.

RELATING DECISION MAKING AND ORGANIZATIONAL BEHAVIOR

In this chapter we highlight some of the major influences on decisions made in organizations. Analyzing decision processes from the perspective of a unitary decision maker, as was our emphasis in the preceding chapters, has proven useful in many situations. It is important, however, to place decisions made in organizations within an organizational context. Clearly, it is impossible to understand the behavioral processes involved in handling information and choosing in organizations without considering the impact of powerful organizational influences.

Although both the professional literature pertaining to managerial decision making and that pertaining to decisions made in organizations are voluminous, relatively little has been done to relate these literatures. Yet, the desirability of doing so appears generally accepted among those working in each field. A conference on "New Directions in Decision Making" held in March, 1981 at the University of Oregon reflected an interest in integrating the literatures of managerial decision making and organizational behavior (Braunstein & Ungson, 1982). In the spirit of the "New Direction in Decision Making" conference, we explore in this chapter a few of the major influences on decision making imposed by organizational contexts of problems.

We begin this analysis of the organizational context of decision making by examining some of the main theoretical viewpoints that have attempted to explain how choices are made in organizations. Following this, three challenges to decision making presented by characteristics of organizations are analyzed. These characteristics are:

1. multiple decision makers with conflicting objectives
2. specialization and division of labor, and
3. separation of decision making and implementation functions

These issues were selected as the focus for our discussion of organizational influences on decisions because they appear to be central to understanding decision making in organizations. Implications for making and implementing decisions are then derived from an examination of the research literature related to each issue and strategies for improving decision making in organizations are suggested.

THEORIES OF CHOICE IN ORGANIZATIONS

A great many theories have been proposed to represent the manner in which choices are made in organizations. In one taxonomy of theories for analyzing decisions, Allison (1971) has suggested that decision making in complex systems can be understood only when the theoretical framework for the analysis is appropriately selected. He has proposed theories of decision making which are suitable for examining decision processes at three levels. At the first level, called *rational actor theories,* analysis focuses on the components of the decision process (goals, alternatives, consequences, and choices) and the decision maker is expected to behave so as to maximize the payoff. *Organizational theories* represent a second level of analysis which expands the rational actor level by describing the organizational processes which may influence the decision. At the third level, the *societal processes* (sociopolitical) that may influence decision making are included in the analysis.

Theories of choice in organizations, generally, are of three types. In addition to the rational decision theories discussed earlier in this volume, and which forms the basis for many of the concepts and decision-making methods reported in the literature on judgment and choice, two other types of choice theories are examined below. These are conflict resolution theories and nondecision (artifactual) theories (Olsen, 1976).

Rational Decision Theories

Many of the theories and techniques of decision making discussed earlier in this volume are based on some form of rational decision theory (e.g., Simon, 1965). This theory represents the most constrained and rigorous view of decision making and, typically, assumes that decisions can be described adequately by analyzing a rather restricted range of variables; frequently with objective and quantitative measures. The theory implies that actions must be explained, behavior reflects intention or purpose, actions are chosen as calculated solutions to strategic problems, and that decisions can be understood by demonstrating that the decision maker was pursuing goals and that the actions are reasonable choices in view of these goals.

Rigorous forms of rational decision theories require that rather complete information be specified regarding the components of the model. The goals of a decision maker must be explicitly stated and criteria representing each goal must be specified for judging the alternative courses of action, all important courses of action must be listed, and the consequences of choosing each course of action must be known. While the rigorous forms of the rational actor theory (e.g., maximizing or optimizing) require the acquisition of much information, less rigorous forms (e.g., satisficing) require less information. In analyzing decisions from the rational actor point of view, an organization would be viewed as a single decision maker; thus, one may speak of the "organization's decision."

Implications of Rational Decision Theories for Decision Making in Organizations

The rational decision theories provide useful ways to analyze many decision processes. At times, it is convenient to simplify a decision problem in order to deal more precisely, and quantitatively, with the variables of interest. In using Multiattribute Utility Analysis (MAU), for example, it is clear that not all variables can be included in the analysis. However, as long as the variables which have the greatest potential to influence decision outcomes are included, the approach provides a reasonable approximation of the values a decision maker gives to various courses of action, and a method for determining which action is most valuable. The danger, however, is that omitting important aspects of the decision problem (e.g., social or political features) may lead to serious errors in assigning values to decision alternatives.

The rational decision theories fail to completely model the complex set of variables that affect choices made in organizational contexts. Yet, rational decision theories are useful when the parties to a decision are in agreement regarding desired outcomes and are virtually certain about the linkages between courses of action and outcomes (Thompson & Tuden, 1959); under such conditions it is appropriate to use computational decision strategies in attempting to maximize choices within certain constraints (e.g., Friedland, 1974). But, when disagreement exists regarding preferences or outcomes or there is uncertainty about outcomes resulting from the actions that may be taken by a decision maker, then it is necessary to reach decisions through compromise or judgments regarding the likely outcomes (Thompson, 1967).

The approach taken in analyzing choices made in organizations has a marked effect on insights into the choice process and the strategies used in attempting solutions. The rational decision theories recognize as a major challenge to making choices the diversity of preferences that typically exist in organizations. They make explicit the preferences and values of organizational members (including quantitatively measuring their risk-taking tendencies), provide methods for aggregating preferences, and identify organizational policies which influence choices. This viewpoint is extremely effective in highly structured and routine choice situations, and some forms of the rational decision model take the limited and biased information-processing skill of humans into account in formulating the notion of a satisficing decision maker.

Conflict Resolution Theories

Conflict resolution theories extend the rational decision theories by incorporating societal and organizational influences on decision makers. They recognize that choices in organizations, typically, are not made by single, unitary individuals or by groups acting in unison. Frequently there is no internal consensus among parties to the decision regarding goals and objectives of the organization. Instead, multiple goals exist and, often, the goals are not compatible with one another. In addition, the parties to a decision may be in fundamental disagreement concerning the preferred goals. Hence, uncertainty is avoided by focusing on solving immediate problems rather than long range problems, attempting to reach satisficing solutions, and use of standard operating procedures (SOPs), plans, or industry traditions to solve problems.

The conflict resolution theories can be used to analyze influences on decision making external to the organization. From this perspective, the influence of governments, consumers of goods and services produced by the organization, or public groups advocating special interests on choices made in organizations can be identified.

Important influences on decisions made in organizations are exerted by political behavior of major coalitions in society; as well as by the ideologies and the belief systems held by members of a society (Allison, 1971, Gouldner, 1970). Our focus in this volume, however, is primarily the influence of an organization on choices made by its members. Those interested in further treatment of the societal and governmental influences in organizational changes are referred to Gouldner's (1976) insightful discussion.

Conflict resolution theories, then, permit an analysis of decision problems that incorporates relevant features of the social and political context of decision making. Among the conflict resolution theories which have been used to analyze decision making in organizations are: (1) cognitive consistency theories and (2) game theory. Although we shall not discuss it further here, disjointed incrementalism (described in Chapter 3) is a conflict reduction model that focuses on a social-political level of analysis.

Cognitive Consistency Theories

Cognitive consistency theories specify that people attempt to eliminate any inconsistencies that may exist among their feelings, beliefs, cognitions, and behaviors in order to reduce the psychological discomfort and tension that imbalances produce. Although the various cognitive consistency theories differ in the manner of explanation, they all attempt to specify the cognitive adjustments that people make to reduce these imbalances.

But keep in mind that people in organizations are subject to many tensions and do not live in the tension-free environments of the psychological laboratories. They may have to accept imbalanced states that are beyond their control. Yet, even in the midst of conflict and competition, it seems likely that people will attempt to simplify the world around them. One way to do so is to strive for cognitive balance.

What causes cognitive inconsistences? You may like a teacher, but not find the content of the course that teacher teaches interesting. This situation would, according to cognitive consistency theories, produce an imbalance state that you would be motivated to reduce. There are several reasons suggested for the existence of imbalanced states (McGuire, 1966):

1. Inconsistencies may be produced because you occupy competing roles (teacher and evaluator of student performance; boss and friend, etc.)
2. inconsistencies may be produced by our logical fallacies—for example, inability to use sound logic because of wishful thinking
3. your environment or situation may be altered while your beliefs remain the same, resulting in your being out of touch with the reality of your situation (participating in a volunteer program to bring assistance to an underdevel-

oped country may place you in an unfamiliar culture; a divorce may produce the unfamiliar situation of being single again

4. also, external social pressures to behave in ways that are inconsistent with your attitudes may be exerted (e.g., teenagers may be pressured by their peers to engage in behaviors which are considered antisocial or illegal).

How can cognitive inconsistencies be reduced? What can a person faced with one of these types of inconsistency do about it? Festinger (1957) suggested a number of ways to reduce cognitive inconsistencies that may be used. These include:

1. **Forgetting the situation.** This seems like an easy solution, but seldom seems to be possible in actual life.
2. **Bolstering.** This involves placing the inconsistent events into a larger body of consistent events, thus reducing the effects of the inconsistent events, for example, saying that the inconsistent events are not too important in the "big picture."
3. **Differentiation.** You may try to keep the inconsistent events separated in your mind. You may dislike your boss, but feel that charity work is important. If your boss is very active in charity work you may experience tension due to these inconsistent events. "Boss" and "charity work" may be placed in separate mental categories to avoid dealing with the inconsistency.
4. **Distorting your perception of the situation.** Much of the research on cognitive consistency has dealt with how the inconsistent events that produced dissonance are perceptually altered to bring them into balance. In the above example, you may conclude that the particular type of charity work your boss does is not as desirable as other forms of charity work.
5. **Leaving the situation.** At times, it may be possible simply to avoid or leave situations that produce dissonance. If you view yourself as attractive to other people but are a poor dancer, you may avoid dances. Or, in the above example, you may find another job. In many real-life situations, of course, leaving has consequences that you may not be willing to face.
6. **Selectively expose yourself to information about the situation.** By seeking information that makes events appear more consistent, and avoiding information that would emphasize their inconsistent aspects, one can reduce tension concerning the events. Reducing cognitive inconsistencies in this way appears to be widely used in rationalizing choices after they have been made.
7. **Reduce the importance of the sources of inconsistent events.** You may challenge the credibility of the source of information about the inconsistent events. A rumor implying something unfavorable about a friend may be attributed to someone being jealous of your friend. Consequently, the rumor may be discounted or denied.
8. **Change your attitudes about the inconsistent events.** If you are asked to publicly advocate a political party that you did not initially favor, your attitude toward that political party may become more favorable. The bulk of research on cognitive consistency has dealt with the effect of behavior on attitude change, and it appears that changing attitudes is one of the major ways in which people attempt to achieve cognitive consistency.

Implications of cognitive consistency theories for decision making in organizations. Any or a combination of these avenues may be used to reduce inconsistencies, but cognitive consistency theories say little about which way will be used in any given situation. From the standpoint of applying cognitive consistency theories this is a serious omission. In fact, in complex organizations—with many factors beyond our control—it is likely that we simply tolerate a great deal of inconsistency by considering it outside our area of expertise or concern. Reading a newspaper account of an atrocity committed in another country may be viewed with initial shock and horror, then dismissed as not within our area of responsibility. Yet, the fact that inconsistency can be tolerated does not violate these theories—no doubt, an ordered, cognitively consistent world would be a desired state for everyone, but is unattainable. Still, within the limits of our situation we may continue to strive for consistency and the striving will be reflected in our decisions.

Cognitive dissonance theory. One of the most thoroughly researched cognitive consistency theories is the cognitive dissonance theory advanced by Festinger (1957). Although we shall not attempt to summarize all the research addressed to testing this theory, a brief description of its major features may help to illustrate both this theory and cognitive consistency theories more generally. As in other consistency theories, dissonance theory holds that when beliefs, feelings, cognitions, and behaviors are out of balance, a person will attempt to reduce the cognitive tension that results from the imbalance. Relationships among these aspects can be consonant (in balance), dissonant (out of balance), or irrelevant (not related to each other). While irrelevant and consonant situations would be tolerated by a person, dissonant relationships would be expected to motivate the person to make the relationships consonant. People would attempt to, first of all, avoid situations which are dissonant. If this is not possible, then they would use one of the avenues for dissonance reduction mentioned above (i.e., seek information that will justify the situation).

In organizational decision making, dissonance frequently is associated with goals or objectives. This can take two forms. Prior to choosing among courses of action a decision maker may experience dissonance regarding the inconsistent objectives that a decision is attempting to attain. Hiring an employee who is qualified for a salary which the firm can afford may be viewed as a case of incompatible objectives. The resulting compromise in employee quality or salary may produce dissonance that could lead to viewing the applicant as better qualified or the job as less responsible than is actually the case.

After making a decision, cognitive dissonance can also enter in the form of "postdecision regret." Frequently, postdecision regret leads either to seeking information to bolster or justify the decision already made, or avoiding information that would make the choice appear less justified. For example, people have been found to read only pamphlets describing the virtues of a car they have purchased and to ignore pamphlets extolling the virtues of cars they decided not to purchase (e.g., Ehrlich, et al., 1957). Through this process, the chosen alternative tends to become more attractive to a decision maker and the alternatives not chosen become less attractive—hence, justifying the decision. It seems very likely that decisions made in organizations are subject to this type of postdecision justification. This may, in part, explain why decision makers have been found to prefer decision rules which can be easily explained and justified to other people.

Effect of dissonance on attitudes and behaviors. Dissonance theory has shown that both attitudes and behaviors can be affected by cognitive dissonance. Dissonance theory specifies that behaviors change first, followed by changes in attitudes. When attitudes are to be changed by altering a person's behaviors, dissonance theory posits that three elements must be present: (1) prior commitment, (2) volition, and (3) task relevance. If a person has no choice in taking an action, no dissonance will be produced and no attitude change will ensue. However, if the person is free to choose whether to perform the behavior (volition), then dissonance can be produced. The more a person is pressured to perform a behavior contrary to one's attitudes, then, the less the dissonance that would be produced. Public commitment is also important in producing dissonance. The greater the public commitment (by making speeches in favor of a cause that the person did not initially endorse) the greater the dissonance produced and the more behavior becomes irrevocable. Finally, if behaviors are seen as trivial no dissonance will be produced; important behaviors, on the other hand, can lead to attitude changes.

Equity theory. Equity theory (Adams, 1965) is a form of dissonance theory built on the idea that exchanges are made among individuals in a group. The idea of exchange implies that when two people feel that it is to their mutual advantage to do so, they will agree to trade resources between themselves (Gergen, 1969). For example, you may agree to do work for another person in exchange for pay or other benefits. Basic to the idea of equity is the notion that each person compares what they are putting into an exchange with what is being received. In addition, they are comparing their ratio of inputs and outcomes with those of other people in similar situations.

Implications for satisfaction with pay and job performance. Striving for "equity" has been suggested to serve as the basis for satisfaction with pay in organizations. Finding an imbalance when comparing your inputs to the job (education, experience, hours of work, etc.) and outcomes (salary, benefits, etc.) with those of others in similar jobs will cause cognitive tension that you will attempt to reduce. A balanced relationship would exist when your ratio of inputs to outcomes is the same as the ratio for others in similar jobs. An imbalance would be dealt with by taking action to reduce dissonance. You might ask for a raise, leave the job, or decide that you are not really working as hard as the other person in the social comparison.

Bribes vs. gold stars. Equity theory predicts that subjects who are paid a smaller amount would regard a task more favorably than would subjects who were paid more to perform the task. This suggests that large incentives to perform tasks will have less effect on attitudes toward the task than would small incentives.

This finding is in contrast to a prediction of incentive theory, which predicts that large payments would tend to produce larger shifts in attitudes (Elms, 1967). One resolution to this contradiction has been suggested in terms of when the reward is given (Linder, Cooper, & Jones, 1967). Money given prior to an action which is contrary to a person's attitudes would be viewed as an incentive. In this situation, dissonance theory would apply and the larger the incentive, the less attitude change would result. Money provided, however, after a person is committed to an action would be viewed as a reward and incentive theory would apply. In this instance incentive theory would predict that the larger the reward the greater would be the attitude change. The way in which a person interprets the meaning of the reward is essential to attitude change in either situation.

Steiner (1972) attempted to explain this apparent contradiction in the following manner. An incentive that is offered prior to the act, and can be declined, is viewed as a bribe. The larger the bribe, the less will be attitude change and dissonance theory would explain this situation. A reward given after the action, with no opportunity to decline it, would be viewed as a gold star. In this instance, greater reward would produce greater attitude changes and incentive theory would apply. One interpretation of this finding is the *insufficient justification hypothesis*. A person who receives money for a behavior can adequately justify the behavior on the basis of money. In this case, there would be no need to attribute the behavior to the person's own beliefs. However, when a person does not expect to receive sufficient rewards to justify the behavior, then the person needs to justify the behavior in terms of one's own beliefs.

Game Theory

The theory of games provides a formal analysis of decision making that, although it cannot encompass all features of complex decisions, is applicable to organizations. Game theory has some features in common with the rational decision theories discussed above, in that it attempts to formally define the decision situation and to specify an optimal solution. However, game theory can be classified more appropriately as a conflict resolution theory. It specifies outcomes that depend upon the joint actions of a number of people and, in some types of games, the goals of these people are in conflict.

In the typical game, each player chooses a course of action without communicating with other players. Then, the choices are revealed simultaneously and each party is informed of what payoff was received according to the values in a *payoff matrix*. Hence, the payoff matrix represents the outcomes resulting from the combined choices of the players.

Pure competition games. A joint payoff matrix for a two-person game is shown in Exhibit 6.1. In each cell of the matrix the left-hand number is the payoff for player A and the right-hand number is the payoff for player B. For example, if both players choose alternative 1, then player A receives $10 and player B loses $10. Research on game theory has investigated many aspects of the nature of payoffs accruing to each player.

EXHIBIT 6.1. Payoff Matrix for a Pure Competition Game

		If B Chooses	
		1	2
If A Chooses	1	10: – 10	0:0
	2	15: – 15	– 15:15

The payoff matrix described above represents a game of pure competition (also called a *zero-sum game*) since whatever one player wins the other player must lose. For example, if A chooses alternative 2 and B chooses alternative 1, then A will win $15 and B will lose $15. But B is not likely to let this happen. B would prefer to choose alternative 2 and have A also choose alternative 2; thus, B would gain $15 and A would lose $15. A, however, is unlikely to be willing to accept this situation. The usual decision in this game is for both A and B to choose alternative 2 with no gain or loss for either player. A game of pure competition does not permit a combination of choices which could benefit both players. This game is also a *determinate game* since the outcome for a rational player is always the same. Persuasion and negotiation will not influence the outcome of this type of game.

Mixed-motive games. When the payoff matrix is changed as shown in Exhibit 6.2., then social influences on the game can have an effect. In this situation, players can employ communication, persuasion, and deception to try to increase their gains. The more information a player has about the preferences of the other players the greater the possible advantage the player would have. This *mixed-motive game* is relevant to choices made in organizations, because elements of both competition and cooperation are involved. In mixed-motive games there is a cooperative solution which would benefit both players, but does not represent the greatest gain for either player.

EXHIBIT 6.2. Payoff Matrix for Prisoner's Dilemma Game

		If Prisoner A	
		Confesses	Doesn't Confess
If Prisoner B	Confesses	5:5 years	0:15 years
	Doesn't Confess	15:0 years	1:1 years

The prisoner's dilemma. The payoff matrix shown in Exhibit 6.2 represents a game that has been called the *prisoner's dilemma* (Rapoport & Chammah, 1965). In this game, two people suspected of committing a crime are picked up by the police. Although there is no real evidence of their guilt, the district attorney attempts to persuade each suspect to confess by offering the "deal" shown in the payoff matrix. Each suspect is told that by confessing and giving evidence against the other suspect, you will be pardoned and set free and the maximum sentence will be given to the other suspect (15 years). If both confess, they will each get a moderate sentence (5 years) and if neither confesses, they will each get a light sentence (1 year).

The dilemma is that the best strategy for both suspects is for neither to confess, but taking this strategy requires that they trust each other. If one adopts this strategy and the other confesses, of course, the trusting suspect will receive the maximum sentence. Since the suspects are not permitted to communicate, it is hard to develop the mutual trust needed to adopt the best strategy.

Many decisions made in organizations and in society can be viewed as mixed-motive games. For example, a firm being pressured by the government to install pollution control equipment may be better off financially to ignore the pressure, thus saving the expenditure for the equipment. The government agency responsible for pollution control, representing the public suffering from acid rain, may prefer very expensive pollution control equipment which would completely eliminate air pollution from the plant. In fact, there may be a compromise position involving less expensive pollution control equipment that the company could afford and that would meet the government's permissible levels of air pollution. Further reading on game theory is provided by Rapoport (1960, 1970).

IMPLICATIONS OF CONFLICT RESOLUTION THEORIES FOR DECISION MAKING IN ORGANIZATIONS

A central issue related to decision making in organizations addressed by the conflict resolution theories is the manner in which influence attempts shape choices. These theories suggest that influence attempts figure importantly in the processes by which choices are made and in the resulting choice. Several key concepts that are used in conflict resolution theories to explain decision-making behaviors are described in this section: power, coalitions, and conformity.

Power

Conflict resolution theories suggest that it is futile to attempt to understand decision-making behavior in organizational situations where conflict exists without considering the role of power (its distribution and use by parties to decision making). Power influences the behaviors of actors in exchanges as well as choices and outcomes (e.g., Child, 1972; Pfeffer, 1977). The importance of the concept of power for understanding decision processes in organizations has been demonstrated in the context of university administration. University administrators were observed to employ political influence to shape the criteria used for allocating their departmental budgets; rather than using the computational methods suggested by the rational decision viewpoint.

Power is important in understanding how decisions are made in organizations because of the competition among organizational members for the scarce resources that generally exist in organizations. Power of organizational members may be due to their charisma or their expertise in skills valued by other organizational members (e.g., French & Raven, 1959). Organizational positions held by participants in decision making are very important in determining their power. In addition to level in the formal authority structure (Pfeffer, 1977), power resulting from organizational positions can be linked to: (1) a power-dependency relationship resulting from the capacity of one organizational member or unit to reduce uncertainty for another (Hickson, et. al., 1971), (2) extent to which a person or unit controls resources, and (3) having information valued by others (Mechanic, 1967).

Power and uncertainty reducing. As decisions are made in organizations, Thompson (1967) has suggested that the organizational members or units will attempt to reduce uncertainty by striving for a higher level of power than that held by others in the organization. Individuals or units with high power have greater discretion to influence outcomes toward their preferences. The concept of uncertainty reduction discussed in the organizational theory literature appears very similar to the decision theory view of uncertainty that we discussed in Chapter 5—that is, possessing insufficient information upon which to base a sound decision.

Power and resource dependency. A form of dependency that provides a basis for power in organizational relationships is needing resources held by other members of the organization. A great deal of research has investigated power distributions and the findings have implications for the manner in which relative levels of power can be altered. The balance of power can be shifted by acquiring resources or by making joint agreements with other people to share their resources in order to attain mutually desirable objectives.

Power and information dependency. Many resources can be used to reduce uncertainty (e.g., money, materials), but a form of uncertainty reducer with direct implications for decision making in organizations is communicating information needed by other individuals or units (Galbraith, 1973). Influence attempts and other messages are transmitted through communication channels. Experimental research in the laboratory has demonstrated that information networks have strong influences on choices made by groups, and that groups frequently alter communication channels to attain their objectives.

Information dependency can offset, to some extent, the formal level of hierarchy in determining the balance of power in organizations. For example, lower-level organizational members may increase their power (and correspondingly increase their influence on choices made by organizations) by controlling access to information desired by higher ranking organizational members. This strategy can involve attaining centrality in organizational communication networks and/or acquiring expertise needed by the organization (Mechanic, 1967).

Coalitions

The concept of coalition is central to understanding decisions from a conflict resolution viewpoint. Coalitions of individuals or groups are comprised of organizational members who have been drawn together to serve their shared interests, and the various coalitions compete for the generally scarce resources of the organization. Allocation of resources in this situation is bargained, therefore power and political behavior figure importantly in choices when plurality of interests and conflict among organizational members exist. A number of conflict resolution theories have been developed to describe organizational choices (e.g., Cyert & March, 1963; Baldridge, 1971; Pfeffer & Salancik, 1978).

Types of coalitions and implications for decisions in organizations. Among the types of coalitions that have received theoretical and research attention are *minimum winning size coalitions* and *stable coalitions.* The minimum winning size coalition (e.g., Gamson, 1964) has advantages for its members, since each member stands to gain more from this type of coalition than from any other coalition. This is because the minimum winning size coalition—the coalition that wins by the smallest margin—permits the winnings to be distributed among the fewest people. The winnings, as specified by the minimum resource theory, are divided among the winning coalition members in proportion to the resources the members bring to the coalition; to commit resources greater than what is required to win would simply diminish the value of the resources for each coalition member. When the theory of minimum resources was empirically tested, it received some confirmation. Payoffs were found to be positively related to resources in a simulated political convention where members of a winning coalition divided patronage jobs among themselves (Gamson, 1961). Results of analysis of coalitions in presidential nominating conventions since 1900 were inconclusive, since it is necessary for the backers of the nominee to receive the rewards (Gamson, 1962). Losing candidates, of course, had no rewards to distribute.

Although a coalition including all members of an exchange would be very stable (i.e., no members would be attracted away by more lucrative offers), in most instances coalitions that do not include all members yield higher payoffs for at least some of the members (MacCrimmon & Taylor, 1976). Stability of a coalition would offer a decision maker the advantage of a more predictable decision environment. Yet, should coalitions change in such a way as to make the coalition no longer the most advantageous manner of relating to the other parties, the decision maker would be advised to form other coalitions or, if strong enough, to personally control the decision. The implications of stable coalitions are relevant to a variety of decision situations. For example, what joint actions would be mutually advantageous, what should be the duration of contractual agreements to reduce conflict (e.g., treaties for trade or mutual defense), and what are the immediate and longer range consequences of withdrawing from such coalitions?

The coalitions which develop in organizations also affect the exercise of power in decision making. When coalitions are large, or when the members of a coalition are nearly equal in power, the preferences of more people must be accommodated in the resulting decision. In addition, the characteristics of the members of a coalition will be likely to affect how decisions are defined, the range of alternatives considered, the objectives sought, and the manner in which a decision is implemented (e.g., Luce & Raiffa, 1957; Kormorita, et al., 1968). Coalitions may also influence decision making by redesigning the organization or by altering its goals and objectives (e.g., Pfeffer, 1977).

Conformity

Choices in complex organizational problems typically require that many people contribute to reaching solutions, since no one decision maker can handle all the information required. Moreover, seldom does power, authority, and responsibility reside in one person. Even if a decision maker could make a choice unilaterally, the support of others would be needed to carry it out. For these reasons, the influence of group processes on choice in organizations is difficult to understand and no theory has been developed to account for the success or failure of decision-making groups. However, it is possible to analyze interpersonal processes that influence choices made by groups. One interpersonal process that has been found to exert considerable influence on the decision making of groups is examined here, the process of conformity.

Strong pressures for groups to move toward uniformity of opinion and compliance with group norms exist. This point is illustrated by the observation that most groups made unanimous decisions about complex problems and that members of unanimous groups were more satisfied with their decisions than were members of split groups. Moreover, this finding held even when the unanimous decision was incorrect (Thomas & Fink, 1961). When a solution is urgent and alternative choices are similar, social pressure toward agreement may be advantageous. When free exchange of ideas is necessary for sound choices to be made in complex problems or when minority views have value, the tendency for group members to seek consensus may hamper decision-making performance (Hoffman, 1965).

Conformity and group cohesiveness. The cohesiveness of a group generally has been defined in terms of the sum of the forces that act to cause members to remain in the group (e.g., Sherif, 1966; Festinger, et al., 1950). Three factors which figure prominently in descriptions of group cohesiveness are: the duration of past associations among group members, the attractiveness of the group, and the extent to which the group can contribute to attaining goals valued by its members. Members who are highly attracted to a group have been found to attempt to reconcile differences of opinion among other group members (Back, 1951). Also, groups composed of members who liked other members tended to communicate more, to reach consensus on a group position more quickly, and to use group pressure on deviant members to force compliance (Lott & Lott, 1965). This is not surprising, since many studies have noted that highly attractive groups exert strong influences on the opinions and behaviors of their members (e.g., Festinger, et al., 1950; Berkowitz, 1954).

It has been found that stress, threat, and competition exerted on the group by an external force tends to increase internal group cohesion (e.g., Julian, et al., 1966; LeVine & Campbell, 1972). Here, group cohesiveness generally is defined as lack of internal conflict, rather than as attraction to a group. The apparent internal conflict in the form of disagreement has been shown to increase the cohesiveness of the group under some conditions (Lombardo, et al., 1972). While attraction and social cohesion may be partly due to attitude similarity, these outcomes may also be attributed to the reinforcing effects of being able to reply to another group member's comments in cases where disagreements occur. Being able to reply—open verbal communication—is important in reducing the disagreement and, based on learning principles, may increase attraction to another person. In a group decision-making situation, this would tend to enhance cohesiveness.

Groupthink. The effects of conformity pressures were noted in our discussion of creativity-stimulating techniques and in the risky-shift phenomenon. Another decision-making situation in which conformity plays an important role is when high status groups attempt to react quickly to alleviate a crisis. Under these conditions, the group members may feel that they have more knowledge about the problem than anyone else and that other reasonable people would agree with their actions. In avoiding minority opinions and the views of outsiders, these groups may adopt a high degree of conformity within the group and engage in *groupthink* (Janis, 1972; Janis & Mann, 1977). Groupthink appears to rely most heavily on the definition of group cohesiveness as attraction to the group. Cohesiveness in the form of attraction to the group is one of the preconditions of groupthink; whereas, stress on the group leads to a second type of cohesiveness—the lessening of internal conflict and seeking consensus.

Groupthink is defined by Janis and Mann (1977) as a collective pattern of defensive avoidance through bolstering. Bolstering can take place through six processes:

1. favorable outcomes are exaggerated
2. unfavorable outcomes are minimized
3. aversive feelings associated with unfavorable outcomes are denied
4. after a decision has been made, the length of time that will occur before action on the decision will need to be taken is exaggerated
5. the degree of social surveillance required in enforcing the decision is minimized
6. personal responsibility for the decision is minimized

The main difference between bolstering of individual decision makers and by decision makers in cohesive groups is that the group provides social support or disapproval for the actions. It should be noted that bolstering may be useful under some conditions. When a thorough search and appraisal of alternative choices has been made and the best choice has been selected, bolstering the decision may be valuable in increasing commitment to the choice.

Symptoms of groupthink. The result of groupthink is poor quality decision making, characterized by a tendency to avoid controversial issues and failure to challenge weak arguments. Eight symptoms of groupthink, which reflect the extreme pressure for conformity typically found in cohesive groups, are summarized by Janis and Mann (1977). These symptoms are:

1. an illusion of invulnerability
2. a feeling of moral correctness
3. avoiding warnings of danger by use of rationalizations
4. shared negative stereotypes of the enemy as evil, stupid, or weak
5. use of pressure on members viewed as disloyal
6. self-censorship of deviations from the group's consensus
7. shared illusion of unanimity
8. emergence of self-appointed "mind guards" against negative information

These reflect a poor decision-making process. Assuming that the critical evaluation of as many alternatives as possible in the time available and within the information processing constraints is most likely to lead to a high quality decision, groups afflicted by groupthink are likely to operate at a suboptimal level. Failure to heed warnings, unrealistic optimism, and misperceptions of the opponents all suggest ineffective procedures for processing information and reaching decisions. Poor decisions may also result from isolation from outside opinions, the leader stating a preferred solution at the beginning of the discussion, permitting strong group pressures to be exerted against those with deviant views, and the use of "mind guards."

Critique of groupthink theory. Groupthink theory was developed on the basis of case studies, and few attempts have been made to empirically validate the theory. Laboratory experiments have been conducted by Flowers (1977) and Courtright (1978) with inconclusive results. Flowers, for example, found that leadership style affected the processes used in reaching decisions, but groupthink appeared to have no effect. With the exception of Tetlock's (1979) reanalysis of the cases upon which the concept of groupthink was formulated, there is little empirical evidence to support the existence of groupthink.

Nondecision Theories

The major distinction between nondecision models such as Weick's (1977) concept of choices in enacted organizations and the models described above is that, in nondecision models, it is not assumed that events are the realization of the purposes of organizational members. In the rational decision models, events are viewed as rather direct outcomes of decisions made by individuals or groups, and the conflict resolution models represent events as negotiated outcomes of individuals' or coalitions' exercise of power. In nondecision models, outcome events are viewed as ". . . an unintended product of certain processes having dynamics of their own" (Olsen, 1976, p. 83). Decisions, then, are after-the-fact reconstructions of events and their causes by observers. Using this approach to analyzing "choice" in organizations, one would assume that choices are the relatively extraneous product of a set of simultaneous and independent activities, with little management or planning having occurred. The nondecision models appear to have little to offer those interested in normative implications; whereas, the rational decision models suggest rational behavior as the mechanism for improving decision making, and the conflict resolution models offer the effective use of power and influence.

Implications of Nondecision Theories for Decision Making in Organizations

The nondecision models differ sharply from rational decision and conflict reduction models in the manner in which goals are viewed. The latter two models of choice assume that choice behaviors are purposive, that is: (1) behavior and attention follow belief and attitude; (2) beliefs and attitudes are stable enough so that attention remains constant during the choice process; and (3) various levels of attention can be predicted from the content of a decision. Therefore, as long as the resources available are attractive to organizational members, they will engage in decision-making behavior. According to the nondecision view of the "garbage can model" (Cohen, March, & Olsen, 1972), however, involvement in decisions is not always attractive to organizational members. While people have a great many beliefs and attitudes, they have limited time and energy with which to act upon these. Since there are many alternative choice situations, the flow of attention depends upon the relative attractiveness of the choice situations available to a person.

People move in and out of choice situations, and it gives a false sense of orderliness to describe choices in organizations as involving a sequence of processes ranging from information input to implementation. Instead, it is more accurate to describe choices as outcomes or interpretations of relationships among four relatively independent streams of elements: (1) choice opportunities, (2) problems, (3) participants, and (4) solutions. What has been called a choice, then, is simply a chance convergence of these streams. Even in the garbage can model, some order appears to exist since organizational members tend to find the same types of problems and apply the same types of solutions as they move about the organization. While these nondecision models of choice have few implications for improving the manner in which choices are made, they do serve the purpose of pointing out that choices made in complex organizational situations may be advanced by de-emphasizing the importance of goals in directing decision-making activity.

CHARACTERISTICS OF ORGANIZATIONS THAT INFLUENCE DECISION MAKING

Decisions made in organizations are characterized by special features that must be considered if decisions are to be effective. In this section three features common to organizations that would be expected to have an impact on decision making are discussed. These features are:

1. many people are involved in decision making, frequently with conflicting objectives
2. due to specialization and division of labor, decision-making activities performed by organizational members must be linked by effective communication channels
3. those who are primarily responsible for making a decision must rely upon other people to carry it out

Many Decision Makers with Conflicting Objectives

When decisions are made in an organizational context, the outcome depends not only upon the actions of a single person, but on the actions of other people involved in the decision situation. At times, people are protagonists who attempt to pursue their own gains at the expense of others. Or, they may be partly cooperative and everyone may gain if they can agree upon a mutually beneficial course of action. Even when they are not directly engaged in decision-making activities, organizational members and people in its environment may serve as an audience and influence decisions by subtle—or not so subtle—pressure. A boycott of the products of a firm by a consumers group can influence decisions made on behalf of the firm. Although some degree of shared commitment to the welfare of an organization may exist among its members, competition for the resources of an organization can lead to conflicting decision objectives. Hence, choices made in organizations frequently involve negotiation of actions that accommodate the conflicting preferences of parties to these choices. When decisions are made in organizations, new and interesting processes come into play, and the opinions and actions of other people become as important as the formal costs and gains of the decision situation.

Specialization and Division of Labor

To meet the demand for efficient production, most organizations have abandoned the craft technology and have differentiated their operations. Hence, organizations are characterized by specialization, division of labor, and differentiation of responsibility. Differentiation, or breaking decision tasks up into subdecisions, requires coordination and control to integrate the decision-related tasks for effective choices. This requirement for differentiation and integration necessitates the development and use of information systems to supply the needed decision inputs and to coordinate the various subdecisions. And, as organizations become large and more complex, the importance of information-processing systems increases. Many organizations have installed highly sophisticated computerized information systems to ensure that decisions are made effectively and efficiently.

Separation of Decision Making and Implementation Functions

Decisions made in organizational contexts generally require that people who make decisions must rely upon other organizational members to effectively implement the decisions. The scope of many decisions is such that a manager who is responsible for taking effective action to solve a problem does not have the time or skills required to personally carry out the decision. Typically, subordinates are assigned tasks that must be done to implement a decision and the manager monitors the performance of these tasks. At times, however, the decision maker must coordinate with peers in other departments and even with those higher in the organization to effectively implement a decision.

STRATEGIES FOR AIDING DECISION MAKING AND IMPLEMENTATION IN ORGANIZATIONS

The theoretical positions taken by researchers in their attempts to understand how decisions are made in organizations suggest methods to assist decision makers in coping with the challenges implied by the organizational features mentioned above. The challenges, then, are the following:

1. dealing with conflicting preferences of decision makers
2. acquiring and processing decision-related information
3. implementing decisions in organizations

In this section, we suggest strategies pertaining to each of the challenges that the reader may find useful in improving decision-making practice.

Dealing with Conflicting Preferences for Decisions Made in Organizations

Since the many people typically involved in making decisions in organizations seldom agree about the objectives a decision alternative should attain, it is important to find ways to deal with conflicting preferences.

The strategies discussed in this section for coping with conflicting preferences of decision makers can be classified in the following manner. They can assist decision making by eliciting and making explicit the preferences held by decision makers. Strategies of this type are the use of the Devil's advocate, the dialectic, Delphi, and the Nominal Group Technique. Other strategies operate by combining the preferences of decision makers in a manner acceptable to them. Here we discuss multiple-objective methods for aggregating opinions, voting procedures, bargaining, and strategic negotiations.

Eliciting Preferences

When many people are involved in making decisions it is important that the preferences held for various decision alternatives and outcomes be stated. Among the techniques for eliciting preferences in decision-making groups are the use of a Devil's advocate, the dialectic approach, Delphi, and the Nominal Group Technique. The latter two techniques also have implications for combining preferences in making a group decision, a topic we will discuss in the next section.

Devil's advocate. To counteract the tendency for groups to apply pressure toward conformity upon its members, strategies for encouraging the expression of divergent viewpoints can be used. Two of the more useful methods for constructively using divergent opinions in organizational decision making are the *dialectic* and the *Devil's advocate* (Mason, 1969). If only one side of an issue is advocated by those involved in decision making, the Devil's advocate approach specifies that someone must be found to present the other side. By presenting the favorable aspects of a plan first, then the unfavorable aspects, the hidden assumptions and biases in the plan can be revealed. This approach assumes that truly high quality plans will withstand the most forceful opposition, and that sound judgment regarding a plan occurs when the plan is criticized. One must guard against a tendency for criticism to be so negative in its focus on what is wrong with the plan that better plans are not suggested to replace faulty plans; such a tendency can lead to "safe" plans or decisions.

Dialectic. Based on the thinking of Hegel (1964) and Churchman (1966), Mason (1969) has proposed that the dialectic approach may be useful in presenting and evaluating both sides of a decision. Presenting two opposite points of view can be dialectic if the decision is examined completely and logically from both points of view. The method begins by presenting a decision and its underlying assumptions. Next, a search is made for another plausible alternative—the counter decision. This may be one of the courses of action rejected earlier in the decision process.

The major principle in this approach is that decision makers learn about the basic assumptions of their decisions through a structured debate between opposing views. The most forceful presentations of the two opposing decisions are given, with the only constraint being that both arguments must be based on the same data bank and that the data must be entirely used in making each argument. As each item in the data bank is discussed, the advocates of each position attempt to enlist it as support for their position. The process continues until all data have been exhausted. From this debate a new decision alternative will be developed (i.e., a synthesis) which includes the best of both the decision and the counterdecision. As has been pointed out by MacCrimmon and Taylor (1976), this approach should counteract the tendency observed in social psychological experiments for decision makers to avoid information that may contradict their positions (e.g., Mills, 1968).

Delphi method. Project Delphi conducted by the Rand Corporation in the 1950s for strategic military forecasting introduced the survey which became known as the Delphi method (Helmer, 1977). This method is a means of communications within a group, the members of which do not come into face-to-face contact. The technique exploits collective intelligence and knowledge to facilitate a consensus by using the simple pen-and-paper method as opposed to speech and person-to-person interaction. A coordinator, or a coordinating group, interrogates a panel of experts on a well-defined topic. The interrogation follows this scenario: (1) the first part is inquisitive and heuristic, and probes the thinking of the members of the panel with regard to some aspects of the future in relation to the topic in question; (2) the group responses are fed back to the panel after the first round—permitting panel members to gauge their relative position within the group; then, (3) a second round of inquiry is sent out—allowing the members to join the group's opinion or to maintain their own, and to substantiate their decision; and (4) this procedure is repeated until some form of consensus is reached or until the subject is considered explored.

Characteristics of the Delphi method. The Delphi method has three distinguishing characteristics compared to other group methods for gathering opinions:

1. **Anonymity.** There are two levels of anonymity. First, the members of the panel may be anonymous to one another, thus most of the sociopsychological pressures common to face-to-face meetings may be eliminated. The second level of anonymity guarantees that no response can ever be traced to any member by the coordinator. This anonymity is particularly important when, in certain studies, the members are taken from an available organization, and are known to one another. In such cases, anonymity will allow the members to respond according to their own beliefs—free from influence of the dominant members of their group. The higher level of anonymity guarantees that not even the coordinator could trace the responses back to specific members; the intention being that such total anonymity would encourage candid and unguarded responses.
2. **Controlled feedback of the responses.** The returns of each round of inquiry are presented to the members, allowing them to assess their relative standing within the group. On subsequent rounds they can either maintain or modify their original responses. When Delphi is used to identify the factors responsible for changes in opinions, then anonymity must be reduced so the coordinator will know the responses of the panel members and be able to make comparisons.
3. **Statistical group decision.** A consensus is typically the outcome of a Delphi exercise. The group judgment may not represent the best judgment, but rather a compromise. An artificial consensus (e.g., median or mean responses) may be appropriate in certain circumstances (e.g., in establishing

organizational objectives or public policies). However, when Delphi is used to examine differences of opinions, statistical group decisions would not be useful.

The panel is one of the most important features of the Delphi exercise. The quality of the output of the Delphi exercise appears to depend largely on the expertise of the panel and on the ability of its members to predict future events. The definitions of *expert* used in Delphi applications are very diverse, ranging from anyone who can contribute relevant inputs (Pill, 1971) to "a man of knowledge in the sense that he brings to the problem at hand a body of specialized information and skill acquired through formal education and/or training on the job" (Wilensky, 1970, p. vii).

These definitions permit a coordinator to assemble a group that would be likely to support the coordinator's position. Little is said in the literature about panel selection, other than the suggestion that the reliability and accuracy of the judgments of experts be identified from public expressions (e.g., publications, lectures) prior to selecting them (Helmer, 1977). Panel selection biases have led to considerable criticism regarding the reliability and validity of the consensus reached in Delphi. Concern has been expressed about the biases that may result both from pressure to reach a consensus and lack of standardization of the procedure (Hill & Fowles, 1975). The danger is that the narrow outlook that may be used by members of the panel with similar training and/or experiences may lead to forecasts which reflect their biases (Albertson & Cutler, 1976).

Critique of the Delphi method. The effectiveness of the Delphi method in controlling the social biases present in small groups has been examined by several researchers. The argument that it reduces or eliminates the psychological forces in face-to-face meetings was refuted (Van de Ven & Delbecq, 1974). They found that the group median reported in the feedbacks between rounds may be viewed as "authority." Use of the method in manpower forecasting (Milkovich, et al., 1972) demonstrated that Delphi results were more accurate than the conventional regression methods in predicting the manpower policies adopted by firms. However, this study does not demonstrate that the actual policy adopted by the firm was the best policy.

Within large organizations, Lachman (1972) found that Delphi technique allows for the formulation of a democratic opinion, thus reducing sharp oppositions. He concluded that Delphi is a useful management tool, but that it must be used with infinite caution, because the consensus obtained cannot necessarily be equated with an optimal choice. Comparing the characteristics of conferences, interviews, controlled sample population polling, and computer-assisted meetings with the Delphi method, suggested that each method has some advantages. A method should be selected on the basis of the information sought, the users of the information, and the time and costs involved. At times, combinations of these methods may be useful.

Delphi studies are used for planning in the fields of manpower, social policy, urban affairs, corporate environment, health and other areas in which intuitive and value judgments have great influence. Reliance upon subjectivity appears acceptable because the outcome desired is a form of democratic consensus. Whereas the method generally is very lengthy, the use of the computer will readily alleviate this problem. Computer conferencing, making use of anonymity in order to encourage the generation of ideas and liberated discussions, and exploring the divergences of opinions are likely to become the most popular features of the Delphi technique.

Nominal Group Technique. The Nominal Group Technique (NGT) was developed by Delbecq and others (1975) to facilitate generating ideas from groups. The technique capitalizes upon the advantages of groups over individuals, yet attempts to control biases resulting from social processes. The structured format for group interaction consists of four major stages:

1. The individual members independently list ideas on a problem in writing.
2. A "round-robin" session follows in which each group member—one at a time—describes one to the group. The ideas are listed on a blackboard without discussion.
3. Once all ideas have been listed, they are discussed for clarification and evaluation.
4. Individuals silently and independently vote on the ideas, using a decision rule involving rating or rank ordering. The group decision is the pooled outcome of individual votes.

Critique of the Nominal Group Technique. Although the NGT has been used in many situations, little research evidence regarding its effectiveness has been reported. A study by the authors of NGT (Van de Ven & Delbecq, 1974) found NGT to be superior to Delphi and interacting groups both in the number of unique ideas developed and in the satisfaction of participants with the process. In view of the limited evidence regarding the effectiveness of these techniques, choosing between NGT and Delphi should be based on the urgency of the solution and the feasibility of assembling the group members in one location. When it is possible to bring the group members together for a meeting, the NGT can be used; whereas Delphi permits polling their opinions by mail, telephone, or other means. The Delphi method generally requires more time, due to the number of rounds and the delays in communication, than does NGT.

Combining Preferences

In addition to eliciting preferences held by decision-making groups, most models of decision making require some method for aggregating these diverse preferences into a stated *group preference* value. Methods for combining preferences that appear useful in organizational contexts include the use of multiple-objective decision-making techniques, voting methods, bargaining, and strategic negotiations.

Multiple-objective techniques. Drawing upon the behavioral research concerning social influence on decision-making groups, a number of methods for eliciting and combining information and opinions from members of the group can be developed. It should be noted that many of the strategies for dealing with multiple objectives (discussed in Chapter 3) can also be used in multiple-person situations, since any group member may impose preferred objectives. Strategies of this type include using linear regression to build simple models of the attributes of decision alternatives (bootstrapping), applying subjective weighing models in which members of a group can suggest preferences to be included as coefficients, or setting preference constraints specified by group members and seeking a course of action that satisfies these constraints. Additional quantitative methods for assessing group preferences are provided in the literature (e.g., Seaver, 1976).

Voting. One of the most direct strategies for making decisions in groups is to vote. A number of voting rules have been proposed for transforming individual choices into a choice for the group (e.g., Arrow, 1951, Buchanan & Tullock, 1962). The rule generally is selected on the basis of the external costs that may be either imposed or presented depending on the rule that is used.

Voting methods differ from bargaining in that the former requires the parties to the decision to specify a formal rule for resolving the conflicting interests. The requirement that the rules must be viewed by all parties as representative and fair can be a quite demanding one. Yet, there are obvious limits to the size of the group with which the bargaining strategy can be effectively used.

SPAN voting. A voting method that may have some usefulness for committees is the SPAN technique (MacKinnon, 1966). Each individual is given some fixed stock of votes, say one hundred, which the individual can allocate among the alternatives or can give to other individuals so they can allocate them. In SPAN voting a person may choose to cast all available votes on one decision. Allowing the individual to split votes among the alternatives gives an opportunity to hedge on some alternatives where the person's preferences are not strong, and permits transfer of votes to individuals who may have some expertise on a particular issue. Although the method has not been widely used, it offers potentially valuable applications in decisions made by committees and panels.

Logrolling. One attempt to combine certain advantages of voting and bargaining strategies is logrolling (Buchanan & Tullock, 1962; Coleman, 1966). Its use is appropriate when there is a sequence of votes on different issues. With logrolling, votes on unimportant issues can be traded-off to obtain votes on issues viewed as more important to groups representing minority interests. In contrast to SPAN voting, each person initially has only one vote on each decision. Additional votes must be acquired from other people.

In a sequence of decisions, such as votes on a number of issues being taken by a committee, the practice of logrolling can allow for intensity of preferences and, particularly, for the strongly held views of a minority to be expressed. In applying the logrolling strategy, committee members would be permitted to trade off votes on issues which they consider relatively unimportant—but which other members may consider very important—in exchange for future votes on issues which they feel are very important. By use of this method, even a relatively noninfluential committee member (not aligned with a coalition) can express some personal preferences. The advantage of formalizing the procedure is to ensure that many neutral votes will not mask the strong preferences which are held by a few committee members. If no members feel strongly in favor of an issue, it will not be accepted.

Bargaining. A great many strategies for bargaining have been discussed in the literature. When reduced to its most basic form, bargaining consists of two parties—interdependent for information and outcomes and with at least some conflicting preferences for outcomes. Bargaining involves both cooperation and competition. It is cooperative because the two parties—say, a buyer and a seller—must reach a mutually agreeable price if the transaction is to be successful. Yet, since the optimal outcome for one party seldom is the optimal outcome for the other party, each party competes to try to maximize its own gain.

Usually the parties are permitted to communicate with each other regarding quantity and price, but the parties are not permitted to know the payoff matrix of the other party. Influence attempts in bargaining may involve use of threats, persuasion, or making concessions, and the parties may form coalitions in their attempts to gain an advantage. Frequently, the parties attempt to gain information about their opponents' position while concealing or giving misleading information about their own payoff matrix and resources.

Fair vs. ruthless bargaining strategies. Research on bargaining has identified two major strategies that can be used (Siegal & Fouraker, 1960)—"fair" and "ruthless." The advantage of using each of these strategies has been found to depend upon the amount of information a player has. For example, the fair strategy involves striving to achieve a price and quantity that will equalize profits for both parties, but this strategy can actually be detrimental for a player who knows the payoff matrix of the other player. The reason for this is that the player who knows the payoffs to the other player and tries to be fair, would tend to start the bargaining at a moderate price and quantity. The other player, not knowing about the first player's payoff matrix, would tend to start at an extreme level of price and quantity. Since the first player would, then, offer concessions, this would encourage the second player to press for an even more favorable position. Hence, in experiments on bargaining with a fair strategy, it has been clearly shown that having too much information can be a disadvantage.

On the other hand, a player using a ruthless strategy (i.e., attempting to maximize personal gain) can benefit tremendously from having information about the opponent's payoff matrix. By offering an initial position that is very unfavorable to the opponent—and demanding large concessions for even a small increase in the opponent's profit—the well-informed and ruthless player can systematically exploit the situation. An interesting finding of research on this strategy is that the opponent can be manipulated into a position of feeling very relieved about being permitted even a very small profit. So relieved, in fact, that they are willing to play, and even lose, again.

Strategic Negotiation in Organizations

In making decisions in organizations, seldom is bargaining as constrained as the laboratory situation described above. For example, in labor-management relations the sides negotiate with each other using tactics which are much more sophisticated than would be permitted in the laboratory. Generally, each side has a good deal of information about the payoff matrix of the other side and the communication channels can be opened or closed at will by the parties. This permits the use of tactics employing promises and threats. Schelling (1963) has provided a very insightful discussion of how these tactics can be used in negotiations. In strategic negotiations, having power, being "rational," and keeping communication channels open may become liabilities. Let's consider why.

Limitations of power, communication, and rationality in strategic negotiations. Having power to make a decision may be a disadvantage in negotiating. Sending people to negotiate who cannot commit the side to a position can be an advantage because the representatives cannot be persuaded by the arguments of the other side. After getting the best position of the other party, the representatives can take the offer back to their side and, if the offer is rejected, extract even further concessions. Having union membership reject management's best offer made to the union's negotiating committee permits reopening negotiations and, possibly, gaining further concessions.

Manipulating channels of communication can be useful as a negotiating strategy. Frequently, the side with the most efficient communication can be at a disadvantage. A kidnapper's ransom note is of no value unless it can be delivered to the person who is being asked to pay the ransom. If a threat is not heard and understood it will be ineffective. A party with ability to open communication channels only when it wishes to communicate a message generally would have the advantage in using threats and counterthreats.

Finally, Schelling points out that even being seen as rational people can be a disadvantage in negotiating. The accepted procedures of negotiating assume that each party will consider costs and gains in a rational manner and will attempt to maximize their own position. If, however, one side is seen as unwilling or incapable of this type of rational evaluation, the "irrational" side can be at an advantage. If a mugger threatens you with a knife and demands your money, are you more likely to comply when the mugger appears irrational? Or, would airplane hijackers be more likely to receive cooperation from authorities if it appears that the hijackers place a low value on human life—including their own lives? Irrationality in this sense may also imply a commitment to carry out a threat. Schelling demonstrates that such commitment is essential to the effective use of a threat; at least, the other side must believe that the commitment exists. Although some of the strategies Schelling describes are illegal, others are widely used in organizations and should be considered in making effective decisions.

Acquiring and Processing Decision-Related Information in Organizations

Making effective decisions in organizations depends upon gathering information to evaluate, choose, and implement a prescribed course of action. Generally, information relevant to a decision is developed by departments or individuals in an organization, or somewhere outside of it, then transmitted to the person or group responsible for making a decision. For example, in choosing a new product to develop, a Research and Development Department may call upon a Sales Department member for information about the market for various new products, inquire of Production Department members to find out what the production costs for products may be, and consult with specialists in technical areas to determine how to design new products.

Those responsible for selecting new products, then, need to know what information is required, where it can be obtained, how to judge the quality of the forthcoming information, and how to integrate the information inputs from various sources in choosing courses of action. Clearly, making decisions in organizations requires efficient information search and processing mechanisms.

Information processing and communication. Information processing and communication are used interchangeably in our discussion of information exchange in organizations. Keep in mind, however, that a distinction generally is made between these terms. While information processing refers only to receiving information from various sources, communication involves both sending and receiving messages. Many definitions of these terms have been advanced, but the definition offered by Porter and Roberts (1972) captures the essence of information exchange in organizations; communication ". . . seems to imply an attempt to share meaning via transmission of messages from senders to receivers" (p. 1554). The information-processing aspect of communication entails searching, receiving, evaluating, and integrating messages as decisions are made. To adequately understand information exchange for decision making in organizations, both communication and information processing must be included in our analysis.

Strategies for improving information exchange. Research on information exchange has identified two major types of dysfunctions related to both the amount of information that is exchanged and its content. These dysfunctions are: (1) selective filtering or screening of information, and (2) inability to cope with excessive information-processing requirements in solving complex problems. While much of the research on these topics is based on laboratory experimentation, implications for improving decisions made in actual organizations are discussed in the next section.

Dealing with Selective Filtering of Information

As we mentioned earlier in this chapter, a person in an organizational hierarchy may use this position to distort information exchange in furthering one's own objectives. One dysfunction in organizational information exchange is the tendency for information communicated up the power hierarchy to become distorted. Individuals in power hierarchies tend to filter or screen information prior to transmitting it upward and to withhold information that may be threatening to the communicator (e.g., Porter & Roberts, 1972). Downs (1966) has contended that, "When information must be passed through many officials, each of whom condenses it somewhat before passing it on to the next, the final output will be very different in quality from the original input; that is, significant distortion will occur" (p. 269).

The existence of selective filtering of information in organizations has been well-documented in the research literature (e.g., Cohen, 1959; Athanassiades, 1973). Typically, these studies investigated the influence of a message recipient's status in an organization, and the ability to influence the career of a message sender in the extent to which the message sender modified a message before sending it. Possible message modifications that have been studied include revision of the message format, not sending the message at all, and substituting an incorrect message. The results of these studies have been summarized in several review articles (Ference, 1970; Porter & Roberts, 1972; Huber, 1982).

Similar findings have been observed in laboratory studies using communication networks, and have been attributed to the low status person having learned what information is likely to be reinforced by the high status person (e.g., Collins & Guetzkow, 1964). The process of selective filtering has been hypothesized to take place during every transmission, and not just at the boundaries of an organization (i.e., when information enters or leaves the organization) (March & Simon, 1958). Two major influences on message distortion in organizations have been found to be how much the sender trusts the recipient and the sender's perception of how favorable the message will be judged by the recipient.

Trust and message accuracy. A series of studies by O'Reilly and Roberts investigated the impact of interpersonal trust on information exchange. Examining one of these studies may illustrate the experimental procedures and results. University students were asked to communicate upward, downward, and laterally in making group decisions (Roberts and O'Reilly, 1974). The influence of interpersonal trust in superiors, peers, and subordinates—as well as the direction of communications flow—on the degree to which messages were modified was examined. Little support was found for the hypothesized influences of communication direction. But, it was found that senders who trust recipients sent more information that was important to the recipient, sent more unfavorable information, and, overall, transmitted more information.

Based upon these experimental research conclusions and his own survey of organizational processes, Athanassiades (1973) reported a number of factors that appear to contribute to more accurate organizational communication. Among these factors were:

- Rules and regulations should be defined clearly.
- Authority structures should be impersonal.
- Competition among message senders should not arouse fear.
- Work should be standardized and simplified.

These research conclusions may suggest ways to reduce communication distortion in specific situations. The main principle, however, to remember, is that increasing interpersonal trust tends to lead to more accurate communication.

The MUM effect and message accuracy. The second influence on message distortion in organizations found in the research literature is the impact of message favorableness. A series of laboratory studies have investigated differences in the manner in which good news and bad news are transmitted. Although these experiments used college students as subjects, two research conclusions appear relevant to information exchange in organizations. Rosen and Tesser (1969) identified what they called the *MUM effect* (keeping Mum about Undesirable Messages). Most of their subjects appeared very reluctant to communicate bad news, even when they would have no further contact with the recipient and no rewards or penalties would result. In addition, a subsequent experiment found that a recipient of good or bad news also was reluctant to pass along bad news to another person. In contrast, subjects in this experiment were willing to give bad news to a disinterested bystander. It appears that, even when any possible rewards or penalties are removed, senders tend to modify messages to avoid distressing the recipient. Or, as Ference (1970) concluded, "Information. . . will tend to fit the transmitter's perceptions of the recipient's needs."

Dealing with Information Demands

It has been argued that every communication distorts, accenting some things and remaining silent on others; thus, all news censors as well as exposes, and suppresses as well as expresses (Gouldner, 1976). MacCrimmon (1974) reported several fallacies in information processing that he found in a simulation exercise with business managers. Managers were found to acquire more information than they actually needed or could adequately process and to pay little attention to other people's needs or capabilities to produce information. It is one thing to train decision makers to make better decisions when they have control over their analyses; but the situation is more challenging when a decision maker must rely on other people to acquire information, generate alternatives, or to accomplish other aspects of decision making. In the latter situation, effective communication becomes essential for making successful decisions.

Since effective decision making in groups requires efficient exchange of information among its members, the arrangement of channels of communication is an important feature of decision-making systems in organizations. However, the study of communication in organizations has been isolated from the decision-making literature (Connolly, 1977). For example, Allen and Cohen (1969) analyzed the flow of communication in research and development laboratories, but did not consider the implications of information flows for decisions. It would be helpful to integrate decision making and communication in organizations within a single framework in which the impact of information on decision makers and the communication networks which connect multiple decision makers could be analyzed. One approach for doing this is the concept of the diffuse decision process (Connolly, 1977), which is characterized by lack of an identifiable decision maker, an extended time period, and the importance of mechanisms for structuring and linking decision makers. This process reflects the situation that exists in most organizational decisions.

Communication networks and information-processing capabilities. The net of communicative activities in which participants are embedded is important to decision making in organizations. The long accepted practice of organizational planners to assume that a hierarchical structuring of communication channels is most efficient has been challenged by research initiated by the early work of Bavelas (1950) and Leavitt (1951). Subsequent research studies have shown that the arrangement of communication channels in a group influences leadership emergence, morale of group members, and quality of decision making. Although most of this research has been conducted with ad hoc groups studied in laboratory experiments using imposed communication patterns, research findings pertaining to centrality in communication structures have implications for communication in organizational decision making.

In the laboratory studies, a communication network refers to a consistent pattern of exchange during the course of decision making. Communication networks typically are imposed upon a decision-making group to determine the impact of the net on group processes and outcomes. Group members are placed in cubicles connected by slots through which messages may be passed. The communication nets studied, shown in Exhibit 6.3, have included the wheel (only the single member at the hub can communicate with other group members), a circle (each member is connected with two other members), the chain (all members in a line), and the concom (completely connected). Two basic patterns have been shown to develop in nets—centralized and decentralized (Shaw & Rothschild,

1956). The decentralized net has been found to be most efficient when the group solves complex problems. A centralized net is most efficient when the group solves simple problems (e.g., Shaw, 1976). Since most of the problems that groups deal with in organizations are much more complex than the laboratory tasks, it is evident that a decentralized network is most likely to be effective in such situations.

EXHIBIT 6.1 Communication Networks

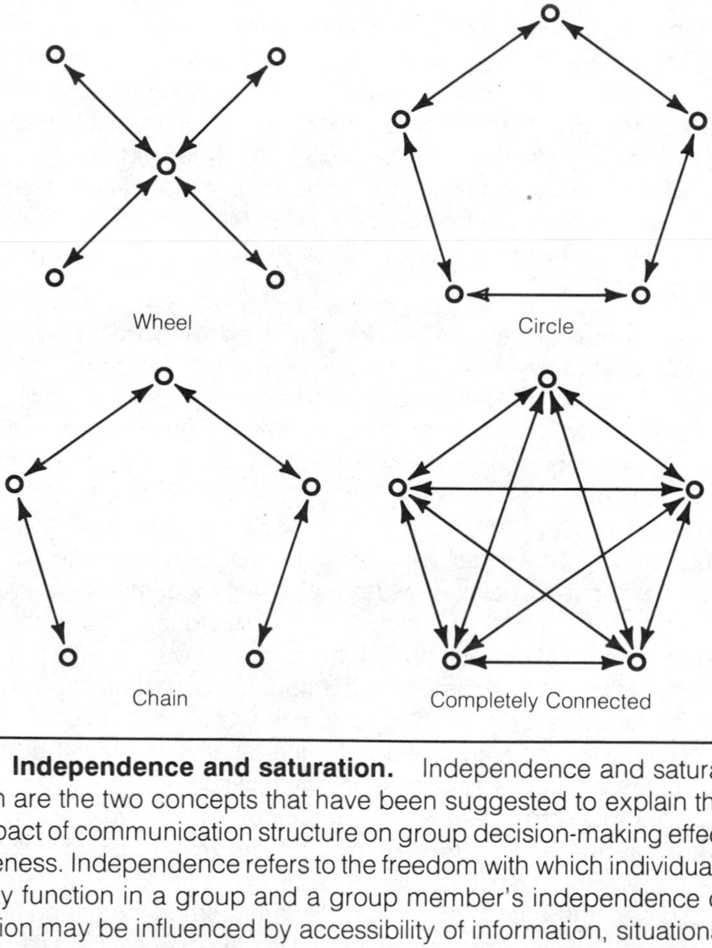

Independence and saturation. Independence and saturation are the two concepts that have been suggested to explain the impact of communication structure on group decision-making effectiveness. Independence refers to the freedom with which individuals may function in a group and a group member's independence of action may be influenced by accessibility of information, situational factors, by actions of other group members, and by one's perception of the situation. Independence has been found to be related to both group efficiency and member satisfaction, although it appears to have its strongest effect on satisfaction (e.g., Shaw, 1954).

Saturation refers to communication overload experienced by group members in centralized positions in networks. When the number of messages that must be handled by a position passes a certain optimal level, the communication requirements begin to interfere with the effects of being in more favorable positions in the network. It has been found that the greater the saturation in a network, the less efficient the group and the less satisfied the group members, but saturation appears to have a greater influence on effectiveness. Two types of saturation have been identified (Gilchrist, et al., 1954)—channel saturation (i.e., the number of channels with which a position must deal) and message unit saturation (i.e., the number of messages that a person must handle).

The notion of saturation accounts for many of the research findings in communication networks and appears to correspond to cognitive strain in individual decision makers. For example, the central position in a wheel network is more vulnerable to saturation than is any position in a decentralized network, such as a circle. The communication requirements are light when the group deals with a simple task and the central position does not become saturated. Hence, a wheel network is more effective for solving simple problems, but in more complex tasks the central position becomes saturated and the efficiency of the group is reduced. Decentralized networks are less subject to saturation and are more effective in solving complex problems. For further details of the experimental results see Glanzer and Glaser (1961), Shaw (1976) and Collins and Raven (1969).

Implications of communication nets for making decisions in organizations. In spite of the great many studies on communication networks, it is difficult to determine implications for designing information networks in organizations. It should be kept in mind that the centralized-decentralized dimension of communication networks does not correspond to centralized-decentralized decision structures (Mulder, 1960), and inferences about organizational communication structures from data on networks in the laboratory should be cautiously drawn.

A major challenge to decision making in organizations is the storage and processing of information. Realizing this, Simon (1973) has proposed that organizational structures should be designed so as to facilitate the decomposition of decision-making activities, rather than on the basis of departments. Lateral, self-contained authority structures for increasing capacity of organizations to process information (Galbraith, 1973) take advantage of the decomposition principle. Complex decision problems are decomposed and subproblems are assigned to self-contained decision units. This approach has the advantages of:

1. reducing the coordination and scheduling within each unit
2. producing a more homogeneous output in each unit since the need to share information across decision units is lessened

3. reducing information distortion and loss due to long communication chains by bringing decision makers closer to information sources

While bringing information sources and decision makers closer together would reduce *uncertainty absorption* (i.e., a false sense of certainty acquired as information is transmitted that was described in Chapter 5), this approach assumes that the subproblems are sufficiently independent to enable choices regarding them to be made independently. Where decisions of one unit depend heavily upon outputs from other units this approach would not be effective.

Using an uncertainty index. The degree of certainty in organizational decision problems can be signaled by an *uncertainty index* (Woods, 1966) in order to reduce the effect of uncertainty absorption. Uncertainty absorption seems to be pervasive in situations involving the transmission of information from those who develop it, to those who use it as a basis for making decisions. While little research evidence on this phenomenon has been generated, it represents a serious difficulty for decisions made in organizations. To ensure that the decision makers are acquainted with the level of uncertainty in the information—resulting from the precision of the measuring techniques or the conditions under which the information was generated—the uncertainty index involves assigning a value to the information indicating the level of uncertainty with which the originator of the information viewed it.

In preparing a report identifying job skills that are expected to be in short supply in the next ten years, a manpower forecaster may feel confident about the forecasts made for some skills and less confident about others. Assigning an index number, ranging from .00 for absolutely no confidence in the estimate to 1.00 for a completely confident estimate, would alert the reader of the report about how much certainty to give to each estimate. Indexing the unreliability of information would enable the decision maker to carefully select and weigh the importance of information used in decisions.

Designing optimal information filters. Sage (1981) has proposed a systems engineering approach for designing optimal information filters in organizations. In this approach three steps are crucial for constructing mathematical models to simulate information flows:

1. the problem must be defined by specifying the elements of the organization to be included in the model
2. relationships among the elements must be identified
3. the parameters of the organizational system must be estimated

Exhibit 6.4 shows a block diagram of this systems engineering approach being used to model a decision about determining organi-

EXHIBIT 6.2 Diagram of a Systems-Engineering Model of Information Filtering in a Policy-Making Decision

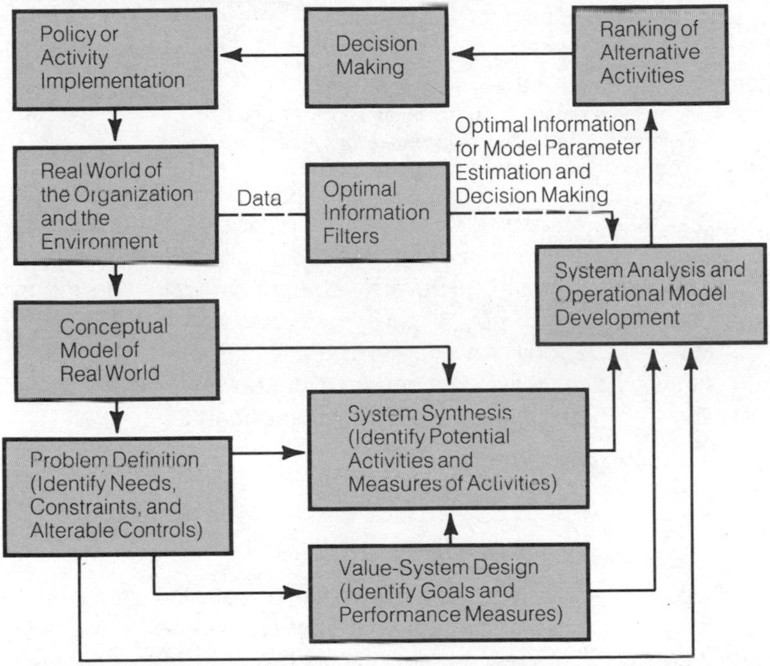

Source: Sage, A.P. Designs for optimal information filters. in P. Nystrom and W.H. Starbuck (eds.), *Handbook of Organizational Design*, Vol. 1, Oxford: Oxford University Press, 1981, 114.

zational policy. This diagram models the activities undertaken as organizations are designed and clearly shows the interrelationships among such elements of decision making as values, objectives, generating and evaluating alternative courses of action, choice, and implementation. The information filters in this model link the real world of the organization and its environment with the systems-analytic evaluation of courses of action. Sage (1981) provides further details regarding how optimal information filters can be specified for a given situation and explains the mathematical formulations that underlie this approach to constructing information flows for decision making in organizations.

Implementing Decisions in Organizations

Why are some decisions implemented successfully while others fail? A major consideration in the effectiveness of decision implementation is the manner in which power is used in organizations to influence other people. In a study of one hundred organizations, Trull (1966) found that decision success was a function of both decision quality and decision implementation. The strategies discussed in previous chapters of this book contribute heavily to decision quality and Trull's findings regarding decision quality are compatible with the appropriate use of these strategies. He found that decision quality was determined by:

1. compatibility with operating constraints
2. meeting the optimal time for a decision
3. using the optimum amount of information
4. the degree to which a decision maker has control over the factors influencing a decision

To a disturbing degree, however, the decision makers he studied showed little concern for determining the optimum time for making decisions; nor did they expend much effort in relating the importance of a decision to cost of the information required (e.g., the marginal value of additional information).

With regard to decision implementation, however, Trull's study indicated that three factors were of major importance:

1. avoidance of conflict of interests
2. appropriate risk-reward factors
3. degree to which those who must carry out a decision understand the decision

Since implementing decisions involves people, the ultimate test of a decision is whether a decision maker can influence others to carry it out. There are few decisions so technically precise that they cannot be undermined by those entrusted to implement them. Finally, perceived involvement in the process of choice was found to be important to successful implementation. The degree of understanding of the decision by those who were responsible for carrying it out was linked to openness of communciation and the participation of these people in the decision-making process. Clearly, efforts made to prepare the organization and the affected members, through communication and enlistment of personal commitments, increased acceptance and successful implementation (Trull, 1966). The type of leadership required to implement decisions successfully involves the voluntary acceptance of its exercise by those who are subject to it (March & Simon, 1958).

Resistance to decisions. "Probably the most universal difficulty arises from people's fears of planned change . . . almost all ambitious plans are intended to produce new patterns of thought and action in the organization. However, as has been said innumerable times, people resist change—or, more accurately, they resist being changed by other people" (Ewing, 1969, p. 44). There are many reasons for resistance to decisions; ranging from fear of change, threat of being manipulated, conflicting interests, constrained freedom of choice in work activities, and failure to see the value of a decision, to increased work load due to decision-making activities. Resistance can take the form of either open hostility or covert sabotage of decision-making efforts. Even the best designed decisions will fail if those who must carry them out refuse to do so.

Considering the values and needs of those involved in decisions is important in implementing decisions. The values and needs of all participants, not just top management, should be accommodated to the greatest extent possible if plans are to guide the behavior of all members in an organization. Whenever possible, implementation of decisions can be facilitated by building in values and objectives which are shared by those who must carry them out. There also is a motivational basis for involving the implementers in the decision process. Goal setting has been found to motivate performance, and self-set goals tend to be more highly motivating than are goals set by others. The more people in organizations participate in the objective-setting process, the more willing they will be to assist in implementing the resulting decision.

Other strategies for overcoming resistance to decisions are implied in Kimberly's (1981) discussion of ways to design organizations to facilitate innovation. The four methods he suggested for dealing with resistance to innovative programs seem equally applicable to other types of decisions. These methods are:

1. **Innovations may simply evolve by processes that naturally occur in an organization and organizational structures may then adapt to accommodate the innovative programs.** This approach to dealing with resistance to decisions has the advantage of not eliciting resistance because the process and resulting decision are seen as clearly within the range of activities acceptable to organizational members. Two examples of this strategy can be seen in the evolution of dual organizational structures (to produce innovations and to implement these innovations) (Duncan, 1976); and the use of self-evaluating organizational units (e.g., units that monitor their own performance and take adaptive actions to insure that appropriate levels of performance are maintained) (Hedberg, et al., 1976).
2. **Innovations may be introduced so that they will be seen as compatible with existing values held by organizational members.** This approach appears similar to incrementalism (Lindblom, 1959) in that innovative programs represent only marginal departures from existing programs. It would be likely to share with incrementalism the limitation that changes would tend to be conservative.
3. **Innovations can be pilot tested on one department or unit of an organization.** If accurate evaluation of the quality of the innovative program is desired, then the unit selected should be representative of the organization, or even present a tough challenge for the innovation. If looking good and encouraging other units to adopt the innovation is the primary objective, then a unit should be selected for which the probability of success is high. In this case, it may also enhance the chances of successful implementation if high status units are used in the pilot test.

4. **Finally, it is important that at least one person in a position of authority in the organization support the innovation.** This person could serve as a buffer to protect the innovative program from attack before its value has been demonstrated.

Use of power for effective decision implementation. A central issue is how a decision maker (e.g., a manager) should use power in exchange with other organizational members to facilitate decision implementation. A great deal of research has been addressed to the styles of behavior that managers should adopt in relation to lower power members of an organization (i.e., subordinates) in order to attain both high productivity and morale.

Since the early experiments by Lewin and his co-workers (1939) suggested the superiority of a "democratic" style of leadership in attaining morale in work groups, many others have attempted to answer the question of what style to use—"employee-centered" and "production-centered" (Likert, 1961), "initiating structure" and "consideration" (Fleishman, 1973), or "task" and "relations" (Fiedler, 1964). Fiedler proposed that contingencies in the leadership situation be considered in adopting a style appropriate to the situation, and House (1971) has suggested that managerial influence attempts are more likely to succeed when they focus on the subordinate's *path-goal instrumentalities.* A leader's major impact, according to this theory, is in clarifying the paths to rewards desired by a subordinate and in making such rewards contingent on effective performance.

These approaches have implications for decision making since, in addition to the features of a decision problem and its environment, the research on leadership styles and behaviors indicates that the relative power held by parties to the exchange can be linked to successful decision making.

Participatory management. One strategy for use of power in decision-making contexts involving power differentials is for the power holder to share the power with relatively low-power members in the exchange to produce a more balanced relationship. As was suggested in our earlier discussion of power, this strategy may aid effective decision making by reducing alienation of low-power members and gaining their cooperation in implementing decisions. Such attempts by managers to involve subordinates in the decision-making process have been widely used and have received some attention in the research literature. Generally, the motivation behind use of "participative management" has been to increase performance and satisfaction of low-power members (e.g., McGregor, 1960; Likert, 1961). Participation, in this sense, refers to ". . . the extent to which subordinates, or other groups who are affected by decisions, are consulted with, and involved in the making of decisions" (Melcher, 1976, p. 314). Hence, participative management is only one component of the "democratic" leadership style mentioned above.

Effectiveness of participatory management. Research evidence regarding the effectiveness of participative management in achieving productivity and satisfaction on the part of subordinates has been mixed. In reviewing research on participative management in three textile mills (Nyman & Smith, 1934; Rice, 1953; Marrow & French, 1945), a parcel post firm (Vroom, 1960), and a General Electric division (French, et al., 1966), Melcher (1976) concluded that:

1. Acceptance of decisions is sharply increased by involving others in decision-making activities. Acceptance is most dramatic when participation in decisions is a sharp change from established norms (e.g., acceptance of cost-cutting methods by union leaders).
2. Only those people actually involved in participation are influenced toward accepting decisions; when some employees are designated to represent a larger group, only these representatives show changes in attitudes.
3. Participation in trivial decisions doesn't affect general attitudes.
4. Personalities of subordinates mediate the impact of participation; those with authoritarian orientations and low need for independence tend to react positively when little participation is used.

It has been speculated that a participative approach to decision making would be expected, and more effective, in small groups or other relatively simple contexts. Other conditions in the organizational situation that appear linked to the feasibility and effectiveness of participation in decisions include low specialization (i.e., it is easier to achieve consensus when decisions do not involve a number of interdependent specialists) and low work demands (i.e., when the pressure is on to get work done, subordinates are more likely to accept less participation in decisions). When the opposite conditions exist—large and complex organizations, high degree of specialization, and high pressure to produce—participation in decisions would be expected to be less effective. It has also been suggested that participation in decisions would be less likely to be effective when: (1) group boundaries are ambiguous, (2) organizational value systems encourage conformity, and (3) group decisions would be expected to be more risky (Campbell, et al., 1970). These speculations, however, have not been empirically tested.

Vroom and Yetton participation tree. On the basis of the research reviewed above, a normative approach has been proposed for determining the conditions under which participation in decisions is advisable (Vroom & Yetton, 1973). The *participation tree* is a decision tree representation of the key elements to consider in determining when to involve subordinates in decision making, and the form this involvement should take.

This normative model provides a method for matching decision processes and problem types. The effectiveness of a decision is determined by three considerations: (1) the quality of the decision, 2) the acceptance of the decision by those who will carry it out, and (3) the time required to reach a decision. The features of decision problems which affect the benefits of involving subordinates in decisions were developed from the work of Maier (1963); he was the first to distinguish between *acceptance-dominant* and *quality-dominant problems.* Essentially, acceptance-dominant problems require that subordinates are committed to implementing them, whereas quality-dominant problems only require sound solutions. Research on the consequences of participation has been presented elsewhere (Vroom, 1960; Vroon & Yetton, 1973) and no attempt will be made to describe that research here.

The model has evolved through several forms, and the current form presents seven questions for a decision maker to answer. These questions are (Vroom, 1976):

A. Does the problem possess a quality requirement?
B. Do I have sufficient information to make a high quality decision?
C. Is the problem structured?
D. Is acceptance of the decision by subordinates important for effective implementation?
E. If I were to make the decision by myself, am I reasonably certain that it would be accepted by my subordinates?
F. Do subordinates share the organizational goals to be attained in solving this problem?
G. Is conflict among subordinates likely in preferred solutions?

On the basis of the answers to these questions, a decision maker works through the participation tree, shown in Exhibit 6.5, to determine the appropriate manner for involving subordinates in a decision. The decision processes represented by the letters to the right of the participation tree branches indicate the feasible set of participation styles appropriate for solving the problem. Choices among the styles included in a feasible set are linked to the urgency of a decision and concern for developing the decision-making abilities of subordinates. When decisions are urgent, the first style listed should be used, whereas if subordinate development is important the last style listed would be most appropriate. Intermediate styles represent a balance of these concerns.

AI and AII reflect an autocratic approach. In AI the problem is solved by the manager using the information available at the time; in AII the manager acquires information from subordinates prior to

EXHIBIT 6.3 Decision Process Flowchart Showing Feasible Set of Participation Styles

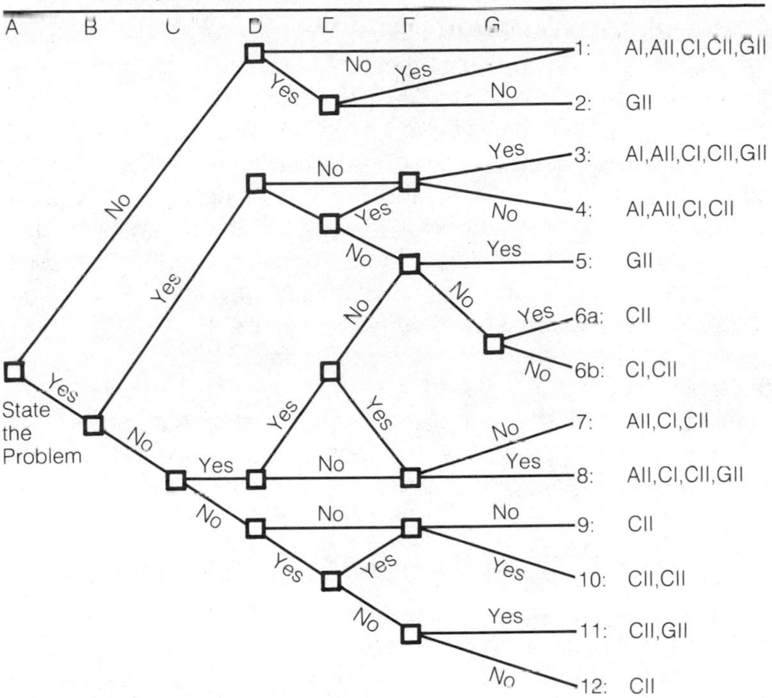

Source: Vroom, V., Can leaders learn to lead? *Organizational dynamics*, 1976, Winter,

making a decision. CI and CII reflect a consultative process. CI involves acquiring information from subordinates individually, along with their ideas and suggestions, before deciding, and CII involves a group meeting in which the information, opinions, and suggestions are acquired. GII involves full participation of subordinates, and the manager chairs a meeting in which the group attempts to reach a consensus regarding the choice.

Effectiveness of the Vroom and Yetton participation tree. The model has been validated by asking managers who were unfamiliar with the model to select two decisions they had made; one successful decision and one unsuccessful decision. These decisions were prepared as cases and the decision processes used were identified. Then, these managers were trained to use the model. They coded the cases so that the research could determine the problem type and the feasible set of methods for that problem type. Some preliminary evidence regarding the extent of agreement between the methods used to make decisions and the model have been reported for forty-six managers. The results showed that when the manager's method for dealing with a problem corresponded with the model, the probability of a successful decision was 65 percent; whereas if the method used disagreed with the model, it was successful only 29 percent of the time (Vroom, 1976).

The research reviewed earlier in this chapter indicated that participation in decision making can facilitate decision implementation. However, the personalities of subordinates mediate the effects of participation; and those with authoritarian personality and low need for independence appear more accepting of decisions in which little participation is used. Yet, little is known about the group processes which may impact upon participation, nor how the participation should be conducted. If decision aids are to be used to aggregate information and preferences of group members, this is a serious omission (Taylor, 1981). In addition, more research is needed to determine the processes such as learning and need satisfaction that may be modified by longer-term exposure to participation, and the long-term effects of participation.

SUMMARY

In this chapter we have expanded our discussion of decision making to include organizational influences. The techniques for improving decisions based on a "rational" model of decision making that have been our focus in prior chapters are extremely useful in many types of decisions. However, it is important to consider more fully the context in which they are used for making decisions in organizations; a context which contains complex social and political influences.

Three aspects of the organizational context of decisions provided the focus for discussing strategies to improve decisions made in organizations. These aspects were: (1) multiple decision makers with conflicting objectives, (2) specialization and division of labor, and (3) separation of the decision making and implementation functions. These aspects represent difficult challenges to effective decision making in organizations. Following a discussion of some of the major theories of decision making in organizations, strategies for coping with these three types of challenges to decision-making effectiveness were suggested.

In the next chapter the "state of the art" in behavioral decision making is critiqued and some more notable advances are indicated. Following this, we suggest future directions in which theory, research, and strategies in the field of behavioral decision making appear likely to proceed or, in our opinion, should proceed.

"STATE OF THE ART" AND FUTURE DIRECTIONS 7

Within the past twenty years, the field of behavioral decision making has made considerable progress. Yet, there is a great deal more to be accomplished if the field is to attain the promise that it holds for understanding how human choices are made in the context of complex organizations, and how they can be made more effectively. In concluding this volume, it appears useful to signal some of the themes that are evident in the advances that have been made; and, in light of the current "state of the art" in behavioral decision making, to suggest some directions that may profitably be taken in future developments in the theory, research, and strategy of this field.

"STATE OF THE ART"

A great deal of progress has been made in understanding the cognitive phenomena of human judgment and choice—particularly with regard to how humans cope with excessive informational demands and seek information in the face of uncertainty. Although the exact nature of the creative process remains a mystery, research on individual differences among people in creative ability has yielded useful findings regarding the origin and development of highly creative individuals; and a multitude of techniques have been used for stimulating the creative thinking by individuals or groups as they reach decisions. A great deal is known about how routine, repetitive decisions can be made effectively and with little expenditure of human resources in their solution. In this regard, there have been significant advances in linking human decision makers and machines in decision systems designed to capitalize upon the strengths of each component.

The technical aspects of decision making have advanced rapidly, with well-developed methods for dealing with the difficulties of incorporating values into the choice process and with the probabilistic features of decision problems. Yet, these advances in techniques for quantifying decision making have also revealed inadequacies in human judgment and choice processes. Although there are some reservations about the implications of these inefficiencies in human cognitive functioning for choices outside the laboratory, it appears that humans seriously distort the information they acquire as they attempt to make choices.

Similar difficulties in making choices exist when groups of decision makers or entire organizations are analyzed. It is not surprising that the inefficiencies in information processing and choice that afflict individuals also afflict groups, and a great deal of attention has been devoted to designing information systems and organizational structures that hold promise for reducing these inefficiencies. Choices made by groups or organizations, however, are subject to additional difficulties imposed by social and political influences on these choices. Understanding the influences of social and political processes on choices made in organizational contexts has just begun. While some theorists have proceeded by expanding the rational model of choice to include a number of participants in the choice, others have approached the difficulty of explaining how choices are reached in organizational contexts by abandoning the rational model of choice—and by proposing very different models. Some have suggested that the central role of goals in rational views of choice (i.e., the use of goals to direct decision-making activity and to evaluate outcomes) be changed—replacing them with either broadly defined directions (e.g., disjointed incrementalism) or by models which do not include goals (e.g., garbage can model, enactment, self-designing organizations). The questioning of traditional approaches to dealing with decision making in organizational contexts appears valuable. These questions have the potential to reveal weaknesses in traditional normative models of rational choice and to suggest ways in which these models can be altered to more accurately reflect psychological, social, and organizational influences.

FUTURE DIRECTIONS IN THEORY AND APPLICATION OF BEHAVIORAL DECISION MAKING

What may be expected of behavioral decision making in the future? Despite the advances highlighted in this volume and elsewhere (e.g., Slovic, et al., 1977; Einhorn & Hogarth, 1981: Cummings, 1982), our understanding of the behavioral aspects of decision making is still very tenuous. It is clear that researchers interested in investigating these issues will have no shortage of important research questions to pursue. There is some urgency in finding answers to the central questions about the behavioral aspects of decision making as ever-larger problems concerning economic, social, international, and environmental issues emerge in the modern world. In view of the complexity and high degree of interconnectedness, solutions to these problems have become even more urgent and solution attempts have the capacity to affect a great many people. In concluding this discussion of the behavioral aspects of decision making, it may be useful to offer some suggestions regarding potentially profitable directions for future advances in theory, research, and strategies in this field.

Advances in Decision-Making Theory and Research

On the basis of the current state of theory and research related to behavioral aspects of decision making, three trends that appear likely to significantly affect future developments are mentioned here. These trends concern: (1) developing alternate models of choice in organizations, (2) reevaluation of research methods traditionally used in investigating behavioral aspects of choice, and (3) grounding theories of individual and collective choice more firmly within the theories of behavioral science.

Developing alternate models of choice in organizations. A normative model of decision making in organizations based on a maximizing principle of rational choice clearly is inappropriate for describing how choices are made, or should be made, in organizational contexts. The information required to justify the assumptions underlying such a model is unavailable, and—even if it could be acquired—it would be too difficult for humans to process in reaching a decision. Even the satisficing view of decision making, which relaxes certain constraints concerning rational decision, may not accurately reflect how choices are made in organizations. Understanding of behavioral aspects of choice in organizations can be advanced by encouraging the development and testing of alternate views of choice. Essentially, the rational model holds that individuals, groups, and entire organizations make decisions in much the same manner. In fact, this may not be so. Even in describing the behaviors of individual decision makers, the rational model has been shown to be inadequate. In addition to failing to meet the assumptions concerning information processing, research evidence has suggested that people may not attempt to maximize expected values or think probabilistically. The ability of the rational model of decision making to accurately model the social and political influences imposed by the features of organizations upon choice seems doubtful.

The alternate models proposed for depicting choice in organizations, thus far, are of two general types: (1) conflict resolution models, and (2) nondecision models (Olsen, 1976). In these views it is assumed that the desires of organizational members largely determine organizational events, just as in the rational models of choice. In the conflict resolution models, however, the organization is viewed as consisting of many rational individuals and subgroups, each with different values, perceptions, capabilities, and resources. Since no single member can determine what decisions are made in this situation, the organizational members bargain, use threats, bribes, or otherwise attempt to arrive at decisions which will best meet their wishes—within the constraints of the resources of the organization. However, considerable conflict may exist among the preferred positions of organizational members or groups and much of the research using this model has examined the ways in which accommodations among the preferences of members are achieved. Central to understanding how organizational choices are made, from this view point, is the emergence of coalitions and the manner in which coalitions divide the resources. This model is evident in the development of game theory (e.g., see Becker & McClintock, 1967), and in disjointed incrementalism (Braybrooke & Lindblom, 1963).

The nondecision models are based on the premise that events are not the realization of individual purposes, nor even the collective purposes formed through bargaining. Outcomes are seen in this view as the unintended product of processes beyond the control of organizational decision makers (Robinson & Majak, 1967). In the "enacted" model of organizational choice (Weick, 1977), events are assumed to occur and, after the fact, decisions to which these events can be logically attributed are identified. It seems fruitful to continue to advance and test a variety of models of choice. A constructive approach proposed by Olsen (1976) involves specifying the circumstances under which each model appears useful and to perform research in these situations using the appropriate model. Certainly, at the present state of development of theories of choice in organizations it appears desirable to pursue research on each model simultaneously, rather than to treat them as incompatible. It appears likely that research performed using alternative models of choice will receive a great deal of attention.

Pursuing research using models of choice other than the rational models offers several advantages. First, this would permit the role of goals in organizational choice to be reexamined. The rational models rely heavily upon stated goals to determine which problems are identified and what criteria to use in making choices. This central role of goals may be dysfunctional due to inability to specify goals in many organizational situations and, as Argyris (1973) has suggested, reliance on goals to guide organizational decisions tends to perpetuate the status quo. This may thwart attempts to achieve greater "humaneness" in organizational decision making (Taylor,

1981). Second, this approach may be useful in attempting to understand the social and political aspects of choices in organizations. It seems likely that power, influence, and motivation, for example, can be better understood if models designed to reveal these processes were used for research on choice. Finally, alternate models may lead to using a range of research methods and permit choice to be viewed through a variety of "lenses"; hopefully leading to a richer understanding of choice processes in organizations.

Reevaluation of research methods for behavioral decision making. To a large extent the research on judgment and choice examined in this volume (e.g., on biases in assessing subjective probabilities) has taken advantage of appealing research paradigms—appealing in that quantitative measures of behaviors can be used, objective norms can be specified for judging the quality of these behaviors (e.g., the Bayes theorem), and the research can be performed using tight experimental control in the laboratory. This approach has disadvantages:

1. Many of the artifacts observed in laboratory research may be due to the nature of the laboratory situation, the use of tight experimental control, or the nature of the tasks used. Little attention has been evident in this research on experimental artifacts which may result from reactions of subjects to the experimental setting, the tasks, or the experimenter; yet these issues have received much attention in experiments done by social psychologists. The research evidence demonstrates that substantial biases can be produced by these reactive effects.
2. The questions of the reliability and validity of measures in studies of judgment and choice, generally, have not been raised. An exception to this was an attempt to determine the convergent validity of a group of measures presumed to measure risk-taking propensity (Slovic, 1962; 1972b). Yet, the reliability of measures places limits on conclusiveness of research findings, and invalid measures can be seriously misleading with regard to what construct has been measured. Research on the behavioral aspects of information system design also suffers from lack of attention to psychometric features of measurement.
3. Important research questions may be neglected because they cannot be researched by tight research designs. Problem identification, for example, is generally regarded as crucial to the decision-making activities that follow (e.g., Connolly, 1977), yet it has received little research. This may, in part at least, be due to difficulties in finding an appealing research framework for the less objectively observed and quantifiable aspects of decision making. The need for research on problem identification has been raised in reviews of the literature (Slovic et al., 1977), and this is likely to be a "hot" area for future research.
4. Experimental designs used in judgment and choices have tended to ignore individual differences among subjects in judgment and choice behaviors. What types of subjects are more prone to use the representativeness heuristic? Which decision makers are more vulnerable to conservativism in revising probabilities? As was pointed out by Cronbach (1957) some time ago, the experimental paradigm tends to treat individual differences among subjects

as error. Alternatively, this variability can be exploited to yield insights regarding individual and organizational influences on choice. This appears to be an important topic for further research.

5. Finally, the predominant use of laboratory experiments has limited the extent to which findings can be generalized to the world outside the laboratory. When the methods are taken from the laboratory to the organization, there remains the question of whether important, real world decisions are biased in the manner found in the laboratory. Increasingly, however, concern for research on important, real world problems has been shown by researchers—with attention being addressed to research on decision making in areas such as technological hazards (Kates, 1977).

Grounding theories of individual and collective choice in behavioral science theory. Many of the conclusions drawn from research on judgment and choice pertain to limited behaviors in specific situations. These conclusions could be more useful both for advancing the scientific knowledge of the field and for improving decision-making strategies if they were integrated into behavioral science theories. For example, the availability heuristic could be understood more fully if it could be integrated into a general theory of the psychological aspects of probabilistic judgment. Finding isolated situations in which judgment behaviors deviate from our expectations is a useful way to empirically generate hypotheses regarding judgmental processes; but understanding these processes depends upon mapping them within the domain of relevant theories of cognitive, perceptual, and/or motivational processes. An abundant literature on cognitive processes is developing (e.g., see Bourne, et al., 1979), and advances have been made in placing human judgment more firmly within the literature on social interaction (e.g., Rappoport & Summers, 1973). Attempts to integrate literature from the various fields related to decision, such as the discussion of findings from judgment and attribute theory research (Fischhoff, 1976), are likely to become more numerous.

Advances in Applied Decision Making

A number of strategies for improving applied decision making have been suggested in this volume. In the future, it appears that strategies for improving decision making are likely to develop in several important directions. Among the future developments that are anticipated are: (1) use of applied decision strategies that consider the needs and capabilities of decision makers, (2) further attention to developing normative strategies based upon behavioral science theory and research, (3) further attention to designing organizational structures and procedures for effective information exchange and decision making, and (4) more extensive use of sophisticated analytic techniques such as Multiattribute Utility Analysis in organizations.

Using applied decision strategies that consider needs and capabilities of decision makers. It appears likely that further attention will be given to accommodating the needs and capabilities of real-world decision makers in specifying decision aids. The research findings from both laboratory and field settings have pointed out that improvements in decision making depend upon providing decision aids which decision makers are both able and willing to use (Brown, 1970). In the use of decision analysis, for example, better estimates of the probabilistic aspects of the decision problem can be obtained if relatively nondemanding methods for assessing subjective probabilities are used and if adequate training in the use of the methods is given.

Similar concerns have been expressed by researchers attempting to "fit" the cognitive styles of management scientists and clients (Doktor & Hamilton, 1973), and in specifying an information system appropriate to the use of the information (Bariff & Lusk, 1977). Concern for the acceptance of decision aids by clients is expected to lead to further attempts to devise ways to reduce client resistance to their use. The key to overcoming the resistance to these techniques may possibly be found by advancing our knowledge of the behavioral aspects of decision making. Decision makers are likely to resist techniques that are not consonant with the way in which the human thought processes work, and it seems likely that decision aids based upon an adequate understanding of the behavioral aspects of human decision-making processes would be better received by decision makers. Development of decision aids which take into account the behavioral aspects of decision makers, and the social and organizational features of their environments, should receive further attention in developing decision support systems.

Developing normative strategies based on behavioral science theory and research. Advances in developing normative decision-making strategies based on bahavioral science theory and research have been very promising. The Vroom and Yetton (1973) participation tree, which specifies how subordinates should be involved in making decisions for which their superiors are responsible, is one such normative strategy. Other normative strategies based upon descriptive theory and research are Delphi (Helmer, 1977) and the Nominal Group Technique (Delbecq, et al., 1975). The latter two strategies prescribe how social influences can be used to facilitate group decision making—and how dysfunctional social influences can be avoided. A common feature of decision-making strategies of this type is that they bridge the gap between the descriptive and normative literatures.

As we discussed earlier, deriving normative strategies from descriptive theory and research presents several difficulties. Frequently, the objective of behavioral science research is to describe relationships between variables in order to better understand the processes involved. For example, research on leadership styles and performance of work groups attempted to correlate these two variables and to conclude that high production work groups tended to be led by employee-centered supervisors. Yet, correlational research of this type does not specify the direction of causal relationships between the variables. Does the leader's style produce high production levels in the group; or do high producing groups bring out certain types of behaviors in their leaders? This distinction is essential to developing normative strategies. One needs to be able to say with confidence that modifying a leader's style by a training program will lead to high levels of production in the leader's work group.

Descriptive research based on experimental designs overcomes this limitation and provides a better foundation for prescribing normative strategies. If a researcher can change one or more of the variables in an experiment and observe the influence of these changes on other variables, then the researcher has more conclusive evidence regarding causal influences. One might conduct an experiment in which people who have various styles of leadership are randomly assigned to work groups, then measure the production levels of the work groups. If other influences on production levels are controlled (e.g., skills of group members), this experiment could provide evidence for specifying a normative strategy for leadership styles. Experimental behavioral science research, then, is important if normative strategies for improving decision making are to be developed.

Other limitations of behavioral science research as a basis for normative strategies to guide decisions made in organizations pertains to the people who are studied and the research sites. Ideally, one would like to specify strategies that would be effectively used by people actually making decisions in organizations. Research using university students making choices in the laboratory presents difficulties in generalizing the findings to people in organizations. Do the university students have the same motivations and abilities as organizational decision makers? Are all important influences on decisions that exist in organizations represented in a laboratory experiment? These and other limitations make it difficult to formulate normative strategies for making applied decisions in organizations on the basis of behavioral science research. Goodman and her coworkers (1978) have discussed difficulties in improving the assessment of probabilities; many other aspects of decision making are similarly limited by research subjects and sites.

Despite the limitations in current behavioral science research, it appears likely that further normative strategies will be prescribed to guide applied decision making—and that behavioral science research and theory will be used in advancing these strategies. How can behavioral science descriptive research provide a more conclusive basis for normative strategies? Generally, confirming research findings in more than one research site (e.g., in the laboratory and in the field) adds to their conclusiveness. Similarly, using both experiments and correlational research designs to study phenomena provides a more convincing evidence.

Perhaps the best basis for developing normative strategies to guide decisions made in organizations is the field experiment. Field experiments involve changing variables of interest in actual organizations and observing the effects of these manipulations on the organization. Although relatively few organizational experiments with implications for decision making have been conducted, it seems likely that more organizational experiments will be done in the future. Developments in quasi-experimental research designs (which supply some evidence regarding direction of causal influences among variables but don't require all features of full experimental research) have made organizational experiments much more feasible than in the past. Taylor and Vertinsky (1981) discuss these issues in greater detail and suggest research designs for experimenting with organizational behavior.

Designing organizational structures and procedures for information exchange and decision making. Another area that appears likely to show considerable development in the near future involves designing structures and procedures for efficient exchange of information in organizations. This, of course, has direct implications for decision making since effective decisions depend heavily upon input of appropriate information. The design of information structures to facilitate managerial decision making has occupied the attention of the field of management information systems and many techniques for aiding applied decisions have been advanced by people working in this field. Similarly, a great deal of research attention has been devoted by organizational theorists to understanding how organizational structures (e.g., matrix structures) influence the behavior and performance of people working in organizations.

To date, however, relatively little effort has been made toward merging these literatures and attempting to derive strategies that can be used in applied decisions. One step in this direction is the work of Galbraith (1973) who has attempted to explain the manner in which information flows influence the effectiveness of organizations. Other researchers have examined how information contributes power to those holding it and have suggested strategies for the effective use of information as an organizational resource. It appears likely that the design of both information systems and organizational structures will be influenced to a greater degree by contributions from organizational behavior. Hence, applied information systems will be developed which take into account the needs and capabilities of both individual decision makers and the social and organizational contexts in which they live.

Use of sophisticated analytic techniques such as multiattribute utility analysis in organizations. Decision analysis has emerged as one of the most promising approaches for improving decisions made in organizations. It provides a systematic method for analyzing complex, dynamic, and uncertain decision situations and represents a merger of the philosophy of decision theory and the systems and modeling methods of systems analysis. In performing a decision analysis, a decision maker typically will decompose and structure a problem, assess the uncertainties and values of the possible outcomes, and try to determine the optimal course of action. A great many applications of decision analysis have been reported (e.g., Howard, et al., 1972; Brown, et al., 1974).

A decision analytic technique that has demonstrated considerable value in applied decision making is Multiattribute Utility Analysis (MAU), which we discussed in Chapter 4. MAU attempts to determine a single measure of overall utility for a decision alternative that has more than one important attribute and, hence, must be judged in the light of more than one criterion. The normative theory of MAU specifies that the weighted utilities for an object be computed and summed across all attributes that characterize the alternative. For example, in using MAU to help teachers find jobs, Huber (1980) described an application in which utilities for various aspects of jobs (e.g., location, type of position, community size, etc.) were summed up. MAU has been widely used in the past decade and has been found to be very robust with respect to omitting minor attributes of decision alternatives. Its usefulness in organizational contexts is enhanced since it appears likely that most of the important attributes can be quantified and included in MAU.

In the future it appears likely that decision makers in organizations will increasingly rely upon sophisticated analytic techniques such as MAU. One difficulty in using these decision-analytic techniques in the past has been due to frictions between decision makers and the decision analysts who advise the decision makers in the use of these techniques. As decision makers become more knowledgeable in the applications of decision-analytic techniques, these frictions may diminish. Applied decision makers who understand decision analysis would be more realistic regarding what it can be expected to do and, in many cases, would be capable of conducting decision analyses on their own. Finally, it appears likely that many of the behavioral and organizational influences discussed in this volume will be built into decision analyses performed in the future.

SUMMARY

In this chapter the current state of behavioral decision making was assessed and some suggestions were made regarding future advances in its theory, research, and practice. Despite the wealth of techniques that are available for making decisions, many of them quantitative, relatively little is known about how these techniques can best be used by human decision makers and in organizational contexts. The merging of decision analysis and organizational behavior reflected in this book holds promise for meeting this need.

Advances in theory and research of behavioral decision making signaled in this chapter include: 1. using a greater variety of models to describe how decisions are made in organizations, 2. reevaluating traditionally used research methods to insure that important issues are not omitted from study, and 3. grounding new theories for decision-making phenomena more firmly within established theories. Advances in applied decision making suggested in this chapter are: 1. using strategies that take into account the characteristics of human decision makers and organizations, 2. basing prescriptions for improved decision making on conclusive findings from descriptive research, 3. further attention to designing structures and procedures for efficient information exchange in organizations, and 4. increasing acceptance and use of techniques developed within decision analysis (such as MAU) for making decisions in organizational contexts.

Behavioral decision making has emerged rather recently, but this focus for understanding and improving decision making is well-grounded both in behavioral science and decision analysis. It represents a timely merging of these fields. Behavioral research has produced many conclusions based on empirical studies that explain how decisions are made and, particularly, how decisions are made and implemented in organizations. The quantitatively based approaches to decision making have developed a number of normative techniques to assist in applied decision making. Behavioral decision making, therefore, has sprung from an awareness of representatives of each field that the time has come to learn and use developments in the other fields. Developing and applying normative decision-making strategies with appropriate understanding of the implications for human decision makers working in organizations holds considerable promise for advancing our understanding and practice of decision making.

APPENDIX

DETERMINING PROBABILITIES

Types of Events

Basic axioms of probability theory can be used to calculate either objective or subjective probabilities for events. An *event* is a single possible outcome of an experimental *trial* (e.g., a roll of a pair of dice is a trial and the two numbers that appear on top of the pair of dice represent an event). Three types of events may occur:

1. Mutually exclusive events—the probabilities of all events can be added to determine the probability that at least one of the events will occur on any given trial.
2. Dependent events—the probability of the occurrence of one event will be affected by the occurrence of another event.
3. Independent events—the probability of the occurrence of one event will not be affected by the occurrence of another event.

In determining probability of occurrence when more than one event is being considered, it is useful to differentiate among *conditional probability, unconditional probability,* and *joint probability.* In indicating these distinctions, it is conventional to use the symbol $\cup$ to indicate "or," the symbol $\cap$ to indicate "and," and to write the conditional probability of an event (X), given the occurrence of another event (Y), as $P(X \mid Y)$. Hence, conditional probability is the probability of one event when another event is known to have occurred. Joint probability is the probability that two or more events will occur, and is written as $P(X \cap Y)$. Unconditional probability is the probability of an event independent of the occurrence of any other event, and is written as $P(X)$.

Rules of Probability

Rules of probability are useful in applying probability theory to decision making. Among the more valuable rules are the *addition rule* and the *multiplication rule.* In calculating the probability of either one or the other of two mutually exclusive events (X or Y) occurring, the addition rule specifies that their unconditional probabilities should be added in the following manner:

$$
\begin{aligned}
& P(X \cup Y) = P(X) + P(Y) \\
\text{If:} \quad & P(X) = 0.2 \text{ and } P(Y) = 0.8 \\
\text{Then:} \quad & P(X \cup Y) = 0.2 + 0.8 \\
\text{And:} \quad & P(X \cup Y) = 1.0
\end{aligned}
$$

The multiplication rule is used to determine the joint probability of events. When two events are independent (X and Y), the product of their unconditional probabilities gives the probability of both events occurring.

$$
\begin{aligned}
& P(X \cap Y) = P(X) \bullet P(Y) \\
\text{If:} \quad & P(X) = 0.2 \text{ and } P(Y) = 0.8 \\
\text{Then:} \quad & P(X \cap Y) = 0.2 \bullet 0.8 \\
\text{And:} \quad & P(X \cap Y) = 0.16
\end{aligned}
$$

To find the joint probability of two events which are not independent, the multiplication rule incorporates the notion of conditional probability. Thus, the conditional probability of event X is multiplied by the unconditional probability of event Y:

$$
\begin{aligned}
& P(X \cap Y) = P(X \mid Y) \bullet P(Y) = \frac{P(X \cup Y)}{(P(Y)} \bullet P(Y) \\
\text{And:} \quad & P(X \cap Y) = \frac{P(X) \bullet P(Y)}{P(Y)} \bullet P(Y) \\
\text{If:} \quad & P(X) = .02 \text{ and } P(Y) = 0.8 \\
\text{Then:} \quad & P(X \cap Y) = \frac{0.2 \bullet 0.8}{0.8} \bullet 0.8 \\
\text{And:} \quad & P(X \cap Y) = \frac{0.16}{0.8} \bullet 0.8 = 0.16
\end{aligned}
$$

Determining the probability of either one or the other of two not mutually exclusive events occurring involves adding their unconditional probabilities and subtracting the probability of their joint occurrence:

$$
\begin{aligned}
& P(X \cup Y) = P(X) + P(Y) - P(X \cap Y) \\
\text{If:} \quad & P(X) = 0.2 \text{ and } P(Y) = 0.8 \\
\text{Then:} \quad & P(X \cup Y) = 0.2 + 0.8 - 0.16 \\
\text{And:} \quad & P(X \cup Y) = 1.00 - 0.16 = 0.84
\end{aligned}
$$

Bayesian Probabilistic Model

To revise probabilities of independent events as traditional information is acquired, another rule can be used. The probability of event X, given the occurrence of event Y, can be found by dividing the probability of the joint occurrence of the two events by the independent probability of event Y. Therefore:

$$P(X|Y) = \frac{P(X \cap Y)}{P(Y)}$$

$$\text{And:} \quad P(X|Y) = \frac{P(X) \bullet P(Y)}{P(Y)}$$

$$\text{If:} \quad P(X) = 0.2 \text{ and } P(Y) = 0.8$$

$$\text{Then:} \quad P(X|Y) = \frac{0.2 \bullet 0.8}{0.8}$$

$$\text{And:} \quad P(X|Y) = \frac{0.16}{0.8} = 0.2$$

When making decisions, generally one has some hunches regarding what is likely to happen (e.g., an item being purchased for a specified price, a stock price going down). Yet, before making a decision a person may gather additional information to be more certain of reaching a high-quality decision. The Bayes theorem, given above in a simple form, represents one approach to prescribing the optimal influence that additional information would be expected to have on a decision maker's judgment about the decision outcome. This theorem, first stated by Thomas Bayes in 1736, permits one to specify the likelihood that a particular hypothesis is correct. The present use of the theorem in probability revision is due to the work of Von Neumann and Morgenstern (1944); Edwards (e.g., 1961) has been influential in communicating the approach to behavioral researchers. In using this method for determining the optimal revision of opinions in the light of additional information, the optimal contribution of each element in a sequence of information is specified by using the posterior probability computed for one item as the prior probability for determining the contribution of the next item to be processed, and so forth for each subsequent item of information.

Given mutually exclusive and exhaustive hypotheses, H, and an item of information, D, the Bayes theorem specifies that:

$$P(H_i|D) = P(D|H_i)P(H_i) \Big| \sum_{k=i}^{n} P(D|H_k)P(H_k).$$

Here, $P(H_i|D)$ is the posterior probability of H_i, taking into account the available evidence D. $P(D|H_i)$ is the likelihood that D would be observed if hypothesis (H_i) were true. The diagnostic impact of the evidence on one hypothesis relative to another hypothesis is represented by the ratio of these likelihoods. The value $P(H_i)$ is the prior probability of the hypothesis H_i. This equation can be expanded to handle several items of evidence.

When two items of information are conditionally independent (D_1 and D_2) the appropriate formula is:

$$P(H_i \mid D_1, D_2) = P(D_1 \mid H_i)P(D_2 \mid H_i) \mid \sum_{k=1}^{n} P(D_1 \mid H_k)P(D_2 \mid H_k)P(H_i)$$

Therefore, the usual form of the theorem is the likelihood ratio. This is also called the odds-likelihood ratio, or the computation of odds. In this form of the Bayes theorem, two possible hypotheses generally are specified and the term *odds* refers to the likelihood of one hypothesis being supported by the data rather than the other hypothesis. To place this in the context of the lens model, when there are two possible states of the world, H_i and H_j, the likelihood ratio of the cue will determine the weight assigned to it. Hence, the relationship between a multivalued cue and a judge's response is shown in the differences among the likelihood ratios of the various values of the cue (D), instead of by a correlation coefficient. The likelihood ratio for the cue is:

$$P(D \mid H_1)/P(D \mid H_2)$$

An example of bayesian opinion revision. To illustrate the manner in which odds can be modified as data are acquired, and the individualistic nature of these probability revisions, consider the views held by two people regarding their health. Jim considers himself to be frail and susceptible to many illnesses. He works as a proofreader for a publishing company and has just completed proofreading an article on heart attacks for a medical journal. He suspects that there is one chance in five that he will have a heart attack. George considers himself to be healthy and has never worried about illness. Yet, he feels that there may be one chance in one thousand that he may suffer a heart attack. The odds for each person, then, are

$$\text{odds (heart attack)} = \frac{\text{p(heart attack)}}{\text{p(not heart attack)}}$$

$$\text{Jim's odds (heart attack)} = \frac{\text{p(heart attack)}}{\text{p(not heart attack)}}$$

$$= \frac{.02}{.08} = .25 \text{ or (1 to 4)}$$

$$\text{George's odds (heart attack)} = \frac{\text{p(heart attack)}}{\text{p(not heart attack)}}$$

$$= \frac{.0001}{.9999} = .0001 \text{ or (1 to 10,000)}$$

Both individuals have annual medical examinations and the tests indicate that both have heart disorders which may lead to heart attacks. The Bayes theorem can be used to determine how to modify their prior probabilities regarding the likelihood of having a heart attack in light of the evidence from the medical examination. The Bayes theorem suggests that the quality of the evidence yielded by the medical tests depends on how likely it is that the evidence would occur given that either hypothesis being considered is true. That is, how likely is it that a positive test indicating a heart disorder would occur if (a) the person *does not* have the heart disorder, or (b) the person *does* have the heart disorder? Since the test for a heart disorder is not perfect, a positive test does not always mean that the patient has the heart disorder. In this particular test, let's suppose that the chance of a positive test is 0.9 when a person does have the heart disorder and 0.05 when a person does not have the heart disorder. Hence, the likelihood ratio for the medical test data is:

$$\text{likelihood ratio (heart disorder)} = \frac{p(\text{positive test} \mid \text{heart disorder})}{p(\text{positive test} \mid \text{no heart disorder})}$$

$$\text{likelihood ratio (heart disorder)} = \frac{0.9}{0.05} = 180$$

The relative odds of a positive test result given the heart disorder are 180 to 1. Next, the prior expectations for Jim and George are combined with the test evidence to find the likelihood of a heart disorder leading to a heart attack, given the initial expectations and the test evidence. The Bayes theorem gives this as:

$$\text{new odds} = \text{likelihood ratio} \times \text{prior odds}$$

$$\text{Jim's new odds (heart attack)} = 180 \times .25$$
$$= 45 \text{ or } (45 \text{ to } 1)$$

$$\text{George's new odds (heart attack)} = 180 \times .0001$$
$$= .018 \text{ or (about 1 to 50)}$$

These results suggest that Jim is almost certain that he has the heart disorder, but that George is more skeptical; yet both received the same medical test results. For Jim the odds of 45 to 1 that he has a heart disorder give a subjective probability of 45/46 or .98; for George the odds are 50 to 1 against having the heart disorder, yielding a subjective probability of 1/51 or about .02. Clearly, the basis for their different subjective probabilities of having a heart attack is their differing initial expectations about how likely it was that they would have heart attacks.

In this method, additional information is used to modify initial expectations concerning the relative probabilities of events and to form new estimates of those probabilities. The quality of the new evidence (i.e., the likelihood ratio) determines the extent of probability revision. This approach to opinion revision is logical in that it reflects changes in expectations as a result of experience. Each item of information may slightly alter our opinion one way or the other. Generally, people who initially hold a skeptical attitude require a great deal of high-quality evidence before they will change their minds; whereas, those who initially believe are hard to convince otherwise. A person with hypochrondriacal tendencies will need only limited evidence to believe that a heart attack is highly possible. On the other hand, a person who expects to have good health will require a great deal of medical evidence to believe that a heart attack is a strong possibility.

Bayes model and optimal judgments: The Accuracy Ratio. The optimality of judgments can be determined with the Bayes theorem by comparing the actual behavior of individuals and the manner in which they use subjective probabilities with the known conditional probabilities of the theorem. Hence, the model can detect systematic deviations of actual behavior from the predictions of the model. An *accuracy ratio* has been suggested (Peterson & Miller, 1965) to directly compare subjective estimates and Bayesian probabilities. The accuracy ratio (i.e., AR = SLLR/BLLR) involves the use of the Bayesian log likelihood ratio (BLLR) and the log likelihood ratio derived from a decision maker's probability estimates (SLLR). This index measures the extent to which an optimal probability strategy is used by a decision maker to revise judgments on the basis of new information. It uses log likelihood ratios to make the optimal responses linear with the amount of evidence favoring one hypothesis over another. This index can be used to summarize departures from an optimal strategy for one or for many items of information.

REFERENCES

Adams, J. S. Inequity in social exchange. In L. Berkowitz (Ed.), *Advances in experimental social psychology* (Vol. 2). New York: Academic Press, 1965.

Albertson, L., & Cutler, T. Delphi and the image of the future. *Futures,* 1976, 8, 397–404.

Alexis, M., Haines, G. H., Jr., & Simon, L. Consumer information processing: The case of women's clothing. In R. L. King (Ed.), *Marketing and the new science of planning.* Chicago: American Marketing Association, 1968.

Allen, M. S. *Morphological creativity.* Englewood Cliffs, N.J.: Prentice-Hall, 1962.

Allen, T. J., & Cohen, S. I. Information flow in research and development laboratories. *Administrative Science Quarterly,* 1969, 14, 12–20.

Allison, G. T. *The essence of decision.* Boston: Little, Brown, 1971.

Allport, F. H. *Theories of perception and the concept of structure.* New York: Wiley, 1955.

Alpert, M., & Raiffa, H. *A progress report on the training of probability assessors.* unpublished manuscript, 1969.

Anderson, N. H. Cognitive algebra: Integration theory as applied to social attribution. In L. Berkowitz (Ed.), *Advances in experimental social psychology,* (Vol. 7). New York: Academic Press, 1973.

Ansoff, H. I. *Corporate strategy.* New York: McGraw-Hill, 1965.

Argyris, C. Some limits of rational man organization theory. *Public Administration Review,* 1973, May-June, 253–267.

Armstrong, J., Denniston, W. B., & Gordon, M. M. The use of the decomposition principle in making judgments. *Organizational Behavior and Human Performance,* 1975, 14, 257–263.

Arnold, J. E. Useful creative techniques. In S. J. Parnes (Ed.), *A sourcebook for creative thinking.* New York: Scribner's, 1962, 251–268.

Arrow, K. A. *Social choice and individual values.* New York: Wiley, 1951.

Arrowood, A. J., & Ross, L. Anticipated effort and subjective probability. *Journal of Personality and Social Psychology,* 1966, 4, 57–64.

Aschenbrenner, K. M., & Kasubek, W. Convergence of multiattribute evaluations when different sorts of attributes are used. In H. Jungerman, & G. de Zeeuw (Eds.), *Proceedings of the fifth research conference on subjective probability, utility, and decision making,* 1976.

Ashby, W. R. *An introduction to cybernetics.* New York: Wiley, 1956.

Athanassiades, J. C. The distortion of upward communication in hierarchical organizations. *Academy of Management Journal,* 1973, 16, 207–226.

Atkinson, J. W., & Feather, N. T. (Eds.). *A theory of achievement motivation.* New York: Wiley, 1966.

Aumann, R. J. Subjective programming. In M. W. Shelley, & G. L. Bryan (Eds.), *Human judgment and optimality.* New York: Wiley, 1964.

Back, K. The exertion of influence through social communication. *Journal of Abnormal and Social Psychology,* 1951, 47, 9–24.

Baldridge, J. F. *Power and conflict in the university.* New York: Wiley, 1971.

Balma, M. J. The concept of synthetic validity. *Personnel Psychology,* 1959, 12, 395–396.

Bariff, M. L., & Lusk, E. J. Cognitive and personality tests in designing MIS. *Management Science,* 1977, 23, 820–829.

Barnlund, D. C. A comparative study of individual, majority, and group judgment. *Journal of Abnormal and Social Psychology,* 1959, 58, 55–60.

Baumd, W. J. *Economic theory and operations analysis* (3rd ed.). Englewood Cliffs, N.J.: Prentice-Hall, 1972.

Bavelas, A. Communication patterns in task-oriented groups. *Journal of the Acoustical Society of America,* 1950, 22, 725–730.

Beach, L. R., Townes, B. D., Campbell, F. L., & Keating, G. W. Developing and testing a decision aid for birth planning decisions. *Organizational Behavior and Human Performance,* 1976, 15, 99–116.

Becker, G. M., & McClintock, C. G. Value: Behavioral decision theory. *Annual Review of Psychology, 1967, 18, 107–186.*

Bellman, R. E., & Dreyfus, S. E. Applied dynamic programming. Santa Monica, Calif.: Rand Corporation, 1962.

Benbasat, I., & Dexter, A. S. Value and events approaches to accounting: An experimental evaluation. Working Paper No. 488, Faculty of Commerce and Business Administration, University of British Columbia, 1977.

Benbasat, I., & Taylor, R. N. The impact of cognitive styles on information system design. *Management Information System Quarterly,* 1978, June, 43–54.

Berkowitz, L. Group standards, cohesiveness, and productivity. *Human Relations,* 1954, 7, 509–519.

Bettman, J. A graph theory approach to comparing consumer information processing models. *Management Science,* 1971, 18, 114–129.

Birkin, S. J., & Ford, J. S. The quality/quantity dilemma: The impact of a zero defects program. In J. L. Cochrane, & M. Zeleny (Eds.), *Multiple criteria decision making.* Columbia, S.C.: University of South Carolina Press, 1973, 517–529.

Block, J., & Petersen, P. Some personality correlates of confidence, caution, and speed in a decision situation. *Journal of Abnormal Social Psychology,* 1955, 51, 34–41.

Bouchard, T. J., Jr. Personality, problem-solving procedure and performance in small groups. *Journal of Applied Psychology, Monograph,* 1969.

Bouchard, T. J., Jr., & Hare, M. Size, performance and potential in brainstorming groups. *Journal of Applied Psychology,* 1970, 51–55.

Bouchard, T. J., Jr., Barsaloux, J., & Drauden, G. Brainstorming procedure, group size, and sex as determinants of the problem-solving effectiveness of groups and individuals. *Journal of Applied Psychology,* 1974, 135–138.

Bourne, L. E., Dominowski, R. C., & Loftus, E. F. *Cognitive processes.* Englewood Cliffs, N.J.: Prentice-Hall, 1979.

Bowers, K. S. The psychology of subtle control: An attributional analysis of behavioral persistence. *Canadian Journal of Behavioral Science,* 1975, 7, 78–95.

Boyd, D. W., Howard, R. A., Matheson, J. E., & North, D. W. *Decision analysis of hurricane modification.* Menlo Park, Calif.: Stanford Research Institute, 1971.

Bransford, J. D., & Johnson, M. K. Contextual prerequisites for understanding: Some investigations of comprehension and recall. *Journal of Verbal Learning and Verbal Behavior,* 1972, 11, 717–726.

Braunstein, D., & Ungson, G. R. (Eds.). *Decision Making,* Kent Publishing Co., 1982.

Braybrooke, D., & Lindblom, C. E. *A strategy of decision.* New York: The Free Press, 1963.

Brengelmann, J. C. Abnormal and personality correlates of certainty. *Journal of Mental Science,* 1959, 105, 142–162.

Brown, R. V. Do managers find decision theory useful? *Harvard Business Review,* 1970, 48, 78–89.

Brown, R. V., Kahr, A. S., & Peterson, C. *Decision analysis for the manager.* New York: Holt, Rinehart and Winston, 1974.

Bruner, J. S., Goodnow, J. J., & Austin, G. A. *A study of thinking.* New York: Wiley, 1956.

Brunswick, E. *Perception and the representative design of experiments.* Berkeley, Calif.: University of California Press, 1956.

Bryan, J. F., & Locke, E. A. Goal setting as a means for increasing motivation. *Journal of Applied Psychology,* 1967, 53, 274–277.

Buchanan, J. M., & Tullock, G. *The calculus of consent.* Ann Arbor: University of Michigan Press, 1962.

Campbell, J. P., Dunnette, M. D., Lawler, E. E., & Weick, K. E., Jr. *Managerial behavior, performance, and effectiveness.* New York: McGraw-Hill, 1970.

Carroll, J. S. Analyzing decision behavior: The magician's audience. In T. S. Wallsten (Ed.) *Cognitive Process in Choice and Decision Behavior.* Hillsdale, N.J.: Erlbaum, 1980, 125–148.

Carter, E. E. The behavioral theory of the firm and top-level corporate decision. *Administrative Science Review,* 1971, 16, 413–429.

Cattell, R. B. *A universal index for psychological factors.* Urbana: Laboratory of Personnel Assessment and Group Behavior, University of Illinois, 1953.

Cattell, R. B. The personality and motivation of the researcher from measurements of contemporaries and from biography. In C. W. Taylor & F. Barron (Eds.), *Scientific creativity: Its recognition and development.* New York: Wiley, 1963.

Cattell, R. B., & Butcher, H. J. *The prediction of achievement and creativity.* New York: Bobbs-Merrill, 1968.

Child, J. Organizational structure, environment, and performance: The role of strategic choice. *Sociology,* 1972, 6, 1–22.

Churchman, C. W. *Hegelian inquiring systems: Space sciences: Lab social sciences project.* University of California, 1966.

Churchman, C. W., & Ackoff, R. L. An approximate measure of value. *Journal of the Operations Research Society of America,* 1954, 2, 172–187.

Churchman, C. W., Ackoff, R. L., & Arnoff, E. L. *Operations Research.* New York: Wiley, 1957.

Churchman, C. W., Auerbach, L., & Sadan, S. *Thinking for decisions: Deductive quantitative methods.* Chicago: Science Research Associates, 1975.

Clarkson, G. P. *Portfolio selection: A simulation of trust investment.* Englewood Cliffs, N.J.: Prentice-Hall, 1962.

Cofer, C. N., & Appley, M. H. *Motivation: Theory and research.* New York: Wiley, 1964.

Cohen, A. R. Upward communication in experimentally created hierarchies. *Human Relations,* 1958, 11, 41–53.

Cohen, A. R. Situational structure, self-esteem, and threat-oriented reactions to power. In D. Cartwright (Ed.), *Studies in social power.* Ann Arbor, Mich.: Institute for Social Research, 1959.

Cohen, D., Whitmyre, J. W., & Funk, W. H. Effect of group cohesiveness and training upon creative thinking. *Journal of Applied Psychology,* 1960, 319–322.

Cohen, M. D., March, J. G., & Olsen, J. P. A garbage can model of organizational choice. *Administrative Science Quarterly,* 1972, 17, 1–25.

Coleman, J. S. The possibility of a social welfare function. *The American Economic Review,* 1966, 56, 1105–1122.

Collins, B. E., & Guetzkow, H. *A social psychology of group processes for decision making.* New York: Wiley, 1964.

Collins, B. F., & Raven, B. Group structure: Attraction, coalitions, communications, and power. In G. Lindzey, & E. Aronson (Eds.), *The handbook of social psychology.* Reading, Mass.: Addison-Wesley, 1969.

Connolly, T. Information processing and decision making in organizations. In B. M. Staw, & G. R. Salancik (Eds.), *New directions in organizational behavior.* Chicago: St. Clair, 1977.

Courtright, J. A. A laboratory investigation of groupthink. *Communication Monographs,* 1978, 45, 229–245.

Cronbach, L. J. *Essentials of psychological testing* (3rd ed.). New York: Harper & Row, 1970.

Cronbach, L. J. The two disciplines of scientific psychology. *American Psychologist,* 1957, 12, 671–684.

Cronbach, L. J., & Gleser, G. *Psychological tests and personnel decisions.* Urbana: University of Illinois Press, 1965.

Crovitz, H. F. *Galton's walk.* New York: Harper and Row, 1970.

Cummings, L. L. Organizational behavior. *Annual Review of Psychology,* 1982, 33, 541–580.

Cyert, R. M., & DeGroot, M. H. Multiperiod decisions models with alternating choice as a solution to the duopoly problem. *Quarterly Journal of Economics,* 1970, 84, 410–429.

Cyert, R. M., & MacCrimmon, K. R. Organizations. In G. Lindzey & E. Aronson (Eds.), *The handbook of social psychology.* Reading, Mass: Addison-Wesley, 1968.

Cyert, R. M., & March, J. G. *A behavioral theory of the firm.* Englewood Cliffs, N.J.: Prentice-Hall, 1963.

Davis, G. A., & Manski, M. E. An instructional method for increasing originality. *Psychonomic Science,* 1966, 6, 73–74.

Dawes, R. M. Graduate admissions: A case study. *The American Psychologist,* 1971, 26, 180–188.

Dawes, R. M., & Corrigan, B. Linear models in decision making. *Psychological Bulletin,* 1974, 81, 95–106.

Dearborn, D. C., & Simon, H. A. Selective perception: A note on the departmental identification of executives. *Sociometry,* 1958, 21, 140–144.

Delbecq, A. L., Van de Ven, A. H., & Gustafson, D. H. *Group techniques for program planning.* Glenview, Ill.: Scott, Foresman, 1975.

Dillon, P. C., Graham, W. K., & Aidells, A. L. Brainstorming on a 'hot' problem: Effects of training and practice on individual and group performance. *Journal of Applied Psychology,* 1972, 487–490.

Divesta, F. J., & Walls, R. T. Transfer of solution rules in problem solving. *Journal of Educational Psychology,* 1967, 58, 319–326.

Doktor, R. H., & Hamilton, W. T. Cognitive style and the acceptance of management science recommendations. *Management Science,* 1973, 19, 638–645.

Downs, A. *Inside bureaucracy.* Boston: Little, Brown, and Company, 1966.

Drake, A. W., & Keeney, R. L. *Decision analysis: A self-study on videotape.* Cambridge, Mass.: Massachusetts Institute of Technology, 1978.

Driver, M., & Mock, T. Human information processing, decision style theory, and accounting information systems. *Accounting Review,* 1975, 3, 490–508.

Drucker, P. F. Managing for business effectiveness. *Harvard Business Review,* 1963, 41, 53–60.

Ducharme, W. M. A response bias explanation of conservative human inference. *Journal of Experimental Psychology,* 1970, 85, 66–74.

Duncan, R. B. The ambidextrous organization: Designing dual structures for innovation. In R. Kelmann, L. Pondy, & D. Slevin (Eds.), *The management of organization design, research, and methodology* (Vol. 1). New York: North Holland, 1976, 167–188.

Dunnette, M. D. *Personnel selection and placement.* Belmont, Calif.: Wadsworth Publishing, 1966.

Dunnette, M. D., Campbell, J. P., & Jaastad, K. The effect of group participation on brainstorming effectiveness for two industrial samples. *Journal of Applied Psychology,* 1963, 47, 30–37.

Edwards, W. The theory of decision making. *Psychological Bulletin,* 1954, 51, 380–417.

Edwards, W. Behavioral decision theory. *Annual Review of Psychology,* 1961, 12, 473–498.

Edwards, W. Conservativism in human information processing. In B. Kleinmuntz (Ed.), *Formal representations of human judgment.* New York: Wiley, 1968.

Edwards, W. Comment. *Journal of the American Statistical Association,* 1975, 70, 291–293.

Ehrlich, D., Guttman, I., Schonback, P., & Mills, J. Post-decision exposure to relevant information. *Journal of Abnormal and Social Psychology,* 1957, 54, 98–102.

Einhorn, H. J. The use of nonlinear noncompensatory models in decision making. *Psychological Bulletin,* 1970, 73, 221–230.

Einhorn, H. J. Cue definition and residual judgment. *Organizational Behavior and Human Performance,* 1974, 12, 30–49.

Einhorn, H. J., & Hogarth, R. M. Behavioral decision theory: Processes of judgment and choice. *Annual Review of Psychology,* 1981, 32, 53–88.

Ellsberg, D. Risk, ambiguity and the Savage axioms. *Quarterly Journal of Economics,* 1961, 75, 643–652.

Elms, A. C. Role playing, incentive, and dissonance. *Psychological Bulletin,* 1967, 68, 132–148.

Ewing, D. E. *The human side of planning.* Toronto: Macmillan, 1969.

Falmagne, R. J. (Ed.). *Reasoning: Representation and process in children and adults.* Hillsdale, N.J.: Lawrence Erlbaum Associates, 1975.

Feldman, J., & Kanter, H. E. Organizational decision making. In J. G. March (Ed.), *Handbook of organizations.* Chicago: Rand McNally, 1965.

Ference, T. P. Organizational communications systems and the decision process, *Management Science,* 1970, 13, B83–96.

Festinger, L., Schachter, S., & Back, K. *Social pressures in informal groups: A study of human factors in housing.* New York: Harper, 1950.

Festinger, L. *A theory of cognitive dissonance.* Stanford, Calif.: Stanford University Press, 1957.

Fiedler, F. E. A contingency model of leadership effectiveness. In L. Berkowitz (Ed.), *Advances in experimental social psychology* (Vol. 1). New York: Academic Press, 1964.

Fischer, G. W. Four methods for assessing multiattribute utilities: An experimental evaluation. *Eng. Psychol. Lab. Tech. Rep. 0372300 6-T.* Ann Arbor: University of Michigan, 1972.

Fischer, G. W., & Edwards, W. *Technological aids for inference, evaluation, and decision making: A review of research and experience.* Technical report, Eng. Psychol. Lab., University of Michigan, Ann Arbor, Michigan, 1973.

Fischhoff, B. Hindsight: Thinking backward? *Oregon Research Institute Monograph,* 1969.

Fischhoff, B. Attribution theory and judgment under uncertainty. In J. H. Harvey, W. J. Ickes, & R. F. Kidd (Eds.), *New directions in attribution research.* Hillsdale, N.J.: Erlbaum, 1976.

Fishburn, P. C. Utility theory. *Management Science,* 1968, 14, 335–378.

Fleishman, E. A. Twenty years of consideration and structure. In E. A. Fleischman, & J. G. Hunt (Eds.), *Current developments in the study of leadership.* Carbondale: Southern Illinois University Press, 1973.

Flowers, M. L. A laboratory test of some implications of Janis' groupthink hypothesis. *Journal of Personality and Social Psychology,* 1977, 35, 888–895.

Franklin, B. A letter to Joseph Priestley, 1772. Reprinted in B. Franklin, *The Benjamin Franklin sampler.* New York: Fawcett Publications, 1956.

French, J. R. P., Jr., Kay, E. J., & Meyer, H. H. Participation and the appraisal system. Human Relations, 1966, 19, 3–20.

French, J. R. P., & Raven, B. The bases of social power. In D. Cartwright (Ed.), *Studies in social power.* Ann Arbor, Mich.: Institute for Social Research, 1959, 150–167.

Friedland, N., Arnold, S. E., & Thibaut, J. Motivational bases in mixed-motive interactions: The effects of comparison levels. *Journal of Experimental Social Psychology,* 1974, 188–199.

Friedman, M., & Savage, L. J. The utility analysis of choices involving risk. *Journal of Political Economy,* 1948, 56, 279–304.

Fructer, B. *Introduction to factor analysis.* Princeton, N.J.: Van Nostrand, 1954.

Galanter, E. The direct measurement of utility and subjective probability. *American Journal of Psychology,* 1962, 75, 208–220.

Galbraith, J. R. *Designing complex organizations.* Reading, Mass: Addison-Wesley, 1973.

Gamson, W. A. An experimental test of a theory of coalition formation. *American Sociological Review,* 1961, 26, 565–573.

Gamson, W. A. Coalition formation at presidential nominating conventions. *American Journal of Sociology,* 1962, 68, 157–171.

Gamson, W. A. Experimental studies of coalition formation. In L. Berkowitz (Ed.), *Advances in experimental social psychology* (Vol. 1). New York: Academic Press, 1964, 81–110.

George, C. Jr. *Management in industry.* Englewood Cliffs, N.J.: Prentice-Hall, 1964.

Gergen, K. J. *The psychology of behavior exchange.* Reading, Mass.: Addison-Wesley, 1969.

Gilchrist, J. C., Shaw, M. E., & Walker, L. C. Some effects of unequal distribution of information in a wheel group structure. *Journal of Abnormal and Social Psychology,* 1954, 54, 554–556.

Glanzer, M., & Glaser, R. Techniques for the study of group structure and behavior: II. Empirical studies of the effects of structure in small groups. *Psychological Bulletin,* 1961, 58, 1–27.

Glucksberg, S. The influence of strength of drive on functional fixedness and perceptual recognition. *Journal of Experimental Psychology,* 1962, 63, 36–51.

Goldsmith, R. W. Studies of a model for evaluating judicial evidence. *Acta Psychologica,* 45, 1981.

Goodman, B., Fischhoff, B., Lichtenstein, S., & Slovic, P. The training of decision makers. *Army Research Institute Technical Report TR-78-B3,* 1978.

Gordon, W. J. J. *Synectics.* New York: Harper & Row, 1961.

Gouldner, A. W. *The dialectic of ideology and technology.* New York: Seaburg, 1976.

Graesser, C. C., & Anderson, N. H. Cognitive algebra of the equation: Gift size = generosity × income. *Journal of Experimental Psychology,* 1974, 103, 692–699.

Granger, C. H. The hierarchy of objectives. *Harvard Business Review,* 1964, May-June, 63–74.

Grayson, C. J. *Decision under uncertainty.* Cambridge: Harvard University Press, 1960.

Guilford, J. R. The structure of intellect. *Psychological Bulletin,* 1956, 53, 267–293.

Guilford, J. P., & Merrifeld, P. R. The structure of intellect model: Its uses and implications. *Report of the Psychological Laboratory,* No. 24. Los Angeles: University of Southern California Press, 1960.

Guion, R. M. *Personnel testing.* New York: McGraw-Hill, 1965.

Haefele, J. W. *Creativity and innovation.* New York: Reinhold, 1962.

Halter, A. N., & Dean, G. W. *Decisions under uncertainty with research applications.* Cincinnati: South-Western Publishing Co., 1971.

Hamburg, M. *Statistical analysis for decision making* (2nd ed.). New York: Harcourt, Brace, Jovanovich, 1970.

Hammond, K. R. Computer graphics as an aid to learning. *Science,* 1971, 172, 908–908.

Hansberger, R. V. Bob Hansberger shows how to grow without becoming a conglomerate. In J. McDonald. *Fortune,* October 1969, 134.

Harleston, B. W. Task difficulty, anxiety level and ability level as factors affecting performance in a verbal learning situation. *Journal of Psychology,* 1963, 55, 165–168.

Harmon, H. H. *Modern factor analysis.* Chicago: University of Chicago Press, 1960.

Harrison, E. F. *The managerial decision-making process.* Boston: Houghton Mifflin, 1975.

Hayes, J. R. *Cognitive psychology: Thinking and creating.* Homewood, Ill.: Dorsey, 1978.

Hedberg, B. L. T., Nystrom, P. C., & Starbuck, W. H. Camping on seesaws: Prescriptions for a self-designing organization. *Administrative Science Quarterly,* 1976, 21, 41–65.

Hedlund, W., Sletton, I. W., Altman, H., & Evanson, R. C. Prediction of patients who are dangerous to others. *Journal of Clinical Psychology,* 1973, 29, 443–454.

Hegel, G. W. F. *The phenomenology of mind* (2nd ed.). London: George Allen and Unwin, 1964 (1820).

Heider, F. *The psychology of interpersonal relations.* New York: Wiley, 1958.

Helmer, O. Problems in future research: Delphi and causal cross impact analysis. *Futures,* 1977, 9, 17–31.

Helson, H. Adaptation-level as a basis for a quantitative theory of frames of reference. *Psychological Review,* 1948, 55, 297–313.

Hickson, D. J., Hinings, C. R., Lee, C. A., Schnuk, R. E., & Pennings, J. M. A strategic contingencies theory of intraorganizational power. *Administrative Science Quarterly,* 1971, 16, 216–224.

Hill, J. Q., & Fowles, J. The methodological worth of the Delphi forecasting technique. *Technological Forecasting and Social Change,* 1975, 7, 179–192.

Hoffman, J., & Peterson, C. R. A scoring rule to train probability assessors. *Engineering Psychology Laboratory Technical Report,* 037230-4-T, Ann Arbor: University of Michigan, 1972.

Hoffman, P. J., Slovic, P., & Rorer, L. G. An analysis-of-variance model for the assessment of configural cue utilization in clinical judgment. *Psychological Bulletin,* 1968, 68, 338–349.

Hoffman, R. L. Group problem solving. In L. Berkowitz (Ed.), *Group processes.* New York: Academic Press, 1965.

House, R. A path goal theory of leader effectiveness. *Administrative Science Quarterly,* 1971, 321–338.

Howard, R. A., Matheson, J. E., & North, D. W. The decision to seed hurricanes. *Science,* 1972, 176, 1191–1202.

Huber, E. Organizational information systems. *Management Science,* 28, 1982, 138–155.

Huber, P. *Managerial decision making.* Glenview, Ill.: Scott, Foresman, 1980.

Hull, C. L. *Principles of behavior.* New York: Appleton-Century-Crofts, 1943.

Hunt, E. B. *Artificial intelligence.* New York: Academic Press, 1975.

Ijiri, Y. Jadicke, R. K., & Knight, K. E. The effects of accounting alternatives on management decisions. In R. K. Jadicke, Y. Ijiri, & D. Nelson (Eds.), *Research in Accounting Management.* Chicago: American Accounting Association, 1966, 186–199.

Janis, I. L. *Victims of groupthink: A psychological study of foreign-policy decisions and fiascoes.* Boston: Houghton Mifflin, 1972.

Janis, I. L., & Mann, L. *Decision making: A psychological analysis of conflict, choice, and commitment.* New York: Free Press, 1977.

Jensen, F. A., & Peterson, C. R. Psychological effects of proper scoring rules. *Organizational Behavior and Human Performance,* 1973, 9, 307–317.

Johnsen, E. *Studies in multiobjective decision models.* Lund: Studentlitteratur, 1968.

Jones, E. E., & Goethals, G. R. Order effects in impression formation: Attribution context and the nature of the entity. In E. E. Jones, D. E. Kanouse, H. H. Kelley, R. E. Nisbett, S. Valins, & B. E. Weiner (Eds.), *Attribution: Perceiving the causes of behavior.* Morristown, N.J.: General Learning Press, 1972.

Jones, E. E., & Nisbett, R. E. The actor and the observer: Divergent perceptions of the causes of behavior. In E. E. Jones, D. E. Kanouse, H. H. Kelley, R. E. Nisbett, S. Valins, & B. E. Weiner (Eds.), *Attribution: Perceiving the causes of behavior.* Morristown, N.J.: General Learning Press, 1972.

Julian, J. W., Bishop, D. W., & Fiedler, F. E. Quasi-therapeutic effects on intergroup competition. *Journal of Personality and Social Psychology,* 1966, 3, 321–327.

Kahneman, D., & Tversky, A. Subjective probability: A judgment of representativeness. *Cognitive Psychology,* 1972, 3, 430–454.

Kahneman, D., & Tversky, A. On the psychology of prediction. *Psychological Review,* 1973, 80, 237-251.

Kahneman, D., & Tversky, A. *Prospect theory: An analysis of decisions under risk.* Unpublished manuscript, 1975.

Kanouse, D. C. Language, labeling, and attribution. In E. E. Jones, D. E. Kanouse, H. H. Kelley, R. E. Nisbett, S. Valins, & B. Weiner (Eds.), *Attribution: Perceiving the causes of behavior.* Morristown, N.J.: General Learning Press, 1972.

Kates, R. W. (Ed.). *Managing technological hazard: Research needs and opportunities.* University of Colorado, 1977.

Kaufman, H. *The forest ranger.* Baltimore: Johns Hopkins University Press, 1960.

Keeney, R. L., & Raiffa, H. *Decisions with multiple objectives: Preferences and value tradeoffs.* New York: Wiley, 1976.

Kelley, H. H. Attribution theory in social psychology. In D. Levines (Ed.), *Nebraska Symposium on Motivation.* Lincoln: University of Nebraska Press, 1967.

Kelley, H. H. The processes of causal attribution. *American Psychologist,* 1973, 28, 107–128.

Kepner, C. H., & Tregoe, B. B. *The rational manager.* New York: McGraw-Hill, 1965.

Keynes, J. M. *A treatise on probability.* London: Macmillan, 1921. Reprinted by Harper, 1962.

Kiesler, S. B. *Interpersonal processes in groups and organizations.* Arlington Heights, Ill.: AHM Publishing Corp., 1978.

Kimberly, J. R. Managerial innovation. In P. Nystrom & W. H. Starbuck (Eds.), *Handbook of organizational design* (Vol. 1). Oxford: Oxford University Press, 1981, 84–104.

Kleinmuntz, B. The processing of clinical information by man and machine. In B. Kleinmuntz (Ed.), *Formal representation of human judgment.* New York: Wiley, 1968.

Kneppreth, N. P., Gustafson, D. H., Leifer, R. P., & Johnson, E. M. *Techniques for the assessment of worth.* Technical paper 254. Arlington, Va.: Army Research Institute, 1974.

Knight, F. H. *Risk, uncertainty, and profit.* Clifton, N.J.: Kelley, 1920.

Kogan, N., & Wallach, M. A. Certainty of judgment and the evaluation of risk. *Psychological Reports,* 1960, 6, 207–213.

Kogan, N., & Wallach, M. A. *Risk taking: A study in cognition and personality.* New York: Holt, Rinehart, and Winston, 1964.

Kogan, N., & Wallach, M. A. Risk taking as a function of the situation, the person, and the group. In G. Mandlu (Ed.), *New directions in psychology,* III. New York: Holt, Rinehart, and Winston, 1967.

Kormorita, S. S., Sheposh, J. P., & Braver, S. L. Power of the use of power, and cooperative choice in a two-person game. *Journal of Personality and Social Psychology,* 1968, 8, 134–142.

Kort, F. A. A nonlinear model for the analysis of judicial decisions. *The American Political Science Review,* 1968, 62, 546–555.

Krantz, D. H., & Tversky, A. Conjoint-measurement analysis of composition rules in psychology. *Psychological Review,* 1971, 78, 151–169.

Kuehn, A. A., & Hamburger, H. J. A heuristic program for locating warehouses. *Management Science,* 1963, 9, 643-666.

Kun, A., & Weiner, B. Necessary versus sufficient causal schemata for success and failure. *Journal of Research in Personality,* 1973, 7, 197–207.

Kunreuther, H. Extensions of Bowman's theory on managerial decision making. *Management Science,* 1969, 15, 415–439.

Kunreuther, H. Limited knowledge and insurance protection. *Public Policy,* 1976, 24, 227–261.

Lachman, O. Personnel administration in a Delphi study. *Long Range Planning,* 1972, June, 21–24.

Lawler, E. E. *Motivation in work organizations.* New York: Wadsworth, 1973.

Leavitt, H. J. Some effects of certain communication patterns on group performance. *Journal of Abnormal Social Psychology,* 1951, 46, 38–50.

Lee, W. *Decision theory and human behavior.* New York: Wiley, 1971.

Lehman, H. C. *Age and achievement.* Princeton, N.J.: Princeton University Press, 1953.

Le Vine, R. A., & Campbell, D. T. *Ethnocentrism.* New York: Wiley, 1972.

Lewin, K., Lippitt, R., & White, R. K. Patterns of aggressive behaviour in experimentally created social climates. *Journal of Social Psychology,* 1939, 10, 271–299.

Lichtenstein, S. C., & Slovic, P. Response-induced reversals of preference in gambling: An extended replication in Las Vegas. *Journal of Experimental Psychology,* 1973, 101, 16–20.

Likert, R. *New patterns of management.* New York: McGraw-Hill, 1961.

Lindblom, C. E. The science of muddling through. *Public Administration Review,* 1959, 19, 79–88.

Lindblom, C. E. *The intelligence of democracy: Decision making through mutual adjustment.* New York: The Free Press, 1965.

Linder, D. E., Cooper, J., & Jones, E. E. Decision freedom as a determinant of the role of incentive magnitude in attitude change. *Journal of Personality and Social Psychology,* 1967, 5, 245-254.

Lindsay, P. H., & Norman, D. A. *An introduction to psychology.* New York: Academic Press, 1972.

Locke, E. A. Motivational effects of knowledge of results: Knowledge or goal setting. *Journal of Applied Psychology,* 1967, 51, 324–329.

Locke, E. A. The ubiquity of the technique of goal setting in theories of and approaches to employee motivation. *Academy of Management Review,* 1978, July, 47–61.

Lombardo, J. P., Tator, G. D., & Weiss, R. F. Performance changes in human conditioning as a function of shifts in the magnitude of attitudinal reinforcement. *Psychonomic Science,* 1972, 28, 215–218.

Long, B. H., & Ziller, R. C. Dogmatism and predecisional information search. *Journal of Applied Psychology,* 1965, 49, 376–378.

Lord, F. M. Cutting scores and errors of measurement. *Psychometrika,* 1962, 27, 19–30.

Lott, A. J., & Lott, B. E. Group cohesiveness as interpersonal attraction: A review of relationships with antecedent and consequent variables. *Psychological Bulletin,* 1965, 64, 259–309.

Luce, R. D. Semiorders and a theory of utility discrimination. *Econometrica,* 1956, 24, 178–191.

Luce, R. D., & Raiffa, H. *Games and decisions.* New York: Wiley, 1957.

Luce, R. D., & Suppes, P. Preference, utility and subjective probability. In R. D. Luce, R. R. Bush, & E. Galanter (Eds.), *Handbook of mathematical psychology* (Vol. 3). New York: Wiley, 1965.

Luce, R. D., & Tukey, J. Simultaneous conjoint measurement: A new type of fundamental measurement. *Journal of Mathematical Philosophy,* 1964, 1, 1–27.

Luce, R. D., & Krantz, D. Conditional expected utility. *Econometrica,* 1971, 39, 253–272.

Luginbuhl, J. E. R., Crow, D. H., & Kahan, J. P. Causal attribution for success and failure. *Journal of Personality and Social Psychology,* 1975, 31, 86–93.

Lusk, E. Cognitive style aspects of annual reports: Field independence-dependence. *Empirical Research in Accounting: Selected Studies,* 1973, 191–202.

MacArthur, L. A. The how and what of why. *Journal of Personality and Social Psychology,* 1972, 22, 171–193.

McClelland, D. C. *The achieving society.* Princeton, N.J.: Van Nostrand, 1961.

MacCorquodale, K., & Meehl, P. E. Edward C. Tolman. In W. K. Estes, *Modern Learning Theory.* New York: Appleton-Century-Crofts, 1954, 177–266.

MacCrimmon, K. R. Descriptive and normative implications of the decision theory postulates. In K. Borch & J. Mossin (Eds.), *Risk and uncertainty.* New York: St. Martin's, 1968, 3–32.

MacCrimmon, K. R., & Toda, M. The experimental determination of indifference curves. *Review of Economic Studies,* 1969, 36, 433–437.

MacCrimmon, K. R. An overview of multiple objective decision making. In J. L. Cochrane, & M. Zeleny (Eds.), *Multiple criteria decision making.* Columbia, S.C.: University of South Carolina Press, 1973, 18–44.

MacCrimmon, K. R. Descriptive aspects of team theory. *Management Science,* 1974, 20, 1323–1334.

MacCrimmon, K. R. Managerial decision making. In J. W. McGuire (Ed.), *Contemporary management: Issues and viewpoints.* Englewood Cliffs, N.J.: Prentice-Hall, 1974.

MacCrimmon, K. R., & Siu, J. K. Making trade-offs. *Decision Sciences,* 1974, 5, 680–704.

MacCrimmon, K. R., & Taylor, R. N. Decision making and problem solving. In M. D. Dunnette (Ed.), *Handbook of industrial and organizational psychology.* Chicago: Rand McNally, 1976, 1397–1453.

Mace, C. A. *Incentives: Some experimental studies.* London: Industrial Health Research Board, 1953.

McGregor, D. *The human side of enterprise.* New York: McGraw-Hill, 1960.

McGuire, W. J. The current status of cognitive consistency theories. In Feldman (Ed.), *Cognitive consistency: Motivational antecedents and behavioral consequents.* New York: Academic Press, 1966, 1–46.

McGuire, W. J. Theory of the structure of human thoughts. In R. P. Abelson, E. Aronson, W. S. McGuire, T. M. Newcomb, M. S. Rosenberg, & P. H. Tannenbaum (Eds.), *Theories of cognitive consistency: A source book.* Chicago: Rand McNally, 1968.

Mack, R. P. *Planning on uncertainty.* New York: Wiley, 1971.

McKeen, R. N. Criteria. In E. A. Quade (Ed.), *Analysis for military decisions.* Santa Monica, Calif.: Rand Corporation, 1964.

MacKinnon, D. W. The nature and nurture of creative talent. *American Psychologist,* 1962, 17, 484–495.

MacKinnon, W. J. Elements of the SPAN technique for making group decisions. *Journal of Social Psychology,* 1966, 70, 149–164.

Maier, N. R. F. Reasoning in humans: II. The solution of a problem and its appearance in consciousness. *Journal of Comparative Psychology,* 1931, 13, 181–194.

Maier, N. R. F. *Problem-solving discussions and conferences.* New York: McGraw-Hill, 1963.

Maltzman, I. On the training of originality. *Psychological Review,* 1960, 67, 229–241.

Maltzman, I., Bogartz, W., & Breger, L. A procedure for increasing word association originality and its transfer effects. *Journal of Experimental Psychology,* 1958, 392–398.

Manski, M. E., & Davis, G. A. Effects of simple instructional biases upon performance in the unusual uses of test. *Journal of General Psychology,* 1968, 78, 25–33.

March, J. G., & Simon, H. A. *Organizations.* New York Wiley, 1958.

March, J. G. Model bias in social action. *Review of Educational Research,* 1972, 42, 413–429.

Markowitz, H. *The utility of wealth in mathematical models of human behavior.* Dunlop, 1955.

Marrow, A. J., & French, J. P. R., Jr. Changing a stereotype in industry. *Journal of Social Issues,* 1945, 3, 33–37.

Marschak, J. Remarks on the economics of information. *Contributions to scientific research in management.* Los Angeles: W.D.P.C., 1959.

Marschak, J. Actual versus consistent decision behavior. *Behavioral Science,* 1964, 9, 103–110.

Marshall, A. *Principles of economics.* London: Macmillan, 1980.

Mason, R. O. A dialectical approach to strategic planning. *Management Science,* 1969, 15, B403–B414.

Mason, R. O., & Mitroff, I. I. A program for research on management information systems. *Management Science,* 1973, 19, 475–487.

Mayfield, E. C. The selection interview: A re-evaluation of published research. *Personnel Psychology,* 1964, 17, 239–260.

Mechanic, D. Sources of power of lower participants in complex organizations. *Administrative Science Quarterly,* 1967, 349–364.

Meehl, P. E. *Clinical vs. statistical prediction.* Minneapolis: University of Minnesota Press, 1954.

Meehl, P. E., & Rosen, A. Antecedent probability and the efficiency of psychometric signs, patterns, or cutting scores. *Psychological Bulletin,* 1955, 52, 194–216.

Melcher, A. Participation: A critical review of research findings. *Human Resource Management,* 1976, 15, 12–21.

Mendelsohn, G. A. & Griswold, B. Assessed creative potential, vocabulary level, and sex as predictors of the use of incidental cues in verbal problem solving. *Journal of Personality and Social Psychology,* 1966, 4, 423–431.

Messick, R. M., & Rapoport, A. A. A comparison of two pay-off functions in multiple choice decision behavior. *Journal of Experimental Psychology,* 1965, 69, 75–83.

Milkovich, G. T., Annoni, A. J., & Mahoney, T. A. The use of the Delphi-procedures in manpower forecasting. *Management Science,* 1972, 19, 281–288.

Miller, D. W., & Starr, M. K. *The structure of human decisions.* Englewood Cliffs, N.J.: Prentice-Hall, 1967.

Miller, G. A. The magical number seven, plus or minus two: Some limits on our capacity for processing information. *Psychological Review,* 1956, 63, 81–97.

Miller, G. A., Galanter, E., & Pribram, K. H. *Plans and the structure of behavior.* New York: Holt, Rinehart, and Winston, 1960.

Miller, J. R. III. *Professional decision making.* New York: Praeger, 1970.

Mills, T. M. *The sociology of small groups.* Englewood Cliffs, N.J.: Prentice-Hall, 1967.

Mills, J. Interest in supporting and discrepant information. In R. P. Abelson, E. Aronson, W. J. McGuire, T. M. Newcomb, M. J. Rosenberg, & P. H. Tannenbaum (Eds.), *Theories of cognitive consistency: A source book.* Chicago: Rand McNally, 1968, 771–776.

Milne, A. A. *Now we are six.* New York: Dutton, 1927.

Minsky, M. Steps toward artificial intelligence. *Proceedings of the I.R.E.,* 1961, 49, 8–30.

Moore, P. G., & Thomas, H. *The anatomy of decisions.* New York: Penguin Books, 1976.

Morgenstern, O. *On the accuracy of economic observations.* Princeton University Press, Princeton, N.J., 1963.

Mosteller, F., & Nogee, P. An experimental measurement of utility. *Journal of Political Economics,* 1951, 59, 371–404.

Mulder, M. Communications structure, decision structure, and group performance. *Sociometry,* 1960, 23, 1–14.

Mulder, M., & Wilke, H. Participation and power equalization. *Organizational Behavior and Human Performance,* 1970, 5, 430–448.

Murphy, A. H., & Winkler, R. L. Forecasters and probability forecasts: Some current problems. *Bulletin of American Meteorology Society,* 1971, 52, 239–247.

Murphy, A. H. A sample skill score for probability forecasters. *Monthly Weather Review,* 1974, 102, 48–55.

Neimark, E. D. & Santa, J. L. Thinking and concept attainment. *Annual Review of Psychology,* 1975, 26, 173–205.

Newell, A. Production systems: Models of control structures. In W. G. Chase (Ed.), *Visual information processing.* New York: Academic Press, 1973.

Newell, A., Shaw, J. C., & Simon, H. A. Chess-playing programmes and the problem of complexity. *IBM Journal of Research and Development,* 1958, October, 320–335.

Newell, A. Heuristic programming: Ill-structured problems. In J. Aronofsky (Ed.), *Progress in operations research.* New York: Wiley, 1970.

Newell, A., & Simon, H. A. *Human problem solving.* Englewood Cliffs, N.J.: Prentice-Hall, 1972.

Nyman, C., & Smith, E. D. *Union-management cooperation in the "stretch out": Labor extension at the Pequot Mills.* New Haven: Yale University Press, 1934.

Ofstad, H. *An inquiry into the freedom of decision.* Oslo: Norwegian Universities Press, 1961.

Olsen, J. P. Choice in an organized anarchy. In J. G. March, & J. P. Olsen (Eds.), *Ambiguity and choice in organizations.* Bergen: Univesitetsforeaget, 1976.

Osborn, A. F. *Applied imagination* (3rd ed.). New York: Scribner's, 1963.

Peterson, C. R., & Beach, L. R. Man as an intuitive statistician. *Psychological Bulletin,* 1967, 68, 29–46.

Peterson, C. R., & Miller, A. J. Sensitivity and subjective probability revision. *Journal of Experimental Psychology,* 1965, 70, 526–533.

Pfeffer, J. Power and resource allocation in organizations. In B. M. Staw & G. R. Salancik (Eds.), *New directions in organizational behavior.* Chicago: St. Clair Press, 1977, 235–265.

Pfeffer, J., & Salancik, G. R. *The external control of organizations.* New York: Harper and Row, 1978.

Phillips, E. J. Characteristics essential for the emergence of problem solving behavior. *Psychology,* 1969, 6, 19–29.

Phillips, L. D., & Edwards, W. Conservativism in a simple probability inference task. *Journal of Experimental Psychology,* 1966, 72, 346–354.

Pill, J. The Delphi-method: Substance, context, a critique and an annotated bibliography. *Socio-economic Planning Sciences,* 1971, 5, 57–71.

Pitz, G. F. Subjective probability distributions for imperfectly known quantities. In L. W. Gregg (Ed.), *Knowledge and cognition.* New York: Wiley, 1974, 29–41.

Porter, L. W., & Lawler, E. E. *Managerial attitudes and performance.* Homewood, Ill.: Irwin Dorsey, 1968.

Porter, L. W., & Roberts, K. H. *Communication in organizations.* Irvine, Calif.: University of California, 1972.

Posner, M. I. Immediate memory in sequential task. *Psychological Bulletin,* 1963, 60, 346–354.

Pounds, W. F. The process of problem finding. *Industrial Management Review,* 1969, 11, 1–19.

Prince, G. M. The operational mechanism of synectics. *The Journal of Creative Behavior,* 1962, 2, 1–13.

Pruitt, D. G. Informational requirements in making decisions. *American Journal of Psychology,* 1961, 74, 433–439.

Radford, K. J. *Managerial decision making.* Reston, Va.: Reston, 1975.

Raiffa, H. *Decision analysis.* Reading, Mass.: Addison-Wesley, 1968.

Ramsey, F. P. *The foundations of mathematics.* London: Routledge and Kegan Paul, 1931.

Raphael, B. *The thinking computer.* San Francisco: Freeman, 1976.

Rapoport, A. *Fights, games, and debates.* Ann Arbor, Mich.: University of Michigan Press, 1960.

Rapoport, A., & Chammah, A. M. *Prisoner's dilemma.* Ann Arbor, Mich.: University of Michigan Press, 1965.

Rapoport, A. *N-person game theory.* Ann Arbor, Mich.: University of Michigan Press, 1970.

Rappoport, L., & Summers, D. A. (Eds.). *Human judgment and social interaction.* New York: Holt, Rinehart and Winston, 1973.

Rasmussen, N. C. *An assessment of accident risks in U.S. commercial nuclear power plants.* Atomic Energy Commission, August, 1974.

Reitman, W. R. Heuristic decision procedures, open constraints, and the structure of ill-defined problems. In M. Shelly, & G. Bryan (Eds.), *Human judgment and optimality.* New York Wiley, 1964.

Restle, F. Mathematical models and thought: A search for stages. In J. F. Voss (Ed.), *Approaches to thought.* Columbus, Ohio: Charles E. Merrill, 1969.

Rice, A. K. Productivity and social organization in an Indian weaving shed. *Human Relations,* 1953, 11, 297–330.

Roberts, K. H., & O'Reilly, C. A. Failures in upward communication in organizations: Three possible culprits. *Academy of Management Journal,* 1974, 17, 205–215.

Robinson, A., & Majak, R. R. The theory of decision making. In Charlesworth (Ed.), *Contemporary Political Analysis.* New York: Free Press, 1967.

Roe, A. *The making of a scientist.* New York: Dodd, Mead, 1953.

Rokeach, M. *The open and closed mind.* New York: Basic Books, 1960.

Rosen, S. & Tesser, A. On reluctance to communicate undesirable information: The MUM effect. *Sociometry,* 1969, 253–263.

Rossman, J. *The psychology of the inventor* (Rev. ed.). Washington, D.C.: Inventors Publication Co., 1931.

Russell, D. G., & Sarason, I.G. Test anxiety, sex and experimental conditions in relation to anagram solution. *Journal of Personality and Social Psychology,* 1965, 493–496.

Sage, A. P. Designs for optimal information filters. In P. Nystrom, & W. H. Starbuck (Eds.), *Handbook of organizational design* (Vol. 1). Oxford: Oxford University Press, 1981, 105–121.

Sarason, S. The contents of human problem solving. *Nebraska Symposium on Motivation,* 1961.

Savage, L. J. *The foundations of statistics.* New York: Wiley, 1954.

Sayles, L. *Managerial behavior.* New York: McGraw-Hill, 1964.

Schelling, T. C. *The strategy of conflict.* Cambridge, N.J.: Harvard University Press, 1963.

Schroeder, H. M., & Suedfeld, P. *Personality theory and information processing.* New York: Ronald Press, 1971.

Schroeder, H. M., Driver, M. J., & Streufert, S. *Human information processing.* New York: Holt, Rinehart and Winston, 1967.

Seaver, D. A. *Assessment of group preferences and group uncertainty for decision making.* Social Science Research Institute, 76-4, University of California, 1976.

Seghers, R. C., Fryback, D. G., & Goodman, B. C. Relative variance preferences in a choice-among-bets paradigm. *Eng. Psychol. Lab. Tech. Report 011313-6-T.* Ann Arbor, Mich.: University of Michigan, 1973.

Shackle, G. L. S. *Expectations in economics* (2nd ed.). Cambridge: Cambridge University Press, 1952.

Shaw, M. E. Some effects of problem complexity upon problem solution efficiency in different communication nets. *Journal of Experimental Psychology,* 1954, 48, 211–217.

Shaw, M. E. *Group Dynamics.* New York: McGraw-Hill, 1971.

Shaw, M. E. *Group dynamics: The psychology of small group behavior* (2nd ed.). New York: McGraw-Hill, 1976.

Shaw, M. E., & Rothschild, G. H. Some effects of prolonged experience in communication nets. *Journal of Applied Psychology,* 1956, 40, 281–286.

Sherif, M. *Group conflict and cooperation.* Boston: Houghton Mifflin, 1966.

Shuford, E., & Brown, T. A. Elicitation of personal probabilities and their assessment. *Instructional Science,* 1975, 4, 137–188.

Shull, F. A. Jr., Delbecq, A. L., & Cummings, L. L. *Organizational decision making.* New York: McGraw-Hill, 1970.

Siegel, S. Level of aspiration and decision making. *Psychological Review,* 1957, 64, 253–262.

Siegel, S., & Fouraker, L. E. *Bargaining and group decision making: Experiments in bilateral monopoly.* New York: McGraw-Hill, 1960.

Simon, H. A. A behavioral model of rational choice. *Quarterly Journal of Economics,* 1955, 69, 99–112.

Simon, H. *Administrative behavior* (2nd ed.). New York: Free Press, 1957.

Simon, H. *New science of management decisions.* New York: Harper & Row, 1960.

Simon, H. A., & Ando, A. Aggregation of variables in dynamic systems. *Econometrica,* 1961, 29, 111–138.

Simon, H. Administrative decision making. *Public Administration Review,* 1965, March, 31–37.

Simon, H. A. *The sciences of the artificial.* Cambridge: M.I.T. Press, 1969.

Simon, H. A. Applying information technology to organization design. *Public Administration Review,* 1973, May-June, 268–277.

Simon, H. A. Rationality as process and product of thought. *American Economic Review,* 1978, 68, 1–16.

Slovic, P. Convergent validation of risk taking measures. *Journal of Abnormal and Social Psychology,* 1962, 65, 68–71.

Slovic, P. Cue consistency and cue utilization in judgment. *American Journal of Psychology,* 1966, 79, 427–434.

Slovic, P., & Lichtenstein, S. C. The relative importance of probabilities and payoffs in risk taking. *Journal of Experimental Psychology Monograph Supplement,* 1968, 78, No. 3, Part 2.

Slovic, P. Analyzing the expert judge: A descriptive study of a stockbroker's decision processes. *Journal of Applied Psychology,* 1969, 53, 255–263.

Slovic, P., & Lichtenstein, S. C. Comparison of Bayesian and regression approaches to the study of information processing in judgment. *Organizational Behavior and Human Performance,* 1971, 6, 649–744.

Slovic, P. From Shakespeare to Simon: Speculations—and some evidence—about man's ability to process information. *Oregon Research Institute Research Monograph,* 12. Eugene, Oregon: Oregon Research Institute, 1972a.

Slovic, P. Information processing, situation specificity, and the generality of risk-taking behavior. *Journal of Personality and Social Psychology,* 1972b, 22, 128–134.

Slovic, P., Kunreuther, H., & White, G. F. Decision processes, rationality and adjustment to natural hazards. In G. F. White (Ed.), *Natural Hazards: Local, National and Global.* New York: Oxford University Press, 1974, 187–205.

Slovic, P., & MacPhillamy, D. Dimensional commensurability and cue utilization in comparative judgment. *Organizational Behavior and Human Performance,* 1974, 11, 172–194.

Slovic, P. Choice between equally-valued alternatives. *Journal of Experimental Psychology: Human Perceptual Performance,* 1975, 1, 280–287.

Slovic, P., Fischhoff, B., & Lichtenstein, S. C. Cognitive processes and societal risk taking. In J. S. Carroll, & J. W. Payne (Eds.), *Cognition and social behavior.* Hillsdale, N.J.: Erlbaum, 1976.

Slovic, P., Fischhoff, B., & Lichtenstein, S. C. Behavioral decision theory. *Annual Review of Psychology,* 1977, 28, 1–39.

Smith, R. D. Heuristic simulation of psychological decision processes. *Journal of Applied Psychology,* 1968, 52, 325–330.

Smode, A. Learning and performance in a tracking task under two levels of achievement information feedback. *Journal of Experimental Psychology,* 1958, 56, 297–304.

Spence, K. W. *Behavior theory and conditioning.* New Haven, Ct.: Yale University Press, 1956.

Spetzler, C. S., & Stael von Holstein, C. A. S. Probability encoding in decision analysis. *Management Science,* 1975, 22, 340–358.

Stael von Holstein, C. A. S. An experiment in probabilistic weather forecasting. *Journal of Applied Meteorology,* 1971, 10, 635–645.

Stael von Holstein, C. A. S. Probabilistic forecasting: An experiment related to the stock market. *Organizational Behavior and Human Performance,* 1972, 8, 139–158.

Staw, B. M. Organizational Behavior: A review and reformation of the field's outcome variables. *Annual Review of Psychology,* 1984, 35, 627–666.

Stein, M. I. *Stimulating creativity.* (Vol. 1). New York: Academic Press, 1974.

Steiner, G. A. (Ed.). *The creative organization.* Chicago: University of Chicago Press, 1965.

Steiner, I. D. Perceived freedom. In L. Berkowitz (Ed.), *Advances in experimental social psychology* (Vol. 5). New York: Academic Press, 1972.

Stouffer, S. A. The American soldier: Combat and its aftermath. *Studies in social psychology in World War II* (Vol. II). Princeton, N.J.: Princeton University Press, 1949.

Stratton, E. P., & Brown, R. Improving creative training by training in the production and/or judgment of solutions. *Journal of Educational Psychology,* 1970, 16–23.

Streufert, B., & Castore, C. H. Effects of increasing success and failure on perceived information quality. *Psychonomic Science,* 1968, 11, 63–64.

Summers, D. A., & Oncken, G. F. The logical consistency of person perception. *Psychonomic Science,* 1968, 10, 63–68.

Svenson, O. A note on the think aloud protocols obtained during the choice of a home. *Psychological Laboratories Report 421.* Sweden: University of Stockholm, 1974.

Swalm, R. O. Utility theory: Insights into risk taking. *Harvard Business Review,* 1966, 44, 123–131.

Swinth, R. C., Gaumnitz, J. E., & Rodriguez, C. Decision making process: Using discrimination nets for security selection. *Decision Sciences,* 1975, 6, 439–448.

Taylor, C. W., & Barron, F. *Scientific creativity: Its recognition and development.* New York, 1963.

Taylor, D. W., Berry, P. C., & Block, C. H. Does group participation when using brainstorming facilitate or inhibit creative thinking? *Administrative Science Quarterly,* 1958, 3, 23–47.

Taylor, R. N. Nature of problem ill-structuredness: Implications for problem formulation and solution. *Decision Sciences,* 1974, 5, 632–643.

Taylor, R. N. Perception of problem constraints. *Management Science,* 1975, 22, 22–29.

Taylor, R. N. Planning and decision making in managing organizations. In H. Meltzer & W. Nord (Eds.), *Making organizations humane and productive.* New York: Wiley, 1981, 159–178.

Taylor, R. N., & Dunnette, M. D. Influence of dogmatism, risk-taking propensity, and intelligence on decision-making strategies for a sample of industrial managers. *Journal of Applied Psychology,* 1974, 59, 420–423.

Taylor, R. N., & Dunnette, M. D. Relative contribution of decision-maker attributes to decision processes. *Organizational Behavior and Human Performance,* 1974, 12, 286–298.

Taylor, R. N., & Vertinsky, I. Experimenting with organizational behavior. In P. Nystrom, & W. H. Starbuck (Eds.), *Handbook of organizational design.* Oxford: Oxford University Press, 1981, 139–166.

Terborg, J. R., & Ilgen, D. R. A theoretical approach to sex discrimination in traditionally masculine occupations. *Organizational Behavior and Human Performance,* 1975, 13, 352–376.

Tetlock, P. E. Identifying victims of groupthink from public statements of decision makers. *Journal of Personality and Social Psychology,* 1979, 37, 1314–1324.

Tharp, R., & Wetzel, G. *Behavior modification of the natural environment.* New York: Academic Press, 1969.

Thomas, E. J., & Fink, C. E. Models of group problem-solving. *Journal of Abnormal Social Psychology,* 1961, 63, 53–63.

Thompson, D. *Numerical weather analysis and prediction.* New York: Macmillan, 1961.

Thompson, J. D. *Organizations in action.* New York: McGraw-Hill, 1967.

Thompson, J. D., & McEwen, W. J. Organizational goals and environments. In A. Etzioni (Ed.), *A sociological reader on complex organizations* (2nd ed.). New York: Holt, Rinehart and Winston, 1969.

Thompson, J. D., & Tuden, A. *Comparative studies in administration.* Pittsburgh: University of Pittsburgh Press, 1959.

Thorndike, R. L. The problem of classification of personnel. *Psychometrika,* 1950, 15, 215–235.

Thurstone, L. L. Creative talent. *Proc., 1950 Conf. Test. Probl., Educ. Test.* Serv., 1951, 55–69.

Trull, S. G. Some factors involved in determining total decision success. *Management Science,* 1966, February, B271–279.

Tversky, A. Elimination by aspects: A theory of choice. *Psychological Review,* 1972, 79, 281–299.

Tversky, A., & Kahneman, D. The belief in the "law of small numbers." *Psychological Bulletin,* 1971, 76, 105–110.

Tversky, A., & Kahneman, D. Availability: A heuristic for judging frequency and probability. *Cognitive Psychology,* 1973, 5, 207–232.

Tversky, A., & Kahneman, D. Judgment under uncertainty: Heuristics and biases. *Science,* 1974, 185, 1124–1131.

Ullrich, J. R., & Painter, J. R. A conjoint-measurement analysis of human judgment. *Organizational Behavior and Human Performance,* 1974, 12, 50–61.

Van de Ven, A. H., & Delbecq, A. L. The effectiveness of nominal, Delphi, and interacting group decision-making processes. *Academy of Management Journal,* 1974, 17, 605–621.

Venn, J. *The logic of chance* (3rd ed.). London: Macmillan, 1888.

Vickrey, W. Measuring marginal utility by reactions to risk. *Econometrica,* 1945, 13, 319–333.

Vinokur, A. Review and theoretical analysis of the affects of group processes upon individual and group decisions involving risk. *Psychological Bulletin,* 1971, 74, 231–250.

Vlek, C. A. J. Multiple probability learning. In A. F. Sander (Ed.), *Attention and performance* (Vol. III). Amsterdam: North-Holland, 1970.

Vlek, C. A. J. Coherence of human judgment in a limited probabilistic environment. *Organizational Behavior and Human Performance,* 1973, 9, 460–481.

Von Neumann, J., & Morgenstern, O. *Theory of games and economic behavior.* Princeton: Princeton University Press, 1944.

Vroom, V. H. *Some personality determinants of the effects of participation.* Englewood Cliffs, N.J.: Prentice-Hall, 1960.

Vroom, V. H. Can leaders learn to lead? *Organizational Dynamics,* 1976, Winter, 17–28.

Vroom, V. H., & Maier, N. R. F. Industrial social psychology. *Annual Review of Psychology,* 1961, 12, 413–446.

Vroom, V. H. *Work and motivation.* New York: Wiley, 1964.

Vroom, V. H., & Yetton, P. W. *Leadership and decision making.* Pittsburgh: University of Pittsburgh Press, 1973.

Wald, A. *Statistical decision functions.* New York: Wiley, 1950.

Wallach, M. A., & Kogan, N. *Modes of thinking in young children.* New York: Holt, Rinehart and Winston, 1965.

Walster, E. Second-guessing important events. *Human Relations,* 1967, 20, 239–250.

Warren, T. F., & Davis, G. A. Techniques for creative thinking: An empirical comparison of three methods. *Psychological Reports,* 1969, 25, 207–214.

Weick, K. E. Enactment process in organizations. In B. M. Staw, & G. R. Salancik (Eds.), *New directions in organizational behavior.* Chicago: St. Clair Press, 1977, 267–300.

Weiner, B., & Seirad, J. Misattribution for failure and enhancement of achievement strivings. *Journal of Personality and Social Psychology,* 1975, 31, 415–421.

White, G. F. *Choice of adjustment to floods.* Chicago: University of Chicago, Department of Geography, 1964.

Whiting, C. S. *Creative Thinking.* New York: Reinhold, 1958.

Wilensky, H. L. The professionalization of every one. *American Journal of Sociology,* 1970, Sept., 137–158.

Wilson, R. C., Guilford, J. P., & Christensen, P. R. The measurement of individual differences in originality. *Psychological Bulletin,* 1953, 50, 362–370.

Winer, B. *Achievement motivation and attribution theory.* Morristown, N.J.: General Learning Press, 1974.

Winkler, R. L. The consensus of subjective probability distributions. *Management Science,* 1968, 15, B61–B75.

Winkler, R. L., & Murphy, A. H. Experiments in the laboratory and the real world. *Organizational Behavior and Human Performance,* 1973, 10, 252–270.

Witte, E. H. The cognitive structure of choice situations. *European Journal of Social Psychology,* 1972, 4, 313–328.

Woods, D. H. Improving estimates that involve uncertainty. *Harvard Business Review,* 1966, 44, 91–98.

Wyer, R. S., & Goldberg, L. R. A probabilistic analysis of the relationship between beliefs and attitudes. *Psychological Review,* 1970, 77, 100–120.

Zarnowitz, W. *An appraisal of short-term economic forecasts.* Occasional Paper No. 104, National Bureau of Economic Research. New York, 1967.

Ziller, R. C. Vocational choice and utility for risk. *Journal of Counselling Psychology,* 1957, 4, 61–64.

Zwicky, F. *Morphological astronomy.* New York: Springer-Verlag, 1957.

Zwicky, F. *Discovery, invention, research through the morphological approach.* New York: Macmillan, 1969.

NAME INDEX

*Numbers in *italics* indicate reference pages.

SUBJECT INDEX